HOPING

FOR THE BEST

Three months in the life of a twin plus one mummy

SARAH BERRYMAN

Matador
9 Priory Business Park,
Wistow Road, Kibworth Beauchamp,
Leicestershire. LE8 0RX
Tel: 0116 279 2299
Email: books@troubador.co.uk
Web: www.troubador.co.uk/matador
Twitter: @matadorbooks

ISBN 978 1785899 485

British Library Cataloguing in Publication Data.
A catalogue record for this book is available from the British Library.

Typeset in 11pt Adobe Garamond Pro by Troubador Publishing Ltd, Leicester, UK
Printed and bound by CPI Group (UK) Ltd, Croydon, CR0 4YY

Matador is an imprint of Troubador Publishing Ltd

Warmest thanks to ...

The midwife who told me that twins only come to those who can handle them.

Child C's preschool teacher who told me that if it wasn't for the lows, you wouldn't get such lovely highs.

Each and every friend who has given me support, encouragement, a smile, a kind word, a shoulder to cry on and a spare baby wipe / tissue / plaster since becoming a mummy. I'd like to name you all here, but that would be a whole book in itself.

My family. Thank you for absolutely everything.

Child A, Child B and Child C. You are my inspiration and I love you more than chocolate, Diet Coke and wine all put together.

Maya Angelou. For igniting my love of the written and spoken word, and for the strength, courage and humour you showed the sixteen year old me.

How it all began ...

When I was sixteen, I read *I Know Why The Caged Bird Sings* – a deeply moving and inspirational account of Maya Angelou's childhood.

She explained that she was "hoping for the best, prepared for the worst, and unsurprised by anything in between".

This phrase has stuck with me for twenty-one years. Since becoming pregnant with identical twin boys, and then welcoming a third addition to the family (another boy), like all parents, I am constantly making things up as I go, hoping that it all goes ok, making contingency plans in case it doesn't and unsurprised if things go a bit off plan. Maya Angelou's take on life gives me hope at the end of a sleepless night, and helps me to see the funny side just a little bit when discovering three unrolled toilet rolls, a carpet covered in Sudocrem and a pencil wedged in a table, having just turned my back to clear up three uneaten meals.

I have real children. They did not sleep through from day one. They did not master baby led weaning. They have all had the norovirus, chicken pox, and two of the three have had nits. They have bitten and been bitten. They did not potty train in a week. One has a hearing aid, one wears splints at night to stop him walking on tiptoes, and one has speech delay, and bears similarities to a small dog. They play a little, bicker a lot, and are friends and enemies in equal measure.

My children do, of course, have names. But for speed of writing as it happened, ease of reading, and to protect their identities should this book go global, become a major motion picture and threaten their careers as a professional cricketer, a premiership footballer / yachting entrepreneur, and a rock star (their choices, not mine), here they are simply Child A, Child B and Child C. Child A and B are identical twins, aged seven, and Child C wants to be twelve but, sadly for him, is two.

Fed up of how-to books, and people with perfect children who do wonderful things all of the time, this is how it really is in our house. It's hectic, it's noisy and it's messy most of the time. But by and large it's a happy house. We laugh more than I shout, and the children spend more time kicking balls than each other.

Read this and feel better about your own household craziness. Read this and feel smug that your children are much more angelic than mine. Read this and show your husband / boyfriend / parents that it's not just you. Read this, locked in the bathroom, in the three minutes you have before the next call of "Mummmmmmm". Read this and warn teenagers against early motherhood. Read this and smile.

This is it. All true and, sadly, non-fiction (the fiction version would have all the kids behaving beautifully while Mummy goes for lunch and to a spa for free). I am, and always will be, hoping for the best, prepared for the worst, and unsurprised by anything in between.

PART ONE: HOPING FOR THE BEST

"Try to be a rainbow in someone's cloud"

Day One (Monday)

3.00 Wake up call. Child C yells out "Where are the baby chicks?" in haunting fashion, repeatedly. Reassure him that there are no chicks in his cot. Attribute this delusion to his attempts to unwrap Creme Eggs by the dozen in the shops last week.

5.30 Up to provide the same child with a *Thomas And Friends Sing Along Songs* book.

Up at 6.15 for shower.

Husband dropped at station at 7.30, return to station at 8.00 to give Husband forgotten phone.

8.05 Find Husband has run home through the woods to retrieve phone from kitchen work top (not there, as in my car with me and three kids). Back to station at 8.10, school run at 8.17, Child B retrieved from puddle covered in mud from head to toe at 8.25, Child A dropped at school at 8.45, back home for more trousers at 8.55, preschool run at 9.00, hospital appointment for Child B's new leg splints (to stop him tiptoe walking) at 9.30, rainstorm at 10.00. Only one coat between one adult and one child (as Child B's coat coated in mud) so share coat, whilst Child B chants "you always get more from the cut price store" (a line from an episode of *Fireman Sam*) to keep our rhythm of walking together and assures me that what we are doing is just like a "two legged race".

Child B dropped at school at 10.20, after discussion in the car about him wanting to become a referee, the meaning of racism and whether he'll be back in time for morning play. Sharing bag of Minstrels consumed by Mummy alone by 10.30.

And so begins Monday.

12.00 Child C picked up from preschool. No accidents (yay). Home for lunch – crumbled bread and two squeezy yoghurts – healthy stuff rejected. Read books, get climbed on, act out story of *The Three Little Pigs* four times, toy with idea of writing a book and do some research on Amazon. Search results return books entitled *Am I Messing Up My Kids?* and *Living With Less So Your Family Has More*. Intrigued and concerned by the first. Second not an option.

14.45 Scoot to school to pick up Child A and B. Have developed technique for scooting while wearing a rucksack, holding a scooter, and supervising another child on a scooter. Must work on thigh strength required to propel me at the same speed as Child C. It's all in the keeping low and keeping momentum … oh and under no circumstances trying to talk to anyone, wave hello or take your eye off your intended path. All quite tricky when you're over the age of thirty-six and your centre of gravity isn't as low or as flexy as that of your kids.

Load up with school bags, water bottles, ukuleles and music books. Note to self to remember that Child A and B require a cereal box turned inside out for Thursday.

15.25 Home. Costume change for Child C who has cup full of water in his wellies and has wet himself on the way home. Try to stop Child C from making balls and "dog bones" of toilet paper and throwing them in the toilet before manically flushing – totally disinterested in my explanations that he is using up all the water and toilet paper, and that he's going to ruin the planet and flood the house.

In attempt to do fun, wholesome, non screen-related after-school activity with children, embark on making chocolate muffins from cookery book that the children received for their birthday. Child A and B keen to add blueberries. Blueberries fly all over the floor, strawberries largely eaten by Child C, and school uniform now needs washing before tomorrow. Have now run out of fruit. Supermarket can't deliver until tomorrow evening. Will attempt shop tomorrow.

Clear up cake mess against soundtrack of "Mum, mum, mum" from three different children, simultaneously. Ponder my idea for a Child Queue Management System which may, one day, make me a millionaire. Basic pitch goes as follows: Ticket machine to be worn on belt by mum, and tickets taken and responded to in turn, in the style of shoe shops, *or* LCD belt showing next customer's / child's name, and a message saying something along the lines of "cashier number four please" *or* a holding message played with a variation on "your call is important to us" … or maybe a combination of all three. Velcro naughty step also part of same product line.

Children despatched to bed. Youngest still playing *Thomas And Friends* tunes, Child A and B decide to share a room. Chapter of book read to Child A and B. The latter assures me that he'll let me know if his new leg splints bother him. Have reminded him that "sleep is the best thing" and to just take them off rather than call down to me.

Wine in fridge left over from Saturday. Would be wasteful not to have a glass.

Called up by Child A who has lost Snuggle, his comfort blanket. Hunt for Snuggle ensues. Can't find it. Child A told to sleep in his own room and stop disturbing others.

Make To Do List for tomorrow – includes cleaning what I think is crayon off the TV, and sorting through the newly appointed lost property box in newly constructed storage unit (part of hapless eternal quest for ultimate storage solution) so that all items can be repatriated to their rightful homes. May take a while.

Diet Cokes: 4.

Chocolate: 1 sharing bag of Minstrels, 2 large bags of buttons, and 1 chocolate muffin.

Glasses of wine: 1.

Day Two (Tuesday)

4.30 Wake up call. Request to "Take off pa pas". Through half closed eyes, go through range of options based on interpretations of Child C's calls, while he becomes increasingly irate. Finally realise that "pa pas" means pyjamas. He seems to think that they are wet. They are not. "Pa pas" changed and back to bed. 6.00 *Thomas And Friends* concert begins.

6.20 Shower.

6.30 Husband reminded that he has a plane to catch.

6.48 Call of "up time" from Child C. Make important choice between jeans with hole in left knee (always just the left knee which goes) and jeans with no hole. Opt for no hole jeans, on assumption that I won't be doing any cleaning today. Check on Child A and B who are deep in Match Attax trading.

Down for brekkie. Slow cooked mince done, and needs freezing. Minor meltdown from Child B as we're out of Shreddies. Put dishes in sink to soak and feel super-organised.

Child A is reunited with Snuggle. It seems that it was "lost" on one side of his bed.

7.40 Car frozen. Husband curses.

8.30 Child C scoots to school wearing adult size England jester hat complete with bells. Noticeably easier to find him in the playground.

7

Succeed in signing up for parents' evening before the first-day-of-the-sales type rush, and get two back to back appointments – hurrah! Remember it is Pancake Day. Have invested in pancake maker, and now need to make sure we have something to put in the pancakes. Since my pancakes are always rubbery and cold, have decided that pancake maker will be indispensable part of kitchen equipment and allow me to entertain and delight in equal measure. Less "expenditure", more "helpful equipment for a multitude of social occasions".

Spend morning researching holiday for May half term. Find perfect place in Guernsey and now just need to convince everyone that it is a good idea. Ring owners to check availability and totally confuse them by saying that we are looking to travel to Germany. Need more sleep. Proposal to be drawn up and submitted to Husband on return from work trip.

Slow cooked mince still needs freezing. Washing up still in (now cold) water.

One hour til preschool pick up. Dash to supermarket and back just in time to collect Child C.

Freeze mince, following attack of conscience in case leaving it any longer means that I poison those who eat it.

13.30 Take executive decision to give Child C's swimming class a miss this week. Legitimately allowed to do so based on the following reasons:

1. Child has already been expelled from his original swimming class for throwing too many uncontrollable tantrums in the water.

2. Child spent so long on the potty last week that we only arrived in time for the last ten minutes of the lesson.

3. Child shouted "get off" any time the teacher went near him last week.

4. Child can't swim anyway, and missing this lesson won't make the slightest bit of difference.

5. Child has a slight cold – could turn serious if we go swimming!?

6. Oh … and need to try out pancake maker so can assume role of pancake making pro for when Child A and B return from school.

Feel slightly bad that have paid already, but his health and happiness are more important, right?

Make vague attempt at doing something useful, by vacuuming lounge floor while Child C makes tower from Tupperware found lying on kitchen floor. Watched *Obsessive Compulsive Cleaners* yesterday and recall some fact about the average lounge floor harbouring more germs than the average toilet seat, so do best to get the worst up. Child C holds onto the other end of the cable shouting "pull pull pull". And Husband wonders why I "don't get much done".

14.15 Do quick practice batch of pancakes, whilst Child C watches *Dora The Explorer*, eat some to check they are OK, and spend rest of afternoon in a comatose Nutella-fuelled state, reading books to Child C whilst trying to keep my eyes open. Figure that lying on the floor and having to tense stomach muscles while he stands on my stomach counts as a form of core workout. Or he may be displacing my internal organs.

16.00 Pick up kids from school. Scoot back to car. Pop into neighbouring old people's home to let them know that a resident is wandering in their garden in a distressed state. Spend next fifteen mins trying to explain dementia to Child A and B. Child A concerned that he might be suffering from it, as he "often writes *my* instead of *me*" in class. Explain that that's not quite it. Drop in prescription request to doc, home for tea and pancakes proper. Pancakes a success, in terms of cooking, but once covered in honey, chocolate, sugar, lemon juice, pineapple and strawberries (and by this stage gone stone cold) might as well be eating cardboard. Child C declares "me no like pancakes", rejects fish fingers, and demands a fruit string for tea.

18.45 Bath, reading, bed. Child B up with "bleeding gum". Reassured that sleep will fix it and sent back to bed. Child A asks if I am tired, as has noticed that I am rubbing my eyes. He suggests that I might have the plague and that I should keep an eye out for green spots under my arms. Helpful.

19.45 Create compelling holiday proposal for when Husband gets back home tonight.

Diet Cokes: 2 (I think … may have lost count).

Chocolate: 3 bags of chocolate buttons, most of a Nutella pancake, grated chocolate leftovers.

Glasses of wine: 1.

Day Three (Wednesday)

1.57 Attend to Child C who is trying to build a K'Nex set in the dark, in his cot and can't find all the pieces.

2.01 Pick up dropped pieces off the floor.

2.04 Reassure Child C that it is time to sleep.

2.16 Help Child C find his water and a "I used the potty today" sticker that has fallen off his pyjamas.

2.33 Respond to screams of "Ma Ma, the ladybirds". Reassure Child C that there are not, and never have been, any ladybirds in his cot. Presume this outburst is thanks to Child A and B bringing home ladybirds from a walk, keeping them in a box, them escaping and Child C now having an aversion to anything even mildly spotty.

2.58 Help Child C go for a wee and advise him not to play with the singing *Thomas And Friends* book, despite his requests. Tempted to use vintage stash of Medised, which always worked beautifully on getting Child A and B back to sleep in emergencies, but alas is now banned. Child C finally relents with a heart-warming "Okay Maaaa Maaaa".

6.10 Shower.

6.20 Children burst into bedroom.

Husband cross at being served crumpets with mould on them (I didn't see it). Also cross at my expenditure on pancake machine and at my not-so-compelling holiday proposal when "meant to be saving". Duplicate breakfast made. Abandon hope of going to Guernsey.

7.25 Child A and B busy planning Fantasy Football teams. Child C sitting on toilet and asking someone to read him a book. Husband wants car de-iced. Hurriedly make sandwiches – no mould.

Kids, football bags, school bags, water bottles, scooters all in car. Forget inside out cereal boxes. Return and school run commences.

8.40 Peel Child C off other children whom he is barging with his head countless times, in the playground. Adopt carpet hold to save other unsuspecting children (Child C under one arm, head forward, legs back, leaving him free to kick and wave without causing harm to other humans). Kiss goodbye to Child A and B and scoot back to car. Let preschool know that Child C keeps prodding my boobs and mentioning "baby in Mummy's tummy" and that, just FYI, I am not pregnant.

Preschool sends note asking which days Child C will be attending in September. Feel bad signing him up for some longer day sessions, but not bad enough not to. Idealised image of lovely autumn walks, kicking through the leaves, stopping to admire nature's beauty, followed by returning home to wholesome lunch before we do some craft, and bake cookies probably not very realistic so decide to bagsy lots of days and cut down if Child C undergoes a personality transformation.

12.00 Speech therapy. Haven't done practice exercises. Feel better that another child in the waiting room is throwing books and shouting "NOOOOOO" while Child C sits nicely. Wonder whether the breastfeeding mothers waiting in clinic, are wondering what they have let themselves in for. Look fondly at newborn babies and think "what if ...", then Child C reminds me why not by climbing over the chairs in his wellies. Child C making improvements from "basically unintelligible" (less than helpful first analysis some months back) to "making some nice sounds". Child C behaves beautifully, then takes ten minutes to get in his car seat (for half of which I am forced to keep my eyes shut counting to five as part of his game, repeatedly), then gets totally worked up with following exchange:

Child C: Me have narnar snack bar cake.
Me: You had banana today?
Child C: Cake.
Me: Was it someone's birthday?
Child C: No cake today.
Me: Oh, no cake today.
Child C: Nooooo cake today.
Me: Oh, ok.
Child C: You no talk to me.
Me: Cake today, ok.
Child C: Noooooo.
Me: No cake.
Child C: Nooooo. Talk to me.
Me: I am listening to you. What do you want to say?
Child C: No cake today cake today.
Me: Yes.
Child C: No.
Me: No.
Child C: Nooooooooooo.

Conversation continues thus for three and a half miles until finally abated by arriving home and seeing some birds on the grass. He may be making "nice sounds" but I still don't have a clue what he's saying most of the time.

13.00 Home for lunch. Fried egg sarnie for me. Selection of toddler friendly delights for Child C who rejects all but a squeezy yoghurt. Allowed to eat it in the lounge in the hope that staring at the TV might make him try different food without realising it. Turn my back for one minute, resulting in need to scrape yoghurt off floor and feed to Child C. Wonder about that germs on lounge floor fact learnt yesterday and pleased I vacuumed in advance of spilt yoghurt. Also wonder how long a child can survive on such a poxy diet. Child A recently informed me, interestingly, that a human can survive for two weeks by eating the sole of their shoe. Need further clarification on whether that is the actual sole, or all the stuff stuck in the sole … or both. Either way, I'd be happy if Child C ate anything even mildly nutritious.

Read and submit gas and electricity readings. Electricity seems quite low. Gas appears huge. Think we may be powering the road. Await bill with trepidation.

Realise have failed as perfect housewife as nothing out for dinner. Grab chicken breasts from freezer, put them in sandwich bag, in a colander, over some boiled water. Worked as a student. May or may not live to see tomorrow.

Pay for school lunches and think about going to Wisley. Decide to leave it for a day when I feel stronger and Child C feels more amiable. Memories currently too raw from last visit when Child C pulled out thirty-two plant names on metal sticks before falling backwards and down two feet into a rotting plant-filled swamp, from where I had to rescue him. All children were banned from talking on the way home, which didn't stop Child A and B asking how babies were made. Gave vague response about eggs. Now both kids unaware that men involved in reproduction in any way. Oops.

16.15 Collect Child A and B from school football. Gather that Match Attax have been banned so Child B reveals he plans to start a secret trading club which will meet "behind the trees". Child A not sure whether he wants to join, or not, on account of possible trouble he might get into. Still don't understand the excitement of Match Attax ... it was never like that with *Smash Hits* stickers. If you only had half of Morten Harket's face you waited patiently til you got the other half. Or just never got it. Pains me that every discarded card around the house represents a discarded 10p.

Zip fallen off Child B's expensive winter coat, so call shop to get replacement. Make call whilst being shouted at by Child C to pull him across the hall and lounge and back again in a large plastic tub containing him and a spacehopper. Liaise with very nice man who sorts it all out and replacement immediately dispatched without further ado. Just goes to prove my theory that more expensive shops *do* have better customer service (albeit, on this occasion, rubbish zips).

Coconut and melted chocolate pancakes for pudding at tea time. Best combo yet.

19.15 Child B goes to bed with "Mum do you want to know an interesting fact? More people have been killed by coconuts in the past two years, than sharks" ... tell him we'll watch out for man-eating coconuts. "Oh and can I have the multi-coloured toenail scissors when you die?"

Child A and B want to share a room. Separated at 20.30 after too much groaning coming from the bedroom. Sent on their way. Peace restored.

Diet Cokes: 3.

Chocolate: 2 bags of chocolate buttons, some melted chocolate, half a piece of Nutella toast.

Glasses of wine: 1. Last one in the bottle. Tomorrow shall be a no-alcohol night, which is probably a good thing after reading article in trashy mag about how mums can easily become alcoholics and should have at least 2 or 3 alcohol free days per week. They haven't met my children.

Day Four (Thursday)

No early morning wake up calls. A blissful six hours uninterrupted sleep. Almost a lie-in.

World Book Day and Mums' Day at school, so take Child A, B and C to school dressed as a penguin, donkey and cow respectively. Deposit Child C with kind friend who takes him to preschool in her "cool car" (Child C's words), and spend an hour with Child B. Children tasked with creating a made up character for their own book. Marvel at teacher's patience and enthusiasm. Child B toys with idea of creating "Mr. Banana" then settles for "Super Seal" who lives "in a lake on Apple Tree Farm". I question how he gets from a lake on a farm to the sea, but that doesn't seem to be of primary concern to Child B. Not wanting to curb his enthusiasm nor his creativity we spend next hour inventing random background for aforementioned seal, and making a teeny weeny model of it in Plasticine. Child B cries when I leave. I try not to.

Next hour spent with Child A doing the same thing (I missed the rocky road session – bad planning on my part). Conclude that most seven year old boys seem very easily distracted and very willing to go off plan. Hope that Child A does not fall into that category, when I'm not around.

Home by 11.40. Quick lunch, then to preschool. Encourage Child C to play in the back garden. Keen to get everything out of the shed, but less willing to entertain himself. Play *Shopping Game* twice (he wins), *Knickerbocker Glory* twice (he cheats) and read three stories about trains.

12.45 Have broken world record for amount of potties emptied in one day – and pants changed when potty not quite reached. Not helped by Child C's assumption that he has to try to do a Number Two every time he does a Number One. Made more painful still by him wanting to save the contents of every potty to show Child A and B for when they get back from school.

Spot life-improving bikini in catalogue that I was about to chuck away in temptation-avoiding move. Ring them about one I have already taken delivery for, and need to change down a size. Hesitate when calling based on current chocolate intake. Must do exercise next week.

16.00 Collect Child A and B from after-school French. Child A has lost his Plasticine model so tears ensue as we retrace his steps to look for an alien no bigger than a child's finger nail. Model not found. Advise him that we'll make an even better one. Child B has left school with another child's rocky road cake, so advise him we'll make that too. But not tonight.

Friend of Child A's calls goodbye to Child B (who he thinks is Child A) on the way out of school. Child B blanks him. Give Child A and B brief lecture on either correcting the person who called them by the wrong name, in instances such as these or replying anyway (if it's a person of supreme authority and / or it's not worth the hassle). Not sure what the twin etiquette is on that, but conclude anything is better than ignoring people and hope my approach won't cause identity trauma in later life.

Child A and B have snacky bits tea – their favourite and my easy option. Child C has five pieces of pasta. Can only presume that he eats the whole of the preschool snack bar (though not the fruit) based on his eating issues when he returns – and the fact that the contents of his potty have to come from somewhere.

Child A and B work on their Fantasy Football teams while Child C has a bath and spends even more time on the potty. *The Three Little Pigs* read twice, *Goldilocks* once. Bedtime all round. Child C goes to bed wearing an elf hat complete with pointy ears. Still wearing it four hours later.

18.50 Read book to Child A and B. Both terrorised. Husband rings to say he is on his way home and is taking tomorrow off. He mentions that he plans to have a lie in. I smile wryly.

19.40 Husband home and opens a beer. Feels like a Friday. Husband has two more beers and falls asleep on the sofa. I wash up from dinner and pack school bags. Alas, not really Friday.

Family visiting for the weekend and Husband's birthday so must transform house into ultra-tidy welcoming environment, and defrost the cake that said "not suitable for home freezing", but I see no reason why. Google "why can't I freeze chocolate cake?" and "why does cake say not for freezing?" None the wiser.

Watch last ten mins of *DIY SOS* and am reduced to tears. Motherhood has turned my brain to mush.

23.00 Hear thumping upstairs. Child B is thumping about in his leg splits getting a drink, and complaining about feeling itchy. Google "how do I know if my child has worms?" None the wiser on that either.

Diet Cokes: 3.

Chocolate: 3 bags of chocolate buttons (but all in one sitting post-helping at school so possibly only count as 1), 2 mini Bounty bars.

Glasses of wine: 1. Wasn't meant to be drinking and out of white wine, but Husband having a beer and feel like I deserve one (apparently that's how the Mummy Alcoholism starts). No white wine, so having rosé. In March.

Day Five (Friday)

Worms are us.

Up half the night with Child B in pain. On closer inspection, and thanks to my Google research, able to conclude that he has worms. Child B fascinated to have a look. I am repulsed.

7.25 Decide to keep Child B off school, as tired and seems a bit mean to send him in if he is uncomfortable, plus, I have seen too many outbreak films to release the germs into the middle of the school. Drop off Child A, go to chemist, buy large bottle of worm medicine, go home and all take it. Child C spits it all down his front so administer extra dose hidden in chocolate milk. Sorted. Operation worm blitz has to be repeated in two weeks I gather, to attack hatching eggs. Nice.

Husband off for the day. Lots of work phone calls to sort, so Husband entertains Child B and Child C for the most part. Child C wets himself approx. ten times. Conclude that this is attention seeking for Mummy working and not being around. Feel bad.

Balance and order go out of the window as Husband at home. Noise and chaotic mayhem levels higher than recommended average.

Read that eggs from worms can end up on pyjamas, towels, sheets, in dust and on carpet … in fact anywhere. Am wishing I had special egg-vision goggles so I could see where they might be lurking. Wash sheets, favourite teddy bear and towels, and draw a line at that. Cleaners coming on Monday so that should get the rest.

Friend (without children) suggests taping up Child B's bottom so that they can't escape. Don't fancy that option so hope medicine kicks in ASAP.

14.45 Husband does school run. Child B complains that he hasn't done anything interesting all day. Quickly blow up balloons, for Husband's birthday weekend.

19.15 Kids in bed. Spend next two hours tidying for arrival of sister-in-law, her husband and children. House looks like a show home.

Diet Cokes: 3.

Chocolate: 2 bags of chocolate buttons, 1 large slice of chocolate cake.

Glasses of wine: 1 prior to visitors arriving (Husband informs me that it is rude to drink before guests arrive), and 4 (less rude ones) after their arrival.

Day Six (Saturday)

Woken at 4.18 convinced we have an intruder. Lie in dark wondering why and how they have come in through the roof. Remember that we have visitors staying upstairs and go back to sleep.

All kids up and playing by 6.30.

Take Child A and B to their swimming class. Chat to other mums about how men don't see the washing up that needs doing, the washing load which needs hanging out, nor hear the children calling out in the night. All reassured that it's same for most families.

10.00 All go, en masse, to football match. We win 8-2. Four goals scored by Child A. Child B dissolves into tears. Upon further investigation, tears due to Husband promising money for goals scored by Child A or B. That was never going to be a happy ending.

12.30 Pizza for lunch. More cake.

Sunny day so kids play in garden all afternoon. Child C develops a fever so I stay inside watching *Peppa Pig* whilst others bask in the sun. At least no need to break up disagreements from inside.

20.00 Curry for dinner. Birthday boy keen to watch a James Bond film. We all fall asleep within ten mins of the film starting. That is why I can never tell any of the Bond films apart. All merge into one once you have slept through all of them on and off. Don't dislike them. They just have a soporific effect. Or perhaps that is films and motherhood in general.

22.00 All woken by James Bond being shot at loudly by A N Other bad guy and escaping on skis* / in flash car* / off a mountain* / on a boat* (delete as applicable).

Diet Cokes: 4.

Chocolate: 2 bags of chocolate buttons, 1 large slice of chocolate cake.

Glasses of wine: Er, somewhere around 5, I'm guessing.

Day Seven (Sunday)

Husband's birthday so kids and I up early with eager anticipation. Husband less so.

Child C reads *Lift The Flap – Castles* in our bed from 5.15 crying out "Ow, ow, get off, hurts me" repeatedly. Try searching questions to determine cause of pain. Decide that it must be a urine infection, though strange that it covers the top of his leg also, and contemplate the prospect of day ahead in the out of hours doctors surgery.

Morning breaks and realise that pain is not from infection but from sunburn-like rash all the way round where Child C's pull ups were. Culprit is Child C himself who must have fiddled in the night and soaked the waistband which doesn't absorb. Day spent without trousers for the most part to let the area get some air.

Husband sort of pleased with gifts, but hard to tell with blokes. Not fussed with main present from me (iPad – ten times more expensive than anything I would have normally bought) due to excessive spending and the fact he is, I gather, "getting one at work". IPad going back to shop – along with a pair of Hunter wellies which are too big.

10.00 Stick lamb in the oven. Take Child A and B to their cricket class.

Rest of day spent in sun – after lunch and more cake.

Even get a little bit of time to relax in the sunshine. As I close my eyes, I catch a funny snippet of conversation between Child C and Child A (who Child C calls "lo lo").

Child C: Lo Lo?
[No answer]
Child C: Lo Lo?
[No answer]
Child C: You Lo Lo?
Child A: Yes.

It had never occurred to me that Child C might, at times, not be sure to which twin he was talking, and how that might be weird for him.

18.00 Visitors head home. Tidy Child A's room and find note which reads as follows:

Dear Mummy.
May I please have a packet of Match Attax

"Mummy" then crossed out and replaced with "God". Obviously thought he would have more luck asking him.

Spend next two hours tidying up for the arrival of the cleaners tomorrow.

Eat too much dinner, and go to bed feeling like Shamu.

Diet Cokes: 3.

Chocolate: 2 bags of chocolate buttons, a slice of chocolate cake and 2 scoops of Baileys ice cream.

Glasses of wine: 0. Da daaaa !!!!

Day Eight (Monday)

Deep sleep. Don't want to get up.

6.15 Get up.

Tantrum from Child C about Child B going downstairs before him. Or maybe just because someone looked at him. Banished back to cot to calm down while Child A and B have breakfast. Feel like cocktail waiter, as Child A orders Coco Pops, Shreddies and Frosties, with a cold banana Nesquik on the side. Child B opts for Mini-Weetabix, chocolate granola, Crunchy Nut Cornflakes and Cheerios, with a hot choc and a straw. Child A throws tantrum at lack of strawberry yoghurts.

Empty bin ready for bin men this morning. Bag splits and Child A spots that I had disposed of his *Beast Quest* cards. Child A distraught. Cards that smell of old beer rescued (for now).

Child C retrieved from cot.

Need to send the football goal list from Saturday to the team manager, so telephone Husband to check who scored. Instantly forget what he told me so check with Child A and B. Child B tells me that I "should have been watching rather than talking". Give stern lecture to Child B about how much I do for him, and ban him from scooting to school today, plus he has to carry all his own stuff. He has a point, but that's not the point.

8.30 Sunny school run (yay!). Children deposited without major incidents. Find dessert spoon sticking out of my pocket on way back through playground. No idea how long that's been there.

Home and continue Project Tidy Up for the cleaners.

9.45 Hide in playroom while cleaners make the house lovely again. Do some work emails and ring round to sort out returning Husband's birthday presents. In quest to carve out more me-time, and because it is sunny (and because I ate way too much chocolate cake at the weekend) decide to go for a run. Get changed and realise that have unwittingly composed garbled text to important work contact, by sitting on my phone, thus unlocking it somehow and then walking up the stairs. Delete hastily.

Feel guilty leaving the cleaners clearing up my mess. Run for approx. twelve mins. Look like I've run a marathon.

In vague attempt to avoid becoming chocolate eating, Diet Coke guzzling lazybones, search on phone for fitness apps. Find one that fits the bill and upload my run. A disappointing ninety-nine calories only for my running efforts. Set target to lose small amount of weight – the bit which equates to my muffin top – and enter food consumed. Only five hundred and forty-one calories allowed for the rest of the day. That's not even two Yorkies.

Opt to see if I can offset food choices with listing physical activity on there. Whilst "walking in a brass band" is listed, am disappointed to see that none of the following feature on the list:

- Scooting (esp while holding additional scooters or wearing rucksuck of Mummy Supplies).

- Holding child in carpet hold.

- Running after toddler in the road.

- Fetching and carrying for all members of the family – with a multiplication factor added in for number of bags and members of family.

- Carrying children to naughty step.

- Wrestling toddler into car.

- Waiting in cold playground.

- Picking up clothes from the floor.

- Stepping over items to get to other items.

- Child related stress.

"Walking carrying load of seven kilograms or small child" is on there ... will bear that in mind.

Scooting to school so put it as walking. Change it to cycling since that counts as more calories.

Have decided on two new apps of my own: *How Much My Children Owe Me* – based on broken items, lost opportunities etc. and *How Much My Children Are Ageing Me* – put in the daily events and factors and see what your real age is. Just need to come up with snappy names, some science behind it, and an app development team.

14.50 I fall off scooter on way to school. Possibly set handlebars too high, plus staring at a van. Child C narrowly avoids being squashed by a car. I recount fictitious tale of fictitious school friend who got run over by a fictitious car, and "missed school and lots of parties" in hope that it will make him stop at the road. Worked a treat with Child A and B. Child C not fussed.

29

Children home – ratty and starving. Child C insists on helping me put the wheelie bins away. Narrowly avoids being squashed by wheelie bin. Child A insists on collecting mud and bringing it inside in a margarine tub. Child A told that he will have to pay for the cleaner if I find any of the mud from the tub anywhere.

15.20 Child A, B and C all want cereal. I relent after they agree that they will stay at the table all night if necessary to ensure they eat their tea. Child A and B eat all their tea, and more. Guess they were quite hungry. Feel a bit mean.

New regime introduced to do homework early. Works beautifully, and computer time delayed until reading homework is all done.

Nose through school bags, to see if anything of interest for today. Cake sale on Thursday.

18.00 Child C in bath, Child A and B working on their Fantasy Football teams. Feel suitably bad that not doing something meaningful with them, but it's Monday and I'm tired. Plus they are being calm and peaceful … savouring it while it lasts.

Return to fitness app and enter steak and wine … That leaves me with just nine calories for the rest of my dinner. Lots of red all over my profile page indicating that I have failed in spectacular style. Must try harder.

20.15 Sit down to dinner. Trip over unemptied potty I didn't realise had been filled.

Do Tesco online shop. Wonder what the fitness app will make of bits I have ordered for girly lunch on Wednesday.

21.30 Arrgh. No clean tops for Child A and B for tomorrow.

Diet Cokes: 3.

Chocolate: 2 bags of chocolate buttons – but one was only a treat size one. Progress.

Glasses of wine: 1. Using up the rosé.

Day Nine (Tuesday)

Woken needing a wee at 4.45. Woken by Husband who can't sleep at 4.55. Woken by Child C screaming with a bad dream at 5.05. Rush to attend to Child C. He tells me to go away. So begins the *Thomas And Friends* concert.

Tesco delivery booked between 7.00 and 8.00, so up and ready for its arrival, just in case it's early. It's not. Delivery man arrives at 7.45, missing brekkie, but in time to provide fruit for Child A, B and C. Unpack cold stuff. Find eight beetroot I didn't order and don't eat. Also eight tomatoes on the vine instead of the one beef tomato I ordered. Guess we'll be eating tomatoes this week. With everything. Feel sorry for the poor person missing their eight beetroot and probably ringing Tesco customer service this very second.

Glad to drop Child C at preschool. Competing for World's Most Annoying Child this week and winning hands down. Insists on wearing a teddy bear's straw boater to school, although it doesn't fit and falls off with every breath. Insists on ultimate supremacy in the playground at all times – even up against the big kids. Insists on listening to the theme tune of *Wonder Pets* in the car on the way to preschool, even though we don't own and have never owned it. Insists on needing a red trampoline (we don't have one). All within the space of one hour. Return home and google "reform schools".

Fill rest of morning with work emails, then squeeze in quick run. Quick, as in didn't take long, not as in faster than the speed of light.

Feel bad about not tackling the mountain of laundry. Rather than free samples of washing powder and vouchers they gave in the Bounty bag at birth, I'd have rather had six washing baskets, and two washing machines. And a form to send back to get one glass of wine delivered every evening for each child that you have … a bit like the milkman.

12.00 Pick up Child C. Still going on about trampoline, but has dropped the *Wonder Pets* rant. Thank goodness.

12.30 Lunch, then take parcels to corner shop to send back poorly selected birthday presents for Husband. Child C takes ten mins to get into the car, and only gets in when I start driving off without him. He moans the whole way there that I left him behind. Manage to get Match Attax for Child A and B while in the same shop.

13.00 Home. Child C won't rest until I play with the Little People toys. Repeated game of plastic sheep getting stuck up a mountain (on back of sofa) and fire engine coming to its aid. Play game eight times before retiring on grounds of breakfast washing up. Child C not convinced and wets himself, probably in protest.

14.40 Scoot the whole way to school to fetch Child A and B. Child C falls off his scooter four times, and crushes the chocolate spread roll I had made at his request. Grump intensifies. Dodge children and adults who clearly disapprove of the scooting ability of Child C and at the seemingly carefree attitude of a parent who scoots behind.

15.20 Home for food, homework and all that.

After the usual exhausting repeated requests and processes, read *Goldilocks* at bedtime for Child C. Story time for Child A and B. Story makes me cry. Have to explain cancer to Child A and B. Child B thinks that a child in his class might have cancer "because she has red spots on her skin". Explain more likely to be eczema.

19.15 Kids in bed. Return to this morning's unpacked shopping.

19.30 Fancy chilli. Find box in freezer. Hope it is chilli, not curry.

20.00 What I thought was chilli was chicken stock. Beans on toast for dinner.

Diet Cokes: 3.

Chocolate: 2 bags of chocolate buttons, 1 line of Fruit and Nut.

Glasses of wine: 1. Still using up the rosé

Day Ten (Wednesday)

5.00 Wake up call from Child C, who is a "bit scared of the bees". Apparently "needs a scarecrow". Faffs for five mins with comfort blankets laying them just so. Leave him to chortle.

6.00 Alarm goes off. Early start as Husband needs to be in work early.

A mere nine requests to Child A and B each to put shoes on this morning while Child C jumps off the arm of the sofa shouting "walk the plank". Cold school run. Child C takes on every child in the playground. Three episodes of carpet holds (tonnes of calories burnt, no doubt). Will only leave with five sticks and then has huge strop as to whether he wants to wear his cow costume to preschool.

Old school friend over for lunch so spend late morning catching up and putting world to rights. Always reminds me that I should do more of this. Living in household of all men distorts one's view of life. In fact, maybe men should be sent on training course to learn how to understand what a woman in a male-dominated household has to endure. Have accumulated a considerable knowledge base on subjects that take up valuable brain space needed for other things … from Teddy Sheringham's Premier League goal total (one hundred and forty-six, in case you ever need to know) to the various afflictions of my sons' genitalia, and exposure to a whole host of films which were never *really* made with girls in mind, but of which every bloke knows the entire script and doesn't see why you "just don't get it".

However, despite my best efforts, the men in this house show mostly disdain for my favourite things:

- Anything from John Lewis.

- Anything pink.

- Nail varnish colours.

- Shoes.

- Practical yet classic clothing items, which wash well, and are more of an investment than a splurge.

- Worthwhile lifetime investments e.g. pancake maker.

- Practical storage solutions and cool stationery.

Not fair, surely?

Calorie counting on hold as tuck into large lunch, and very-bad-for-you-but-tastes-yum cheesecake. Can't find the tab on the fitness app where you can enter "friend round for lunch so calorie intake can be justifiably doubled for the day".

Child C spends the afternoon speaking well and weeing all over his trousers. Conclude that I can't have it all. And there was me thinking that we had the potty training thing all sewn up. Google "going backwards in potty training". According to Netmums, Huggies and host of other experts, regression is quite normal.

Email preschool and see whether Child C can start his Friday sessions a bit earlier than planned. Have master plan that we will spend afternoons doing fun activities together, if I get an extra morning to do all other mundane jobs. Will become a housewife and mother extraordinaire – all just by gaining a mere three hours (two and a half if you count the pick up, drop off and washing up from brekkie) in a day.

18.00 Tea, bed and final chapters of book for Child A and B. One of the funniest, but also the most heart-wrenching books of all time. Now finished, and I only got asked to stop crying three times. Topical discussions on cancer ("is it worse than the plague Mummy?", "how many people do you actually know who have had it?", "can children get it?"), funerals ("what goes inside the coffin, Mummy?"), hospices ("can they still give you medicine?"), and what it's like to drive past your deceased grandparents' house. Drink please.

Child A and B excited about using a telescope they received today as a late Christmas present from a friend. Don't trust them not to spy on the neighbours overnight, so confiscate it til they are asleep.

19.15 Put chicken in the oven.

19.30 Medicinal wine administered. There should be a word in the English dictionary for when children drive their parents to drink. Alcotherapy? Demonicbehaviourrewardism? Either of them would do. Alas it isn't compatible when your kids have Upwiththelarkitis.

Check emails and see that Child A and B have an away football match on Saturday, after swimming. Husband away that day so will be taking all three to Child A and B's swimming lesson. Will need to draw up battle plan and pack large range of waterproof activities to stop Child C from throwing himself / toys in the water or running off and deciding he'd rather go home.

19.45 Get roast chicken out of the oven, and remember that I was meant to be making casserole with the chicken stock from last night.

20.30 Watch documentary about poverty and my fitness regime seems rather shallow.

Diet Cokes: 3.

Chocolate: 2 treat size bags of chocolate buttons. Large slice of Millionaire Cheesecake.

Glasses of wine: 1. Last glass of the rosé.

Day Eleven (Thursday)

Deep sleep again. Have decided it may be due to my tartan pyjamas. Or Child C wearing me down into the ground. Or due to extra energy expended growing grey hairs.

Eat breakfast with curtains closed as Child C "bit scared of the fog". Totally blame *Peppa Pig and the Foggy Day* episode. Has freaked out two of my three children over the last seven years.

Child C in full Extreme-Toddler Mode. Tantrums many, varied and for nonsensical reasons:

• Mummy asks Child B to unclip the seatbelt of Child C. He kindly does so. Child C wants Mummy to unclip it.

• Mummy does not unclip the seatbelt in the correct manner.

• Child C scoots into bushes on purpose and Mummy won't pick him up.

• Child C gets up, but Mummy will not retrieve scooter from bushes (Standoff ensues with large percentage of onlookers thinking that he has lost me. Fat chance).

• Mummy does not place scooter on the "right part" of the fence, outside the playground.

• Child C wants snacks (at 8.40, just an hour after breakfast).

- Five cheerios have dirt on them from him putting them down on the playground.

- Other children speak to Child C.

- On the way to preschool (giving another child a lift today) Mummy makes the mistake of joining in with *The Wheels On The Bus* which Child C is singing.

Seriously. Working in an office brings pressures of its own, but no human should have to endure all of that in the space of forty-five minutes. Apparently Husband only threw one tantrum in his childhood. Definitely doesn't come from my side of the family, so can only presume that it is some clashing of DNA. Hope beyond hope that it results in him becoming a genius rather than a psychopath.

Children deposited and return home to comfort of a Diet Coke and chocolate. Check emails. Love the togetherness of Boden email arriving seconds after their catalogue drops through the door. Wonder whether buying more Boden clothes might automatically make my children more wholesome and smiley. Not a grumpy child or ratty mum in sight in their catalogues. Wonder where I could apply for funding for my research.

Do some work emails then decide to go for quick run. Notice considerably greater number of grey hairs on tying hair back. Always quite lucky until now, but I reckon one new grey hair a day at the mo. Mental note to work out how to tackle that one (highlights, or colour … hmmm) and must plan grey hairstyle in case in all happens v quickly … can't see me with a shampoo and set.

Pick up Child C from preschool. Teacher hands me six pairs of wet trousers and says she thinks he might have a urine infection. Great. Last week worms, this week infection. Spend next hour pumping Child C full of water, and waiting for it to pass through. Finally fills the potty. Have to fish out accompanying poo with a spoon, hope it doesn't contaminate the results, and pour into sample pot.

13.50 Turn up for "sit and wait" appointment. Starts at 14.00 but hoping that getting there early might stand us in good stead. It doesn't. Child C alternates between playing nicely with trains, and trying to make paper aeroplanes out of back issues of *The Lady*. Another mum looks on, and comments that "I'd have stopped at my daughter if I'd known what boys were like". Yep. Her son (aged four) complains that Child C is hurting his ears.

Doctor takes swabs of nose (not sure what that's going to prove) and sends off wee. Doctor asks kindly if he seems uncomfortable. I explain that he has been wiggling quite a bit and saying "get off" but that he is always playing with himself so it is hard to tell whether there is anything wrong or not. She smiles and we agree that that is just boys. No infection it seems. In that case he is just a pain in the backside. Contemplate asking doctor if they do anything for that.

14.40 Child C falls asleep in car on way home from doctor. Hurrah on the one hand. On the other, how long should I leave him to sleep? Wonder if anyone has ever worked out the formula as to child's time spent sleeping in day and how much that eats into evening sleep. Probably not, but I bet there is one.

Wake Child C to put him in buggy to collect Child A and B. Instantly hungry. Give him a fruit string. Still hungry. Root through bag and discover, amongst other things, an old packet of chips from Wimpy. Don't remember going to a Wimpy since about 1983. Child C proceeds to scream for the next thirty minutes, prompting other school children to ask Child A and B "what's wrong with your brother?" before moving as far away from him as possible. Another parent suggests I "should have brought something for him to eat". I reply that I did. Refrain from letting her know that the little sod should have eaten his lunch, which was left untouched and partly trodden into the lounge carpet, while I tried to encourage him to wee for the sample. Mystery solved as I remember that Child A and B went to a party at Wimpy about this time last year. Pretty bad bag maintenance. Even by my standards.

17.00 Tea time. Grandma rings to return my call to her earlier, when they were out. Can't talk at our end over the noise. All children so vile, I leave the room. Fighting gets louder so I return. Feel like a zookeeper. Or a referee in WWE Smackdown. Everything calms down once food has been absorbed into their bodies. No one ever warned me how horrible children become when they are hungry. Actually wonder what they eat at school. Pretty sure that they eat plenty but they come out SO starving and behave so awfully you'd think they'd never been fed. Ever. Or maybe that they'd just been fed a load of E numbers and sugar. Heaven help me when they grow up and discover alcohol. Trip over box full of craft buttons and spill all over floor. Bend down to pick them up. Child A, B and C think I've left the room again and start yelling for me.

18.00 Just when I think it can't get any more chaotic, noisy and wee-soaked, it does. At one point in the space of six minutes there are six items in the queue, as follows:

1. Child A performing his school dance – in the style of a building being burnt down by the Great Fire of London, to an Ellie Goulding song on YouTube on iPad.

2. Child C requesting to watch *Peppa Pig* on iPad rather than listen to Ellie Goulding.

3. Child B wanting to save picture he has created on the CBeebies website.

4. Child C wanting me to read him a story about Mrs. Christmas (read it once already in the bath).

5. Child B wanting to perform his robotic dance, without YouTube, but while he sings *The Popcorn song* (that der der der der der der one) – mostly over Ellie Goulding.

6. Child C wanting to switch *In The Night Garden* back on, after I presumed we weren't watching it what with everything else going on.

All at the same time. Literally. As I repeat often and loudly, there is only one Mummy and three children. How in God's name do the families on *Sixteen Kids And Counting* manage? Perhaps it's just my kids. Hearing loss or no hearing loss, I actually don't think they hear each other. Or me. Highly skilled in the art of zoning out interference in the form of any other family members talking. I can actually feel the grey hairs sprouting.

Children all dispatched to bed. Child C goes to sleep surprisingly quickly. Either actually ill or exhausted from all that crying. Just when I'm ready to crumble Child A and B try out a new formula of delaying tactics:

• Can we read more chapters of the book? (No, Mummy's had a bad day).

• I need to look for my Match Attax (You should have done it earlier).

• I think I have something in my eye.

• I only just found your note about not looking at the sun through the telescope (Great load of use that was then. Just as well it was a foggy morning).

• Can I have a hot water bottle? … I'll wait (Yes you can … and no you won't).

- When's Daddy coming home? (Late).

Then told off four times over the course of an hour for talking. Peace at last.

20.15 Dinner. Wash up. Sort school bags. Work out which school clothes can make another day.

22.33 Remember friends coming with Child C-aged children in morning for play / fighting over toys while we all moan about our children. Make Rice Krispie cakes and vacuum floor. Remind myself that apparently children don't remember a tidy house. That may be so, but they might remember a hideously untidy one.

Diet Cokes: 4.

Chocolate: 10 Minstrels, 2 large bags of chocolate buttons, 1 large bag Milky Bar Buttons, 1 chocolate Rice Krispie cake. Feel sick.

Glasses of wine: 1.5.

Day Twelve (Friday)

Alarm goes off at 4.30. Damn. Set Alarm Two instead of Alarm One on my clock.

5.00 Am sure I can hear talking. 5.10 go to investigate and find Child A and B up and playing. Tell them it is too early and to go back to bed. 5.30 hear them up again. Can't face getting up again.

On getting up properly at 6.20, advise them that I will be telling their teachers about their lack of sleep. Child A not fussed. Child B terrified. Also warn them that I will not be in a good mood today as result of them waking me up too early. Child B cross that I didn't tell them "not to get up at a time starting with a four". Nice try.

Print off document Husband needs for work trip. Sort breakfast. School run.

Washing machine repair man scheduled to be round between 9.11 and 12.11. How do they work that one out? Coming to put back on emergency door release that I inadvertently pulled off completely when wet clothes got stuck inside the machine.

Two other mum friends come round with their boys, same age as Child C. Surprisingly they play nicely. Not surprisingly they stuff their face with all the biscuits and tip all toys out all over the floor of every room. That's what having fun is all about when you're two isn't it?

Washing machine man arrives. Stays in the toilet for a suspiciously long time, fixes machine quickly and leaves.

Pop to big Sainsbury's with Child C hoping to get a few non-food bits in the trolley, which will thus go undetected on shopping bills. Whole non-food section shut for refurb. Still manage to spend over £70 on not very much. Child C runs off to try on sunglasses and promptly wets himself. Not sure what the rules are about changing children's clothes in a supermarket aisle (can't recall ever seeing it done) so tell him he'll have to stay in his clothes til we're at the car. Every passing shopper looks at him, then looks at me, as if to say "don't you realise your son has wet himself" and with an air of disgust, like he might be dripping all over the floor. He isn't.

15.00 Collect Child A, Child B and friend from school. Friend's parents in Dubai for a few days. Well jell. Home, tea and drop at Beavers. I explain that they have to wear sports kit tonight to raise money for Sport Relief. Impressed at wisdom of boys' friend who declares proudly that his mum knew to pack him sports kit "cos she just knows everything – she is a mum" – excellent training on her part. Less impressed at Child B who asks, earnestly, whether they are going to be playing games pretending to have no legs. Not quite the point. I give long explanation on poverty. Think I lose him somewhere into second sentence.

Car discussion reveals that all the girls in Child A's class think that he is their boyfriend. He is confused as to which one to pick but rules out one "for starters" as she has said "she'll just find another person to marry". Love the simplicity. I do wonder whether these girls know which twin they want to be their boyfriend. Not sure they do.

17.30 Child C bathed, and pick up Child A and B again. Child A walks into wing mirror. Nose bleed follows.

Child C now developed upset tum, and running from toilet, around in discomfort, and back to the toilet again. What next? Dispatched to bed early.

Read chapter of new book to Child A and B, while they eat and spill two bowls of dry cereal. Then bed for them too. Child B imparts useless knowledge about QPR, Swansea and Reading going up a league, and then being relegated. See ... more football knowledge I don't need but can't shake!

20.00 Sweet potato chips in the oven, one child in bed asleep already, glass of wine poured already, and TV remote allllllll to myself tonight. Small matter of two swimming kits, two football kits, directions to football match, selection of entertainment for Child C to source, and entire toy collection to clear. All in good time.

21.18 Child C mumbling upstairs. Find thermometer. Bright red and temperature of 38.6. What was I saying about whatever next?

Last week one child with worms. Yesterday suspected urine infection for a different child. Now same child has the runs and temp of 38.6. Doc instructed me to "have low tolerance threshold if he gets a temperature" (presume on the temperature rather than on his annoying behaviour). Husband in Italy for rugby. Kids meant to be swimming at 7.45 tomorrow. What's that they say about what doesn't kill you makes you stronger!?!

22.35 Called up. Child C distressed about "bugs in cot". Sheets soaked as beaker left open. Full sheets / PJs change. Now to find swimming kit. What happened to my early night?

22.30 Change into pyjamas. Momentary panic on appearance of large wart. Realise it is a Crunchy Nut Cornflake that has been lodged in my bra. Or a Frostie. Hard to tell.

Diet Cokes: 3.

Chocolate: 2 chocolate digestives, 2 large bags of chocolate buttons, licked end of knife covered in Nutella and scoffed the crumbs of the Rice Krispie cakes.

Glasses of wine: 2.

Day Thirteen
(Saturday)

5.38 Woken by Child A and B talking loudly. They do speak loudly, and our rooms are next door to each other but sound so loud I can't get back to sleep so lie there wondering whether:

1. The dividing wall is just a stud partition.

2. There is no dividing wall, just back to back fitted wardrobes.

3. Child A and B have got the wardrobe doors open thus allowing the sound to get through.

4. Child A and B are playing in their wardrobe.

5. Child A are B are playing in my wardrobe.

Figure that it could be a combination of option one and three. Still can't sleep, as their voices become more and more animated. Waiting for one to come in saying that there has been a fight. I would gladly give almost anything for a full night's sleep and to wake up naturally, rather than be woken up.

Child C still asleep, after the whole bugs in cot / temperature thing last night. Up and shower, and sneak downstairs to have breakfast before my shift begins. All goes to plan. Child C still a bit ill, but also a bit better, and all out of the door at 7.50, tripping over train track in hall as we go.

Arrive at pool and, in turning to answer question about cheating in exams from Child A, Child C escapes, slides stealth-like in the manner of a weasel, under the fence of the adjoining school playing fields and pegs it at speed to the other side. Consider whether any of the rest of us can squeeze under a one foot gap, decide against it, and after much negotiation, lure him back with some old chocolate from the bottom of my bag. Manage to survive an hour of swimming lessons without Child C jumping in the pool, or having a relapse. Mentally tick off the parts of the day we have so far encountered, and completed: 8.15 swimming lesson. Check. 8.45 swimming lesson. Check. Must be in car by 9.30. Check. Every minute is a minute survived.

10.15 Arrive at football match. Today's match is in a school playing field. I almost leap for joy on seeing a Child-C-friendly climbing frame right next to the pitch. Spend the next one and a half hours watching the match, helping Child C on the equipment, and pretending to be a troll who will eat children, for Child C and his newly acquired mates on the climbing frame.

Our team wins 8-1. Child B (who never normally scores) scores two goals, Child A (who normally scores loads) doesn't. Child A in a grump, so give lecture on being happy for other people. Endure car ride home with post-match analysis of Saint and Greavesy. Child C drops Wotsits on the car floor, and screams "stop the caaaaaaar" for the full twenty-two minute journey. I repeat several times that I can't stop the car on the motorway. Then I give up and just don't talk.

12.30 Sausages for lunch for Child A and B and me. Discussion over lunch (brought on by them singing *Oranges And Lemons*) about the Old Bailey, the role of a judge, of a jury and the defence team. Child B suggests googling "what are really bad crimes?" I suggest not.

14.00 Unpack car and repack bags for afternoon walk with friends at local National Trust property. Lovely sunny day, and all children enjoy running around in the sunshine. Child C looks for birds with his binoculars, then loses binoculars in the trees. Child A, B and friends terrorise elderly folk genuinely interested in stately houses, by kicking a ball all over the place. Lots of trees climbed. Lots of sticks collected. Happy times. Error to allow Child A and B to wear their new Boden T-shirts. The children in the catalogue do not engage in carrying large clumps of mud across areas of woodland or flipping mud pancakes. Nor do they hide in bushes so prickly that their fun loving, yet immaculate, mothers have to come and get them. Refuse to buy ice creams on the basis that it's not *that* warm.

17.00 Home and tea. Eggy bread for Child A and B. And watermelon, and yoghurt, and fruit salad, and mini Bounty, and dry cereal. Pasta for Child C, but at least he is eating something. Child C has a temperature again, so in bed on time. Story and bed for Child A and B.

Husband texts to say he is on the plane, but that he caused a twenty min delay by leaving his phone in the terminal.

18.30 Child A and B try to hyponotise each other after reading about it in a book. Child B reveals to me that Child A touched his own poo in the toilet once. Child B then reveals that he has done the same. Gross. Boys. Explain that that was probably how he got worms in the first place. He argues that he washed his hands for half an hour later. I am not reassured.

What is they say about "to fail to prepare is to prepare to fail"? Today, we took on the chaos and survived. Eight bags to unpack, three loads of washing to put on, stuff everywhere, but a happy day. Proof that with enough snacks, drinks, wipes and Calpol you can achieve anything.

20.00 Husband arrives home from airport late, comments how tired he is, asks for a drink and for his feet to be massaged.

Check on children before going to bed. Child C has spilt water all over his cot. Change sheets. Finally bed.

Diet Cokes: 2.

Chocolate: 2 large bags of chocolate buttons, 1 chocolate chip brioche (does that count?), 2 chocolate Rice Krispie cakes.

Glasses of wine: 1.

Day Fourteen (Sunday)

4.06 Woken by Child C. 4.44 woken again by Child C. Figure I'll sleep in with him to settle him. He shouts at me to go away. I do.

Child A and B up by 5.18. Both thunder in at 6.30 following a fight. All in our bed for a bit, until it becomes too uncomfortable so I take Child C downstairs, and Child A and B follow.

Take Husband a cup of tea. He has shut the door and is "having a lie in". Sometimes wonder what would happen if I didn't get up either. Idealised image of us spending Sunday mornings reading the paper while the children watch TV in our room, or play games, has not materialised. Lack of TV in bedroom may have something to do with that, but staving off for as long as poss, or Husband and children may never leave bedroom. Ever. Husband has busy week ahead at work and I totally understand that, but I would do anything to put the world on pause and just get a tiny bit more sleep. Or for someone to say "don't worry – I'll do it all this morning".

Child A and B play on computer and Child C builds a train track while I unpick and re-stitch Child C's slippers which I mangled in the washing machine. Sun is shining. All is well. Get garden toys out. Child A and B head outside. Child C too "scared of the bees" to go out. Bodes well for a great summer. Inside.

Take a shower. Husband forced out of bed by Child C shouting "wee wee poo poo" while I'm in the bathroom. Husband takes Child A and B to cricket. I get on with doing the maximum loads of washing possible to make the most of the sunshine. Def a sign of growing old that I get excited by a sunny day, for no other reason than it allows me to hang washing outside on the line.

Husband spots that I'm wearing new trousers and accuses me of spending too much. Explain that I need lightweight trousers, and that I may use them for work. He asks why I don't wear old pre-children suits for work. I launch into explanation about how one's body changes shape, and remind him that he used to say I looked like Simon Cowell in my old trousers anyway. New trousers a little tight. Excellent slimming idea. The Small Trousers, Eat Less Plan.

Ask Child C what he'd like for his birthday. He wants "a red drum and a blue cake". Locate blue cake at Asda. All red drums get awful reviews. Finally locate cheap-ish drum kit at Argos. Not red, but blue. He seems ok with that. Coming in a couple of days. A decision we may live to regret. Or he might be the next Phil Collins. A really angry one.

Ask him if he'd like to go somewhere for his birthday. He suggests seeing Mickey Mouse. We suggest seeing Thomas The Tank Engine. He suggests Thomas Land. We suggest Day Out With Thomas. Poss should have handled that a little better to manage expectations.

12.30 Child C sits at my chair at lunch and declares that he "has lots and lots of jobs to do". Do I really say it that much?

Called to assist in the garden by clearing up a headless dead bird. At same time Child C wees all over the train track on the hall floor, Child B wants me to go and get him some socks, and Child A wants to know exactly where the bird is. Remind Husband that I may spend some of his money but that I more than earn it doing jobs of the clearing up dead birds nature.

Child C plays with sand / water table most of the afternoon, others play and watch football. I get on with clearing and sorting. Spellings and maths games done. Source babysitter for parents' evening next week.

Tea and bath. Two baths for three kids required due to the amount of mud stuck onto their knees. Takes ages. Child C demands I recount *The Three Little Pigs,* four times with three ducks, two seal flips, a squirty fish and a small pot. Child B puts on a demo of how to make waves while under the water. Child A attempts to beat the world record for how long a person can stay submerged in a bath.

Running behind. Big time.

Remember washing. Bring washing in in the dark. The down-side of sunny days.

Enlist Husband's help to listen to Child A and B read in turn while I help with ukulele practice. Objective for next week is to not leave ukulele practice until 19.30 on a Sunday night.

Husband falls asleep on sofa whilst in charge of Child B and C. Child C takes himself to the toilet. Mummy required to wipe bottom. Child B amuses himself on the computer. Mummy required to enter passwords. Child C decides that now is a good time to dress up as a fire fighter. Mummy required to help with costume. All against the backdrop of Child A trying to strum *Daddy's Taking Us To The Zoo Tomorrow.* With loooooong gaps between each chord change. In fact if I had left the jobs until a chord change I could have done each one and been back in time for him to be on the next chord, come to think of it. Or maybe driven to the zoo and back.

19.40 Child C goes to bed dressed as a fire fighter, with hat and costume. Child A and B ask for a story. I explain we are forty-five mins later than we should be in bed. No story.

19.45 Come downstairs to start clearing up. Trip over section of train track and break it.

Clear kitchen. Cook dinner. Manage to wake Husband.

21.35 Coldplay's lyrics "Nobody said it would be easy" playing on repeat in my head. Husband (now awake) working on important presentation. I pack school bags, find stuff, write in homework books, iron, clear kitchen, put the fifty millionth wash on, finish Tesco shop.

22.45 Get ready for bed. Spot first grey eyebrow hair.

Notice still got mark of trousers on stomach when change for bed. Hmmm. Perhaps need to reduce chocolate intake a little.

Husband works on presentation. I fall asleep on lounge floor waiting for him to finish.

Diet Cokes: 2.

Chocolate: 2 large bags of chocolate buttons, 1 chocolate Rice Krispie cakes, 2 mini Bounty bars.

Glasses of wine: 0. Might have been better if I had.

Day Fifteen (Monday)

Monday is just too manic. Every week.

Child C wakes in the night with another nightmare, though not sure what about this time. Probably another form of insect life. Woken by chat about Peter Crouch through slightly open door at 6.12. No one else wakes up, but just special Mummy Powers ensure that light sleep doesn't exist. It's deep sleep or no sleep. Remember getting up for Child C in the night, but now can't remember if it was once, twice, or I thought I heard him once, and then realised I had dreamt it, and just got up for real once. All blurs into one.

Up, shower and dressed. Child A asks why I'm not wearing "nice trousers from yesterday". I give excuse about the weather, rather than the fact the marks have only just faded from my stomach.

Child C back to angry grumpy child. Breakfast. Husband out of the door.

8.25 Gather bags and realise that we have acquired another child's shoes. Pack them, all the bags, instruments and scooters in the car. And a torch – gripped tightly by Child C.

Child C picks heads off the daffodils in the playground while my back is turned and while other kids watch on with amazement. Tell him off. He's not fussed. Tell him just to pick green things.

Child C plays with green things he has gathered, in the car on the way to preschool.

9.05 Work emails then just enough time for a short run. IPod flat, despite it having sat in a drawer for three days doing nothing. Plug it in but never going to charge in time. Changed now, so decide it is fate, and unwrap Pilates DVD received as xmas present. Only time for a fifteen minute workout and already have some crucial reservations:

- The DVD promises weight loss. The instructor is built like a Russian shot putter.

- The DVD keeps highlighting key tips in the style of a Powerpoint presentation. Fine this once, but if I do this very often it's going to start to grate.

- The instructor refers frequently to my "powerhouse" e.g. "keep your powerhouse tight". Am guessing she means the bit where my stomach muscles used to be. Either way, just sounds silly.

- Still not sure whether I've done part of a calorie burning workout or a warm up. Not a good sign.

Look up the DVD on Amazon and it gets good reviews, so perhaps I'm jumping (or stretching) to conclusions too quickly.

Collect Child C from preschool. Back to no accidents – hurrah. Preschool leader tells me that Child C seems to have stopped biting, scratching and pushing. There is indeed hope. Stuff face before work call at 12.30, stick Child C in front of *Balamory* and take call. Finish jobs, take Tesco delivery and find a home for anything that urgently needs one. Settle down to read books with Child C. I read book. He climbs on my head. Phone rings. Go to get it and spill most of a can of Diet Coke in my lap. Soaked. New jeans and underwear required.

Struggling today with Child C's intonation which means "I like" or "I don't like". Provide him with various snacks and each time faced with similar conversation.

Child C: I like this.
Me: You like raisins?
Child C: No I liiiiiikkkke them.
Me: Okay, you don't like them.
Child C: Yes.

This or the reverse version where I wrongly think he doesn't like it.

Brings to mind some African languages or maybe it was versions of Chinese that I learnt about at university, where it's all in the way you say it to convey the meaning. Maybe he's just been born in the wrong continent, and what he has been saying for the past two years makes perfect sense in wherever he really comes from. I read about someone waking up from a head trauma speaking another language. Maybe his language changed in the trauma of birth. Or living with Child A and B. Totally feasible.

14.35 Scoot to school holding another scooter, wearing rucksack, carrying Tesco carrier bag containing snacks, beaker AND balancing a bucket on the handlebars containing a bowl of snacks without which Child C won't leave the house (neither the bucket nor without the snacks).

Child C crosses the road on his own on way home. Give brief two sentence lecture about road safety. Screams in my face.

Child C attempts to plant old conkers in the front garden, while Child A and B get out remote control cars from the box of presents that was put away from their birthday. Put tea on in the hope that all will be in bed super early tonight. Still haven't moved the pyjamas from the lounge floor where they all got dressed this morning.

Then in the space of ten minutes chaos ensues. Scissors and mini screwdrivers required to unpack and power up three remote control cars. Source batteries. Child C needs a wee. Pasta cooks too much. Leave it a bit late to put the french beans on. They end up crunchy. Child C rejects his car (one designed for younger children) on account of it being "too slow". Unpack another car (belonging to Child A). Screwdrivers. Batteries. The full works. It doesn't work.

Meanwhile discover new definition of frustration: opening remote control cars and finding that both controls work on both cars, so one twin can control the other twin's car from a distance of fifty metres away, even through walls and doors and up a flight of stairs. "Stop controlling me" … "NO … YOU stop controlling me" … echoes round the house / garden for the afternoon / evening. As if there weren't enough arguments. Computer rights removed for the evening.

Develop tummy ache from, I presume, the stress and refereeing required. Remote control cars should come with a warning about this kind of incident. Oh, or it could be from keeping my "powerhouse" tight.

17.15 Ask Child B to read a story book to me. Chooses a Mister Maker book. I explain that that is not an option. Finally settles on one. Child C grabs Mister Maker book. Shouts "My Mister Maker book. I stick it to the wall" nonsensically for the full duration of Child B's reading.

Child A reads a school book on pollution. In the course of ten minutes we cover smog, air pollution, lungs and acid rain.

Called by Child C. Stands up from potty. Potty stuck to bottom and run in to catch it before it covers the floor. Knew those beep test / shuttle runs we did at school would be useful for something. Getting to the potty ASAP, retrieving Child C from confrontational situations in the playground … all a piece of cake after the fine training on the netball courts twenty years ago. Although, come to think of it, I was second slowest in the class.

18.00 Put jacket spuds in oven.

Boys allowed computer time after an hour of "good behaviour" (it's all relative). Then bed. Assist Child B with his leg stretches while he tells me about how he is "going to go big in Liverpool this week". Presume this is in reference to Fantasy Football. Child B reads fact book to me and learns all about bar codes and money. I learn quite a lot too. Child A and B intrigued that there used to be prices on everything. Feel old.

Child A and B sharing room. I shout up to tell them to be quiet. Child A calls back "Nighty night indeed I must say". I laugh. He calls out "I like your laughing". Maybe I should laugh more often.

More chatting ensues. Not laughing anymore. Advise them to communicate by telepathy or pack it in.

20.05 Husband not yet left work. Texts to say will be late before big meeting tomorrow. Jacket spuds looking wrinkly.

Go upstairs to get some hangers for the ironing. Child A and B no longer sharing. Child A asleep in his room with all the lights on. Amazed how he sleeps like that. Mind you, could probably give it a good shot myself.

Diet Cokes: 3.

Chocolate consumed: 2 large bags of chocolate buttons, 1 large bag of Milky Bar Buttons.

Glasses of wine: 1.

Day Sixteen (Tuesday)

Birds wake me up. Put pillow over head to ignore noisy birds, and soon to be noisy children.

Child A says that his breakfast tastes funny. Always a sure sign of a temperature with him. True to form he has a slight temperature. Special workshop on at school today so um and ah about whether to send him in.

Child C wants to dress as a doctor and examine Child A. Husband rings from car to chat. I try to chat at same time as washing out water bottles, finding shoes, packing bags, and being screamed at by Child C to empty and clean out a medicine bottle so that he can administer drugs to Child A. Husband wonders why I haven't got much to say, and asks that I don't hold the phone so close when I shout at the children.

Child A seems ok after medicine (from me, not Child C). Don't want him to miss out and then perk up in an hour, and also have lots to do, so school run as normal.

Find *Toddler Taming* book while looking for socks for Child C. Decide that now might be a good time to revisit it, and take out to read. Must track down other parenting books I bought. One about bringing up boys, another about raising twins. Don't think I got past the first chapter with either. Children in question too demanding.

9.18 Return home from dropping off Child C.

9.34 School office calls to say "nothing to worry about" but that Child A has been sick. Collect very teary, weak and vulnerable child clutching sick bowl lined with a Tesco bag. Poor sod. Feel like a bad mummy for sending him to school.

Return home. Child A settles down on sofa to watch Hong Kong vs Afghanistan T20 cricket match. Can't say I knew that either of these were great cricketing nations. Turns out they're not.

Explain to Child A that I have some work to do so have to send a few emails. One hour later he enquires "how many emails *are* you sending?" Explain that this is my job. Don't think he gets it. Feel like bad mummy again for putting work before sick child.

10.14 Delivery of Child C's drum kit, and two bags of sand for the sand pit.

10.25 Delivery of books I had ordered. Quick to explain to Child A that it's not always like this. Don't want him telling Husband that delivery men call round every ten mins.

Uneventful rest of morning. Watch some of the cricket. Struggle to stay awake. Collect Child C who, on seeing Child A, insists that he also has a "tummy ache". Child C covered in orange paint, up his arms and down his legs, inside his trousers. After gentle questioning, am none the wiser as to what art activity is responsible for his orange tinge.

12.15 Having gobbled up a sharing bag of Minstrels, make healthy option of soup for lunch. Well done me.

In between tending to Child A and C, pop for a wee. Leave door open. Look up to see car I don't recognise in the drive reflected in mirror. Look again and realise that gardener is in the driveway. Close door. Doorbell rings two seconds later. Almost 100% probability that he saw everything. Mortified.

Feel sluggish all afternoon and can't decide which of the following is the key contributing factor:

- I have contracted the lurgy carried by Child A, and this is just the beginning. We are all going to catch it and we will spend ten days housebound just like the chicken pox saga the Christmas before last.

- My healthy bowl of soup (albeit with lots of bits in) for lunch was nowhere near enough to sustain me throughout the afternoon.

- Slowing the pace from the normal one hundred miles per hour, to sit with Child A has caused my engines to lose all power.

- Sleep deprivation from children / birds / going to bed too late is catching up with me.

- I have a toxin hangover from my short Pilates DVD sesh yesterday.

- Drinking wine nearly every night is causing a slow creeping attack on my organs.

- Chocolate first thing has provided a sugar high, from which I have crashed and burned.

Child A perks up a bit. Dust off my old Sega Game Gear. Lights come on but it doesn't work. Child A says it doesn't matter and that he likes "looking at things from the olden days". Google it, but can't diagnose the precise problem. Put it down to old technology not surviving modern times. Just like my broken Speak And Spell, barking dog, oinking pig, and flipping rabbit. Gutting. Little Professor is my sole survivor of a forgotten era.

Child A and C play skittles. Child C gets mad. Child A suggests he might like to do a sticker book. Search cupboard. Find *Human Body Sticker Book*. On flicking through, decide not appropriate for child with sickness bug. Could do without discussion on digestion today. Find some other sticker books in another box. Set Child A and C up with stickers. Note to self – must keep more of that sort of thing in.

Feel like I've achieved nothing today. In attempt to have actioned some points from To Do List chase up scaffolding for leaking roof and refund for Husband's birthday present. Call doctor for Child C's urine infection test results. All clear.

15.25 Friend kindly drops Child B home from school. Ask Child B, out of interest, whether he sensed Child A's illness today, like those twins you read about or see on the TV. He doesn't think he did, but mentions that he did have a sore knee just after registration this morning. I don't think that counts.

Afternoon's mission is to get them all to bed early. For their sake and mine. Get fish fingers from freezer. Find four frozen kiwi fruit in the bottom of the shopping bag. Not sure you can eat defrosted kiwi. Not sure it's worth the risk with the current health situation. Could be fatal.

Tea at 16.00, bath at 17.15. All on track. Wonder how early is too early. Vaguely remember getting them to bed by 18.10 before Child C and when Child A and B were young, but terrified that this means they will get up even earlier. If they get up much earlier, they'll be up before I go to bed.

17.35 Child A takes himself to bed. Totally unheard of. In seven years.

Child B won't stop singing *True Colours* at high volume. Keen to practice for school assembly on Friday – that and some other song that involves a rap along the lines of "give it heart, give it soul, give it all you've got" and "give it heart, give it soul, give it mind". Something like that. Not sure how that fits in with the theme of the Great Fire of London. Perhaps a mood lifter at the end.

Heart melting moment when Child C says for the first time ever "I love you". So, I did ask him "can you say, I love you?", so not sure it really counts. And it sounded more like "I love bloooo" since he rolls his tongue and sticks it out to say "you". But very sweet all the same.

School reading for Child B while Child C plays on Husband's iPad. Scary how he is picking it all up so quickly. Must buy bounce proof case. Child C makes three silly Moshling faces, while I learn about Shakepeare's son dying, and the Globe being taken down in North London and rebuilt on the South Bank. Learn something new every day.

18.30 While Child C sits pointlessly on potty since the wee has already gone in his pull ups for the night, Child B finds a spud gun he was given for his birthday (and which was put away until he could use it sensibly). Tells me that it is probably for shooting potatoes. Long explanation follows on how spud guns work i.e. scoop up potato and fire. Still think I'll find him shooting at a potato by the time the summer is out.

18.44 All children in bed. House quiet. Starving after main bulk of lunch being soup – if you ignore all the other bits I grazed on. Opt for avocado as a healthy snack, and a Diet Coke. Avocado counts as good fats, right?

18.55 Still hungry.

House possibly the messiest ever. Don't know where to start. Browse on Facebook instead. Excellent task avoidance.

Check on defrosted kiwi. Total mush.

20.14 Can't get warm. Probably the flesh eating illness taking over. And knuckles bleeding from too much hand washing. Husband late again, but put dinner on. Hope for massive energy burst tomorrow.

Diet Cokes: 3.

Chocolate: 1 sharing bag of Minstrels.

Glasses of wine: 0. Feel too much like I might be harbouring Child A's bug.

Day Seventeen
(Wednesday)

So I don't have the lurgy. Thank goodness. At least not yet. Worse thing ever being a mum and being ill, however lovely it would be to pull a sickie.

Husband can't sleep. Wakes me at 5.18 to tell me someone is playing with a remote control car on the landing. Go to investigate. Child A sent back to bed without remote control car. Accidentally hit him in the eye changing his wet pyjama top.

5.50 Child C wakes for a wee. Send him back to bed with books.

6.23 Noise of toy grabber being hit against cot sides. Jump in shower.

6.35 Retrieve Child C and grabber. He informs me he "has fixed the cot". Fantastic.

Tears from both Child A and B at breakfast. Child B comments that Child A is going to miss football, if he's not at school today. Child A says "I don't mind". No more than two minutes pass. Child A dissolves into tears saying "It's not the football, I just don't know why I feel sad". Cue crying from Child B who is sad about Child A crying and about him missing football. Hug both, and explain to Child A that when you're poorly it makes you want to cry. Remind him of the time I was last ill earlier in the year and had to spend three days in bed with Grandma and Grandpa here to help, and I wanted to cry too. He doesn't remember it. Wonder if they noticed that I wasn't there.

Decide we'll all do the school run. Peaky Child A manages toast, a bowl of cereal, and a brioche for breakfast. Think he'll live. Husband questions allowing him milk and advises that he should be following the BRAT diet. Since Child A doesn't like bananas, or apples, and is unlikely to eat rice for breakfast I had already dismissed that, and opted for the go with What He Fancies And Hope It Doesn't Come Back Up Diet. Fingers crossed.

Child C scoots to school with a Mickey Mouse umbrella, up, "to stop trees falling" on his head. Spends time waiting picking the green plants out of the school flower beds. Not quite what I meant when I told him yesterday just to pick the green stuff.

Other mums fill in the blanks as to Child A's episode yesterday. One child reports that "the teacher and the caretaker left it all day as they were arguing as to whose job it was to clear it up", and that he "splattered" another child. I am hoping that there is considerable fabrication of events on both matters.

9.23 Back home. Child A writes shopping list of things he'd like to eat today. List is comprised of mint chocolate ice cream, peanut chocolate spread, crumpets, honey and grapes. Someone is feeling better. Child A requests that we take a shopping trip prior to collecting Child C "as he can be a bit of a pain". He has a point. We go into town to get key nutritious items. Add to list of my own:

- Send back Child B's coat (which incidentally costs me more than £8 to send). Must remember to call them about refunding postage as promised. I think the bag was half full of air. Should have sat on it first before getting the lady to weigh it.

- Buy more worming medicine, now that the two weeks are up, and if there are any eggs they will be hatching round about now … just now that we've hopefully kissed goodbye to another lurgy.

- Get money out of bank that I "borrowed" from Child A and B's birthday money, and on another occasion from Child B's piggy bank to pay hairdresser.

- Get good hand cream. Fed up of knuckles splitting. Wonder at what point bad hands become a thing of the past. With nappies and sterilising when they were little, potties and wiping bottoms now, occasional housework, constant washing up and a houseful of germs, I don't think my hands will ever recover.

Child A an absolute pleasure to be around. Imagine what it would be like if he were my only child. What a happy, contented life we would all lead. He would tidy up his toys, ask to get down from the table and treat all other children with respect. Lovely to chat to him by himself, and he is really really helpful. Just shows what you can achieve when you are minus two kids for an hour. Buy Child A a football magazine. Feel obliged to buy one for Child B too, or he will ask why he didn't get one when he was off sick. Magazine comes with "free" Match Attax and blow football set. Stupid buying two of the same magazine but no other option to keep things fair. Will most probably get told off by Husband for spending money.

On way home Child A asks whether you can dye your beard.

12.00 Pick up Child C. Tries to run into the car park. Restrained by preschool leader. Throws a wobbly. Chucks grapes and rice cakes all over the car. Here we go again.

House returns to noisy, crazy state. Much as though the children frequently drive me insane, and are doing it again, it will feel very strange when the house isn't a noisy crazy madhouse. I'll become one of those people who chats to younger mothers in the supermarket and says things like "been there", "I've got three boys", "you've got your hands full", "aren't they close in age?" (to mothers of twins) or, my personal favourite – though may have to wait a while, "I've got three sons and sixteen grandchildren". And those mums will, as I do, just smile at me with a mixture of "thank you for understanding" and "you really have no idea".

Desire to interact totally waning this afternoon. Child A perfectly happy to watch anything on TV, and just wants cuddles on the sofa. Suits me just fine. Child C a total pain in the neck. Climbs over the back of the sofa repeatedly, onto our heads, then wees all over my best cushions (albeit £5 each from Sainsbury's, but it's the principle). Banish Child C to the naughty step. Voice echoes in my head about how getting cross with incontinent child only makes their fears and issues magnify tenfold, or something like that. I've done being nice, I've done being upset, I've done being cross. It's all the same to him. It comes down to the fact that if there is anything even vaguely more interesting than sitting on a potty, then he'll just go wherever.

So many jobs to do around the house, and can't do any of them. Love all the children to pieces, but today feel a bit trapped by Child C and his ways. A friend once said to me that as you have more children your patience with them decreases. So true.

13.45 Start thinking about my glass of wine this evening. Does that make me an alcoholic?

14.24 Child A has not stopped talking at me about his Fantasy Football subs for at least twenty minutes. Absolutely none of it has gone in. Trying my best to say "yes", "no", "really?" and "mmm" in all the right places. Child C on an uncharacteristic eating mission (hope it's not worms) and asks for Weetabix on spotting a box in the kitchen. Wolfs down most of that.

14.45 Child C wants more food. Trial the whole Hide Something They Do Want Under Something They Don't technique and get him to eat a banana, as well as two cookies. It works. Yay. Admittedly he takes the banana back to the kitchen first, in a huge strop and the negotiation process takes about fifteen mins but at least something vaguely healthy consumed.

Put jacket spuds in oven for dinner for Child A and B so that tea can be as seamless and easy as poss. Impressed by my forward planning. Collect Child B. Serve up spuds, with (as requested) olives and Serrano ham. That's what happens when you go shopping with seven year olds with eclectic tastes. No one eats any potato. Child A dissolves into those tears that you get when you reach the end of a long day recovering and only eats the olives. Give Child A big hug and make note to save the Serrano ham for the non-recovering people next time.

17.40 Man in driveway on a motorbike. Ask him if I can help. Says he has come to read the meter. Bit odd as I submitted the info the other week. Can only presume that means that the gas reading, which seemed rather high, must have been so high that a special man has to come out and check that I wasn't making it up.

18.30 Bath for Child C. Shower for Child A (against his will, but figure it will do him good before return to school tomorrow). And then shower for Child C (who, has already had a bath but likes the idea of a shower after seeing Child A have one). Pyjamas for all.

Reading with Child B. Child A comes in and asks to listen as he's interested in "learning more about Jack Sparrow". Point out that the book is about William Shakespeare not Jack Sparrow. Put it down to the beard in the illustrations.

Wait for Asda delivery I'm expecting between 18.00 and 20.00.

20.15 Delivery still not here. Ring call centre. Get cut off. Ring again. They promise to look into it. 20.25 They ring back. Apparently it's a new driver and it's taking him a bit longer. 20.45 Shopping arrives. Just as well I hadn't gone to bed or something. As if.

Child C's birthday cake best before date is in two and a half weeks. It is blue and says that it has all natural colours and flavours. How can that be?

Give Husband credit card bill which came and I opened earlier in the day. I pretend not to hear, from the kitchen, when he asks if it is "under £1200". Hear him reeling off names of retailers I have shopped at and "shouldn't have". Think he might be happier if I never went out. Or actually if I always went out. Then I couldn't shop online.

22.30 Sleep. Hands totally covered in new hand cream, and wearing white gloves in the style of Michael Jackson to create overnight miracle (and ensure I don't trash the sheets). Will wake up with the hands of a goddess.

Diet Cokes: 3.5.

Chocolate: 2 triangles of Toblerone, sharing bag of Minstrels.

Glasses of wine: 2 … but Husband had 3 beers so don't feel so bad.

Day Eighteen
(Thursday)

5.18 Woken by Child C hitting cot with toy hammer singing the theme tune from *Bob The Builder*. Gloves off to reveal hands not yet those of a goddess.

Child A and B spend breakfast hours encouraging Child C to say "lots and lots of jobs to do". Child C obliges. I mention that I'll have that on my gravestone. Long conversation follows about what you can put on gravestones. Child A and B fascinated that you can choose. Child A comes up with a long rant. Explain that'll cost him a load of money. Child B disappointed that it isn't free.

Husband asks where his jumper is. Explain that hole in it still needs fixing. He opts to take it anyway, so I tell him to make sure he doesn't raise his left arm. On fixing list. Along with sewing on twelve Beavers badges which have been waiting for over four months. Next time someone tells me they wish they'd had twins, they are getting my sewing pile.

Scooter standoff with Child C at school. Feel better when another mummy tells me her two year old threw a cup of tea across the lounge yesterday. Based on one of my other life mantras, "no regrets", I shan't have any when Child C starts school. Just the same as I didn't when Child A and B started. I might regret him not having a more amiable personality but not the time we spend apart.

Cajole Child C into using big (but very small) toilet at preschool. Insists on flushing it once before starting and pumping the flush after finishing. Staff come in to check that everything is ok. Result though. Despite thinking he would fall down, he didn't and he did a wee. Yay.

9.24 Get home.

Vow to only have a handful of Minstrels. Seems a shame to leave the rest. Minstrels gone. Feel sick.

Do some work. Pilates DVD. Don't feel like I've done anything. Keep remembering the reviewers saying that they lost inches. Not sure how. Order more Pilates DVDs. Justify them as cheaper than going to the leisure centre. And put them on my credit card. Husband can't be upset when I have body of a supermodel.

Take washing out of machine and put in tumble dryer. Can't decide whether I am over tumble drying the kids' clothes or whether they really are growing that much.

12.00 Collect Child C from preschool. Mention tidying up and Child C asks if he can help too. Wonders will never cease. Embark on joint tidy up of lounge. Good job as babysitter coming tonight and don't want him to be disgusted by living conditions.

Order Child A and B shorts for summer term. That'll guarantee a cold wet summer.

15.00 Collect Child A and B from school. Hearing test at hospital for Child A.

15.45 Traffic rubbish. Arrive late. Child B and C annoyed that they can't stay at home by themselves. Park car. Rush inside. Discourage Child A and B from staring at the people entering Accident and

Emergency. Do my best to answer their questions as we peg it down the corridor: "what's oncology?", "Is this our door here?" [gynaecology], "what do you think is wrong with him?" [pointing]. Scold Child C for dangling his feet from the buggy and making it drag.

15.55 Wait whilst names are called, very loudly, for the people awaiting their appointments. Strikes me as ironic that patients' names are *called* out in an audiology waiting room. Louder and louder and LOUDER. Surely there is a better way.

16.00 We are called (not too loudly). Child A is a star and sits patiently doing all the tests, only sliding down his chair towards the end. A funny mixed feeling, as always, when I can hear the beeps that he can't hear, through the headphones on his "bad" ear, which makes me feel sad, and a sense of pride that he takes it all in his stride and very rarely moans about it. Child B and Child C stay in the room with me for a little bit, entertained with a book and my phone respectively. Then Child C starts getting too noisy and fidgety so we wait outside for the test to finish.

16.45 Child A emerges. A slight deterioration from last time but not sure why. Will continue to monitor. A new funky ear mould chosen. And a reminder to look after the "good" ear. Child A looks downcast when I explain that he can't be a drill operator.

17.50 Home and tea. Cook chicken fingers for tea in hope that Child C will broaden his food tastes. Ate turkey numbers well at lunch, so as far as processed meats are going he's making progress. Can add them to the short Will Eat Menu. Not sure how much chicken is in chicken fingers. Not sure I want to look.

18.10 No one likes the chicken fingers. Child A and B tolerate them, Child C has two bites (which is impressive in itself) and then spits them out chewed up all over the table and his chair. Child A and B don't like the new pasta. Tea done in the space of ten minutes. But not quite in the way I had planned.

Lines to practice with Child B, for school performance. Try to encourage him to not jig on tiptoes while talking, in the least pressurised way possible. Don't think he knows he is doing it. Or cares.

Child C wees all over the floor. Again.

Spend twenty minutes looking for black clothes for Child A for same performance. Tries on age five T-shirt. Can just about get away with it. Weird to see how much he has grown, though seemingly mainly in the arms. Smart clothes for Child B. An easier task.

20.00 Parents evening, Proud Mummy and Daddy. Worth it all.

23.15 Remove toy hammer from Child C's cot before going to bed.

Diet Cokes: 3.

Chocolate: Line of Fruit and Nut, sharing bag of Minstrels, ¾ mini bag of buttons.

Glasses of wine: 2.

Day Nineteen (Friday)

6.10 Calls of "Mummy neeeeeed you". Ignore. 6.11 "Mummy neeeeeeed you". Investigate. Child C wants to get up. Brings three puzzles into the bathroom while I have a shower.

Newly washed jeans today. Never a good idea. Always a harsh reminder that no, I haven't lost weight, just that my old ones really needed a wash.

Blow dry my hair – as much as I can in four mins. Child A wanders in and comments on how I "might like to tackle the wash box as it's looking a bit full". Will add that to the list.

School assembly today. Child A and B make most of Husband going in late.

Breakfast for Child B. Brioche and half a bowl of cereal. Take crumpets upstairs for Husband. Breakfast for Child C. Brioche and a bowl of cereal. Breakfast for Child A. Brioche, a bowl of cereal and two crumpets. Looks like he's fully recovered. Breakfast seems easier in rotation than all together. At least that way the diners take it in turns with their requests.

Seem to have lots of time to get ready. Warn Husband that we need to leave at 8.15. Negotiate with Husband for Child B to borrow tie to wear as part of his costume.

8.15 Realise why have loads of time. Totally forgotten to make Husband's lunch. Make lunch quickly. Child C calls repeatedly

"Mummy play with meeeeeee" and gets games out of the cupboard that are too old for him. Point this out. Doesn't care.

Label bags with costumes in. Get everyone in car. To school.

Friend kindly takes Child C to preschool so don't miss any of the assembly.

Lovely assembly. Dances now make sense now in context. Even what Child A and B had described as the "instramenstrual" section makes more sense. Shed a tear at rendition of *True Colours*. Then eighty-two kids play *Mamma Mia* on the recorder. Also enough to make me shed a tear. For a different reason.

Back from performance, for coffee morning. Email from work that needs my attention. Put kettle on. Eat too many cookies. Lovely to catch up with friends. Time goes very quickly.

Collect Child C. Jumper covered in orange paint again. Resembles an Oompa Loompa. Orange tinge to his eyes. Eats lunch. Serve up same lunch as yesterday. Ate it all up yesterday. Rejects it today. Requests "choc choc" sandwiches.

13.20 Not worth starting anything new. Find Beavers uniform and don't do much. House feels quiet without Child A and B and I sort of miss them.

Play Little People with Child C. Discover that two pieces go together that I never realised went together. Child C declares "well done Mum". So lovely that his speech is coming on. Hopefully will go from strength to strength. When starting from such a low point, any progress is so encouraging. Based on the fact that Child A and B were such vile toddlers, there is hope that Child C might turn out to be a well-adjusted child in time. Hope so.

No accidents so far today. Great news. It's the small things.

14.35 Get scooters out of the car. Feel rain drops. Always school run time. Always.

Five minute journey home takes forty-five minutes.

Take it all back about missing them. All totally vile. Child B intent on kicking anything his foot comes into contact with. Not with anger. More subconscious kick in the manner of someone scoring a try or taking a free kick. Old conker, stick, balloon, school jumper, shoes. Nothing is left untouched.

16.00 Ask Child A and B to get changed for Beavers. Both resist.

Serve up tea. Child A and B don't really want it and only eat crisps, olives and a yoghurt. Child C wants crisps and a yoghurt rather than the pasta served for him.

16.20 Still sitting at table. Meant to have left for Beavers.

I eat their leftovers. Must start doing as a friend suggested, and squirt fairy liquid over it the minute they have finished, to stop me eating what's left. Not sure even that would stop me pinching a chip though.

16.25 Decide to sit on a chair until Child A and B can be bothered to put their socks and shoes on, make an attempt at putting their jumpers on and bring their woggles to me to help them put on.

16.26 Child A and B start a game of football.

16.27 Child C needs a wee.

16.35 Leave the house. Child B moans that we are going to be late. Remind him of all the reasons we are late. Mostly starting with him.

16.45 Arrive back home. Run bath for Child C. Find pyjamas which used to belong to Child A and B, but can only find the bottoms. Not sure what happened to the tops. Probably picked by Child B or too much unremovable stainage from Child A. Will probably find them when he becomes too big to wear them.

17.30 Collect Child A and B. They inform me that next week involves making a surprise for mums. Get home. Child C wets himself in the driver's seat. Declares that we need a new car. Might try that one myself. Child B trips up Child A as they enter the house. Vile state resumed. Tell them, with tears, that I don't really want to receive their surprise if they can't behave nicely the rest of the time.

Child A and B both request more food. State they should go back and eat what is left. Then feel bad that they are growing boys, and that making them eat the toasted hot cross buns that they didn't seem to want in the first place and that have now gone cold probably isn't very fair. Make toast for both.

18.00 Put Child C to bed. He is shattered and annoying everyone. First week of five days at preschool and super ratty. Fingers crossed he doesn't wake us all up at 4.00. Asleep within two milliseconds.

18.01 Pour glass of wine. Watch TV on sofa with Child A and B. Silent amends made for the craziness of the last hour.

18.38 Husband calls. Answer in a hushed voice which means "I'm putting the boys to bed and we're in the About To Go To Bed Zone". He puts on a silly voice and sounds like a ninja. He hangs up. Presume is cross with me sounding like I couldn't understand him. Call him back. No reply. Must be really cross.

18.39 Husband calls back. He isn't cross and he isn't pretending to be a ninja. All is well and he's en route. Stress fact that Child A and B are on their way to bed in a we're-nearly-in-bed-please-don't-interrupt-the-flow kind of way. Don't want Child A and B staying up for Husband, or him getting them all awake again.

18.40 Both in bed. After toilet stop, Child B setting off a neighing hobby horse outside Child C's bedroom (question why that would ever be a good idea in the circumstances – apparently he "forgot"), then trying to tell me about / demonstrate an athletic dance routine he has devised.

18.43 Child A and B asleep. That will explain vileness.

Diet Cokes: 3.

Chocolate: 2 large triple chocolate cookies.

Glasses of wine: Friday – can never be too sure. 4? 5?

Day Twenty
(Saturday)

6.04 Woken up by a fight between Child A and B. Presume peaceful compromise reached as noise subsides. Two further fights ensue. Finally give up and go to break up the altercation. Unclear who started it, and don't know who to believe.

Breakfast, manic hunt for swimming kit and Crocs. Disagreement about whose Crocs are whose, and which child owns the ones that were chewed by a fox.

7.45 Leave for swimming, with Child C in tow. Convince myself that it can't be any worse than last week, and am armed with a bag stuffed full of snacks. Watch Child A and B swim while Child C shows no interest in any of the distractions that I brought with us, and plays with the books of another child at the pool. Other kids' toys are always so much more interesting than his own.

Child A and B spend good proportion of the lesson attempting to signal / mouth to me "how long left til the end?" in an over-exaggerated fashion. Tears from Child A. Not himself. Tell them both off for staring at girls, agog, in the changing room.

9.00 Home. Change for footie. Usual wrestle with football socks. Suggest Husband goes ahead with Child A and B. Child C and I follow ten mins after. Cold. Child C sits on damp grass, complains of the cold for an hour, covered in Child A's warm coat over his legs.

12.15 Home for lunch. Child A unhappy again and throws a tantrum about the following:

- Not allowed to use the computer when lunch is being served up.

- Not impressed with menu for lunch.

- His "mean parents" won't get a him a new Build-A-Bear when we go for Child C's birthday tomorrow.

Mid-lunch Child C calls for assistance with potty. Informs me he is "talking to the poo poos". Right.

Child A and B off to a party, so wrap up birthday presents and get cards out for them to write. Child A and B disagree about who gets to choose which card and which present. Normally whoever is in the same class as the birthday child gets first pick, but birthday boy isn't in either class so choices enforced. Child B writes the card to himself "by mistake" and Child A scrawls "I hope you like your presents".

Sit and close my eyes for two seconds. Notice Husband has done the same. There should be a hierarchy for whoever had their eyes shut first.

14.45 Child A and B dropped at party. Supermarket trip for Child C and me. Child C surprises me by not being as bad as expected. Planning faux birthday for Child C tomorrow as Husband away on actual birthday so a few supplies needed. Guarantee that Child C will be totally confused and probably think it is his birthday for the next month.

16.25 Husband goes out for run. I remind him I have to leave at 16.50 to pick up Child A and B.

16.49 Husband not home.

16.50 Husband bursts through the door. Leave to collect two sugar-fuelled children who have eaten their own body weight in marshmallows, argue over party bags, proceed to play catch in the lounge, knock over my pint of orange squash all over the curtains, and blame me for leaving it on the window ledge. Am wishing today over.

19.00 Put children to bed. Embark on Pilates DVD in playroom, while Husband does high energy workout in the lounge. Hard to master my stretches surrounded by Playmobil lifeguards and bits of marble run. Husband suggests I try his high energy workout. I make feeble attempt and go back to my gentler pursuits.

20.00 Cook fish from the freezer, drink the dregs of the left over wine, and doze on the sofa.

Reflect on the fact that I'm best off drawing a line under today. Today was one of those days when Child A and B just wake up looking for a fight. Since every bad day is normally followed by a good one, tomorrow should be a corker.

Diet Cokes: 3.5.

Chocolate: 1 line of Fruit and Nut, handful of chocolate raisins.

Glasses of wine: 1 … left over flat fizz.

Day Twenty-One
(Sunday)

Woken up at 5ish. Tell Child A and B to go back to bed with the light off until something starting with a six.

6.29 Child C calls out.

Child A and B inform me that they managed to sleep in til 5.28. That doesn't start with a six.

Celebrate Child C's faux birthday. Child C happy opening pressies and reads all the cards out loud along the lines of "Dear me ... blurhgladfsdfgsdfsd birday".

Child A and B behave like buzzy bees. Want to get involved in opening everything. Remind them that it is not their birthday. They understand but do a really bad job of putting it into practice. Especially Child B who manages to annoy everyone.

Child C delighted with his drum. Repertoire includes *Twinkle Twinkle Little Star* and *Happy Birthday To Me*. Child A and B declare that "it is too loud". Funny how they don't say that when they are playing. Decide that I am immune to child noise. In fact, think that the drum and cymbal combo drowns out all the other screams and yelps. Can't hear any fighting when there is a drum being played. Marvellous.

Do spellings homework with Child A and B. Luckily, both get them quite quickly this week, though am sure they will be instantly forgotten.

10.40 Child A and B off to cricket with Husband. Peace for a bit.

10.42 Child C: It my birthday today?
Me: Well no it's on Wednesday, but we're celebrating with presents today.
Child C: [Blank look] It my birthday today?
Me: Daddy's not here on your birthday so …
Child C: [Cross look] Noooooooooo.
Me: Ok yes, it's your birthday today.

Child C totally bewildered but can see not getting anywhere with the faux birthday concept. Poor sod.

10.45 Read stories with Child C. Wants to listen to new *Gruffalo* CD on my lap. Runs away scared and wets himself hiding under the table in the kitchen. I suggest putting on new *Peppa Pig* DVD. Wants to put it in the CD player and won't hear otherwise. And won't take off rucksack he has been wearing for three hours, over the two T-shirts he also got for his birthday so that I can attach it to his scooter. My idealised image that birthday child will be happy and smiley and grateful all day is shattered and recognise it would have been much better to fully expect him to cry and be horrible all day.

12.15 Pizza and chicken nuggets for lunch. Followed by ice cream and cake. Child C only wants to eat the blue icing. Tell him that we're planning on taking him to Build-A-Bear. Shouts that he doesn't want to go. Try different ways of saying it. Still doesn't want to go. Decide to not go. Child A starts crying saying that he was looking forward to going. Explain that it's not his day and no point going if Child C is going to scream the whole way round. Child A doesn't eat much. Wonder if he's ill again. Could have more to do with waking up at a ridiculous time every morning.

Afternoon at home. Husband falls asleep on sofa. Despite Child C playing drums.

On the plus side we have time for ukulele practice. Child C watches some TV while Child A and B play cricket in the garden.

18.00 Bath and bed for three tired children. Husband plays maths game with Child A and B. Child C plays on iPad.

18.50 Bid the children goodnight and remind them not to get out of bed until the time starts with a six.

Mention to Husband about going out for the day in the hols to celebrate Child C's birthday. Complains that all I want to do is spend money.

Diet Cokes: 3.

Chocolate: 1 bag of buttons, half a sharing bag of Minstrels ... not chocolate but did have Creme Egg ice cream and cake too.

Glasses of wine: 0.

Day Twenty-Two
(Monday)

5.39 Wake up to the birds rather than the children. Progress.

6.10 Child A comes in recounting a dispute about a Match Attax card. Tell him I'll sort it in the morning.

6.20 Alarm goes off. Ignore.

6.23 Denial not an option so get up.

Walking like a woman three times my age. Presume from workout, but not sure why it has taken two days to take effect. I blame Husband's extreme workout DVD. He blames my freestyling during workout DVD. Reckons if I'd followed the instructor I'd be ok. I think I'd be dead.

6.30 Child A and B come in again. Gather they got up at 6.01. Details a bit unclear but along the lines of Child A tapping Child B on the shoulder at 6.00. Child A says he was awake. Child B says he wasn't.

Gigantic breakfast for Child A and B. Between them the following is eaten:

- Two chocolate brioches.

- Two bowls of cereal.

- One kiwi.

- One piece of honey toast.

- One soft boiled egg and sliced bread.

- One piece of watermelon.

Hope that they might build a cocoon around themselves, stay inside for two weeks, and pop, out will come two beautiful butterflies. Actually surprised that I can get their school trousers on them after that lot.

Child C keen on taking new scooter bag on his scooter to school. Contents include: two ping pong balls, a ball pit ball, a bouncy ball, a toy pig, a plastic coin, a doll sized cup, a toy bowl, a toy pepper pot, a squeaky egg, three birthday badges and a wooden whistle painted to look like Father Christmas.

By the time we leave the playground to go to preschool, the bag also contains seven rocks of varying sizes, in addition to the above. Might have lost some of the initial stuff along the way. Hard to tell. Insists on taking new bag to preschool. Explain it might get lost and he'll have to share – normally both winning arguments. Child C still not convinced and tells me he'll hide it in his basket.

Enquire as to number of people at preschool on day of Child C's birthday. There will be thirty-six children and nine staff. Or was it thirty-nine children? Either way had better cancel all plans for tomorrow for major cake making session. Since little kids only ever eat the icing anyway, am tempted to just turn up with a huge bowl of icing for them to eat and leave the cake out altogether.

9.22 Back home and mammoth tidy up continues for cleaners. Leave bleach and antibacterial spray out so that they can see I do use them. Although, in fairness, hard for them to see where.

9.30 Cleaners arrive (no doubt thinking "how has she managed to make such a mess in two weeks?") Carry on tidying then hide away in playroom to do some work emails. Not sure if they don't know I can hear them, or whether they want me to hear, but two hours later I hear the following snippet:

Cleaner: Now I know what cleaners do, I don't think I'd do it. I feel sorry for them.

Wonder if that is a reflection on the state of the house.

12.05 Collect Child C from preschool. Back for lunch. Child C switches on annoying (but strangely compulsive) penguin toy and complains he can't hear CBeebies. Five min discussion follows on the fact you need to switch off the noisy toy to hear the TV. Eventually he gets it.

Inspired by boiling egg for Child B this morning, have healthy lunch of two boiled eggs. Can't remember how many eggs a day is too many so google it. Apparently there isn't a limit. Should have had three to keep me going.

Prepare tea for this evening, which is super healthy chicken casserole. Can almost guarantee that none of the children will like it. Consider making backup and decide against it. Can't always eat what they want. Character building. Brace myself for dissent.

Get out Aquadraw for Child C – one of his birthday presents – so he can do something which doesn't involve the TV. Turn my back for one second and he unscrews the special pen, pours the

91

water all over the mat, runs to the kitchen and dumps the pen on the floor. Grabs his beaker of water and shakes that over it. Then onto something else. Other mums had recommended it on Amazon as providing hours of entertainment at home, on holiday and on the move. I reckon he maxed one minute. Perhaps he's not mature enough to draw as yet. Or ever.

Scoot to school. Can just about keep pace with Child C. Until he scoots into the road. Give lecture about getting killed. Child C just shouts "NOOOOO" repeatedly. Try different tack:

Me: If you scoot into the road your scooter might get crushed and then you won't have a scooter.
Child C: Oh. No. I see.
Me: So you have to wait for a grown-up to make sure there are no squashed scooters.
Child C: Ok maaamaaa.

Child C wants to climb tree trunk in playground and assures me he'll wait for me there. Chat to another mum. Mid conversation hear a call of "wee wee". Peg it. Just too late. Luckily find spare trousers and pants in bag, and set up travel potty, more as a chair while I change him than expecting anything more to come out. Child C proceeds to do a poo while I change his trousers. No choice but to wipe his bottom in the playground. In full view. While wiping, conclude that I've never ever seen anyone else doing this in the three years that Child A and B have been at school. Beginning to think that this kind of thing only ever happens to me. Um and ah about leaving potty bag in school bin. Decide that it will be ok if I do. Then immediately feel guilty. Too late.

Child B comes out wrapped up and complains of being really cold all afternoon. Uh oh. Doesn't eat bag of cookies I brought for snack. Double uh oh.

Get home. Rush Child B inside. Child C throws nine old conkers down the driveway. Child A has picked some grass and flowers and assures me that he just needs some mud to make a flower garden. Forbid him from bringing mud into our newly cleaned house. Attempt to explain why picked flowers won't grow in a margarine tub while taking Child B's temp. As suspected, temp of 38.2. Here we go again.

Child A claims he is starving. Eats some fruit. Asks what is for tea. Tell him. Melodrama follows.

As predicted no one likes tea. Cook it in such a hurry that forget to do any veg. Child B excused from dinner. Child A promised he can eat whatever he likes if he eats the chicken and mash, and he's allowed ketchup. Child C eats half the bowl before putting it in his mouth then letting it drop off his tongue in big balls onto the table. Child B decides he might eat something. Based on my theory of Eat What You Like When You Feel Ill (within reason) he goes for:

- Plain corn thin.

- Fruit Winder.

- Strawberries and five chocolate buttons.

- Corn thin with peanut butter.

- Dry Shreddies and Coco Pops.

He *has* to be ill, choosing that as his dinner. Let's hope that he wakes up feeling 100% in the morning. Illness today might explain his horrible behaviour yesterday. Always upon always seems to work that way.

17.20 Bath for Child C. PJs for Child A and B. Put away some of the clean washing while Child C in the bath and weed out some of the old clothes which are now too small. Feel suitably sad that no one is ever going to wear them again.

18.15 Bedtime for Child C. Wants to sleep in big bed. Fob him off with explanation that he might fall out. He buys it. Also explain that when we did take the cot sides off and put on cot bed sides he woke us all up at 4.00 and screamed the place down. He acts out screaming place down. No acting required. We all remember. Plan for him to be in a cot til he is ten.

Story time for Child A and B. Opt for reading in Child B's room as he is ill. Child A cries. After various discussions, I take them through the following options in manner of an understanding and rational mother:

1. Read in Child B's room. Child A cries.

2. Read in Child A's room. Not fair on Child B.

3. Don't read at all. Child A's suggestion when asked what he would suggest in the circumstances. When this reduces Child B to tears, he offers that "It is just a suggestion".

4. Read two pages in Child B's room, then go to Child A's room and read the same two pages to him. Rejected by both on the grounds that they only get to hear two pages.

Bet even the UN doesn't have to deal with this constant negotiation. Luckily we go for option one in the end. Child A calms a little and the pages we read are really funny so the mood is lightened.

18.30 All in bed with lights out. Hoping for recharge sleep and all healthy in the morning.

Diet Cokes: 3

Chocolate: 1 large bag of buttons, 1 dessert spoon of Nutella.

Glasses of wine: 0. Don't really feel like it. Hope I'm not pregnant.

Day Twenty-Three
(Tuesday)

Up in the night with Child B.

Fine by morning. Bit off colour, but temperature fine. Dilemma of whether to send him to school or not. Wasn't going to but seems genuinely fine. He is keen to stay home. Make it clear we won't be playing games and playing on the computer all day. Run through all the important things he might miss, whilst also trying to make it clear that if he feels like he is going to vomit then he should stay home.

8.30 Rainy school run. Can't find keys. Take spare.

Drop off kids. Call of "wee wee" from plastic playhouse in playground. Rush over. Bit too late. Child C screams at me to get in the plastic playhouse and set it up as a temporary toilet. Do so with travel potty, but can't get my body in. Other parents drop off and make their way home while my bottom protrudes out of the plastic playhouse assisting Child C through the weeing process. Change pants but used spare trousers yesterday. Must replace. Change trousers and socks in car. Totally drenched from jumping in puddles. Child C insists on keeping an umbrella up in the boot while I change him.

9.15 Home from preschool. Paperwork. Work emails. More paperwork. Print some things off. Put a wash on. Go to get some potatoes. Don't know where the time has gone.

12.30 Lunch with Child C. Tesco shop online.

Tidy playroom so that drum kit can have a home. Put a load of stuff in the garage. Wonder if the kids would notice if we just cleared half the stuff away. Problem with having seven years' worth of toys. Child C throws himself off our bed while I take sheets off to wash. Jumps in every pile of clean laundry that I have. Two baskets down, one to go.

Prepare spuds for tea so I am half organised for this evening.

14.30 Still haven't made cakes for tomorrow or ironed shirts that Husband needs for the morning. Need. More. Time.

14.52 Start preparations for pick up. Not sure what I'm going to find as far as Child B is concerned.

Looks like rain. So gloomy. Tempted to drive, though good chance will have to park further away than we live as every parent in the world will have had the same idea.

15.15 Bag. Check. Snacks. Check. Clean pants and trousers. Check.

Child C goes nuts at the idea of going in the car. Explain that it is just the car then the buggy. Still doesn't want the car. Time check. Just enough. Take buggy. Promise of biscuits once in buggy helps win that argument. Eats biscuits.

15.28 Child C falls asleep waiting for Child A and B. Stays asleep picking boys up, while I chat to another mum, come home and do reading.

16.45 The monster stirs in the vilest of bad moods. Payback for the peace of the last hour or so.

After their pestering, teach Child A and B basics of Powerpoint. Child A starts a story entitled "The penguin that didn't like the cold" and Child B works on one entitled "The three dogs and there (sic) six puppies". Both go to bed extremely excited about the bright new world that Powerpoint has given them. Ask me if I'll teach them how to do flow diagrams and add pictures.

19.05 Make cake with so many ingredients I feel like I'm on the mass catering challenge of *Masterchef*. Enough to put me off eating any of it, when it contains an entire bag of sugar. Could just buy cakes but the need to fulfil a mental image of a perfect mother (ha ha!) is stronger than the desire to just get it done. Want to look back and know that I did all I could. Even if it killed me and filled my children and their friends with too much sugar.

19.40 Husband calls. Early flight tomorrow. Must both be in bed by 21.15. Explain I'm baking cakes. Not sure how that's going to work with one cake tin and sixty million cakes to cook.

19.53 Cake one complete. Out of the tin in one piece. One down. Three more to go. Or more ... not sure how far that mixture will go.

20.02 Resemble one of those comedy chefs, covered in flour. Taste casserole sauce. Predict that Husband will say it tastes of soup.

22.15 Four cakes cooked, stacked and iced. Icing hiding a multitude of crumbliness and thin patches. Shirts ironed. Luckily managed to avoid getting any hint of chocolate on shirts.

Diet Cokes: 4.

Chocolate: 1 or 2 handfuls of Minstrels, lots of cake mixture and icing ... just to check it was ok.

Glasses of wine: 1. Helps with the cooking.

Day Twenty-Four (Wednesday)

4.40 My alarm goes off for Husband.

4.41 Husband's alarm goes off for Husband.

4.42 Remind Husband that he has a plane to catch.

Husband proceeds to get ready for the day. I drift in and out of sleep. Broken only by him blowing his nose, which is akin to a loud fog horn on the foggiest of days, with the wind carrying the sound of the fog horn in my direction.

Husband advises me that Child C is awake. No surprise there. No one could sleep through that. And with our bathroom wall being made from cardboard, or maybe crepe paper, there was no way that he was going to last.

Aware of Child A and B being up and about around 5.00. Heart sinks.

5.25 Husband bids farewell.

5.26 Go in to tell Child A and B to be quiet. They are sitting on the floor, with the lights on writing story plans for their Powerpoint projects. Not what I meant when I said "you can carry on in the morning".

5.27 Doze in and out of consciousness, feeling glum at the time they have woken up. Again.

6.00 Take shower. Then go and wish Child C a happy birthday. He is suitably confused.

Breakfast with a few cards and presents. Burst into tears at the sheer desperate tiredness. Child B accuses me of "being mean by crying". Apparently if I look sad and cry then it makes him want to cry and "that's not fair". Oh, so it's like that. Never mind that he is part of the team that ensures we all get woken at some ungodly hour nearly every day.

Child C keen to do every puzzle and play every game he is given whilst we desperately try and get ready for school run.

8.30 Kind friend gives Child C a present (child's deckchair) as we are getting out of the car. Totally loves it. Carries it to playground. Declares he's going to sit in it "all day long".

Drive to preschool with two large cakes balanced – one on passenger seat and other on the floor. Enlist help of another mum, who is just leaving, to help me carry the cakes in.

Race back home. Work emails before family arrives.

10.25 Tesco shop arrives. Delivery man glances at the hall and asks "ooh have you just got back from holiday?" No I have not. Leave shopping strewn over floor to return to later.

11.00 Grandma and Grandpa arrive.

12.00 Collect Child C from preschool. One and a half cakes left over. Might have over-catered a little then.

Lunch for grown-ups while Child C plays with bubble gun in garden. Child C in silly show off mood. Either the icing or excitement at seeing Grandma and Grandpa.

17.05 Doctor appointment. She says the mouth ulcers I'm struggling with are a virus and that she'll give me some dissolving pills to put on them. Go to chemist. Only half the prescription in stock. Take that, and will collect the rest another time.

Find something to wear for work tomorrow. Shame that the trousers which were too loose aren't anymore. Must start exercise ASAP.

22.30 Teeth cleaned etc. Put pill on my lip to dissolve. Could take a very long time and not sure that I can stretch to doing this up to four times day. That'll be the day gone.

22.46 Half-dissolved pill drops off and falls somewhere. Quick search reveals it is down my dressing gown sleeve. Phew. Reapply.

22.49 Sneeze. Pill falls off again.

22.54 Just too tired to wait any longer for it dissolve. Sleep required.

Diet Cokes: 3.

Chocolate: 1 large bag of buttons, 1 large bag of white buttons, 2 large slices of cake.

Glasses of wine: 2.

Day Twenty-Five
(Thursday)

Up countless times in the night. Child C convinced that there are worms and spiders in his cot and terrified to be in it. The hours seem to blur between the hours of midnight and 2.00 – time spent in his room, time spent in my bed, me dispatched to check for worms and spiders, discussion on how they have got out (won't have it that they weren't there in the first place), needs a wee … by the time I'm told to "go away" I'm very happy to.

5.57 Child B bursts in. Apparently Child A just threw a pencil at his head while they were drawing anti-bullying posters. Child A obviously hasn't got the message then. Send him back to bed.

6.02 Child C calls out with urgency. Go to inspect. His finger nail is falling off, from where he caught it in the door a few weeks back. It went black and now is falling off completely. Tell him I'll sort it in the morning. He takes the bait.

6.17 Call Husband to check he is up. Complain about my bad night's sleep.

Shower and put on smart clothes. Wonder whether they will last the school run. Try and remember where I put my make-up. In taking longer than normal to get ready, kids use it as an excuse to take the duvet and pillows off our bed, and use the spare ones sitting on the landing (waiting to be put away) and make a giant jumping course.

Child A on eating mission again … brioche, cereal, plum, crumpet, banana milk (yuk). Feel extra pressure for them to eat their cereal quickly today. Each delayed mouthful is a potential spanner in the train-catching works. Fight breaks out over *Where's Wally* calendar. Child A accused of "drawing half a circle" around one of the items that is on Child B's list to spot. Long argument follows which results in Child A telling Child B to ignore Mummy, and Mummy refusing to get them dressed as a result. Calendar confiscated. Lecture given on people dying and the futility (though didn't use that word) of arguing over half a circle.

7.43 Smart clothes still clean. Just.

8.14 Child A comments that he likes "my nice shoes" and that he "hasn't seen them before". Explain that I don't normally get the chance to wear boots with heels. Ever. Not to mention the fact that I am so used to wearing flats, that I feel like a man in drag when I wear heels.

8.15 Everyone in the car. Seats rearranged so that Grandma and Grandpa can fit too. Child B cries when asked to sit at the very back. Child A agrees to sit there instead.

First ones in the school playground. Child C slides down muddy bank on his bottom. Totally covered in mud. Rips plaster off sore finger. Repeatedly tries to stick head through the football goal netting. Grandma and Grandpa watch him while I deposit Child A and B. Child B left crying saying he wants to stay with me. Not sure if he's upset about me going to London for a meeting or whether it's more to do with his football team losing 13-4 in the playground. Probably the latter.

Lots of mums comment that they are not used to seeing me looking so smart. Should probably use that as excuse to smarten my attire, but practicality of rescuing child or child's belongings from any given situation more of a priority for now – and probably for the next ten years. Will become smart again when I'm forty-seven. Perhaps.

8.50 Get to preschool earlier than normal. That's what I could achieve if I had a team of helpers every day. Though could not do this every day … at least not very well.

Drop off at preschool. Teacher asks if I'm going to court. Get to station in time for early train – yay. More time to work out where I'm going when I get there. Hate that whole arrive at tube stop, can't find the road signs, stand like a tourist holding my map thing. At least now I have enough time to walk down the wrong road at least twice before finding the right one, and not arrive too late.

Train ticket costs £18.30. That's one and a half children's shoes. For a return to London. Things have changed in the last seven years.

9.18 Train arrives. Get a good spot and a discarded copy of *Metro* – result. Power up computer. Realise screen covered in dust and grime. Put to use, as a duster, the pair of toddler socks I find in my coat pocket.

9.25 Scoff chocolate buttons. Get chocolate all over my hands. Melts. Go to grab baby wipe. Damn. Emergency supply exhausted. Failing at being Office Working Mummy day one.

9.44 Forgot how crowded trains get. Soon cramped up against window with no space to move at all.

Think I must have aged twenty years in the last seven. Arrive at Victoria only to realise I should have looked at the tube map. I had been imagining that I was going to Green Park rather than St James' Park. One more change involved. Totter onto escalator like an old lady. What happened to bounding up on the left hand side wearing my trainers? Squish into carriage with two buggies in it. Children sitting there nicely. Can't imagine Child A, B or C ever sitting nicely in a buggy on the tube. Or anywhere. Maybe they teach that to young children who live in cities.

10.45 Meeting starts. All fine. Actually nice to have a few hours to meet the people I speak to on the phone and to get things sorted in person which can take a long time from long distance. And nice to have some non-child time. And eat shop-made sandwiches. No Pret for a ten mile radius at home, so a real treat.

13.30 Meeting over, do a few emails, sort a few bits. Head home. Get lost, but not as much as last time. Get train. Feet really hurt now. How do people wear heels every day? I have obviously lost the knack. Completely.

15.53 Get train. Get lost in news in the *Evening Standard*. Don't know how much later, realise that I am on totally the wrong train, and am in Surbiton. Get up to leave the train. Ask man getting on where the train is going. Woking. Arrrgh.

Jump off train. Panic. Call Grandpa to tell him to go home and not pick me up as arranged. Devise plan to go back into London and then back out again. Change platform. Quick search on phone. Can catch train to station in next town from my house instead from the platform I was on before. Peg it back just in time to get that one. Now totally paranoid that that is also the wrong train so read nothing, other than station signs. And hope that a ticket collector doesn't ask to see my ticket and charge me hundreds of pounds for having a ticket to a different station from the one towards which I am heading.

Get back. Collected fine. Adventure over. No more berating Husband when he falls asleep on the train and ends up in some random location. Seemingly a fairly easy mistake to make, even when sober.

105

16.45 Home and lovely to see everyone. Tea chaos ensues. Grandma gives puzzle books she has bought for Child A and B. Don't see them for the next hour. Child C is given a sticker book which he throws across the floor shouting "me no like that present". Ungrateful child. Then won't eat tea because he wants to do the stickers. Ungrateful and contrary.

Decide not very good at Office Working Mummy lark. Need to finish today and start afresh tomorrow in Home Mummy mode. Head not in the right place, and can't find anything. And feet still hurt.

18.45 Bath and bed and Husband home early. Child C eventually goes to sleep after long discussion about worms and spiders in his cot. Borrow Child A's lamp so that he can see that there are none there. Child A wants his lamp back and cries. Give him my lamp.

Ask Child B why he was upset when I said goodbye at school this morning. He says he doesn't like me going to London for meetings. Guess I take it for granted how much they are used to me being part of the furniture and the stability it provides. Didn't realise he even noticed I was around half of the time. Not like him at all.

19.45 Chicken korma, glass of wine and an episode of *24*. Lovely. Manage to also sew on six Beavers badges … woo hoo.

22.15 Bed.

Diet Cokes: 3 or 4 (a blur today).

Chocolate: 2 large bags of buttons, 1 slab of chocolate cake.

Glasses of wine: 1.

Day Twenty-Six
(Friday)

5.30 Call for wee wee. Sort that out. Explain not morning. Put blanket over wet patch. Make mental note to return to it later.

6.20 Alarm goes off. All is quiet. Doze.

6.25 Alarm goes off again. Just five more mins.

6.30 Alarm goes off. Still quiet but better get up. Presume that all are still asleep by some miracle. Wrong. All awake, just engrossed and quiet. Can't have it all.

Breakfast. Meltdown from Child B about his sponsorship message not being read out at school for forthcoming Trainer Trek (run round the sports field as many times as you can, and parents donate sponsorship money, with accompanying message of support). Ask what he thinks I should do. He suggests that I sponsor him again. I say that it costs money. He's surprised. Don't think that they quite get the notion of sponsoring. Promise I'll ask at the office if they could possibly read his message out … amongst all the other hundreds of messages.

Running late as can't find anything. Just not where I left it as I wasn't here yesterday. Child A complains that I have put him in Child B's trousers as they are so dirty. Find more. Notice he is also in Child B's jumper as dried snot trailing down the sleeve from yesterday and cuff badly picked, but neither has noticed so keep that one quiet.

8.40 School. Go to office. Ask about message. Child B appeased. Drop off Child A, and take Child C to preschool.

9.25 Physio appointment for Child B. Physio asks him if he's been doing his stretches (not as much as he should have been). He answers "yes". Asks how he's getting on with his splints (tries to wear them as much as possible but getting sores on his legs, and very hot in them). He answers "fine". Asks him to walk across the room in bare feet. He walks very nicely but nothing like his normal walking, on tiptoes, or clumping foot down to over-compensate for the fact he knows he walks on his tiptoes. Physio runs through a range of exercises with Child B to stretch his achilles, and strengthen his core and probably wonders what we're doing there. Have been told that it will all improve with time, as he gets taller, but that he will have to work at it, stretching as he grows. To think that the whole thing only started, in his words, "to be taller than my brother". Seventy million hours waiting in consultant clinics, orthotics clinics and physio sessions, all in the name of twin rivalry.

10.00 Head back to car and use up all my change on the hospital car park. Drop Child B back at school – he's delighted to be back for playtime.

10.30 Home. Emails. Pilates DVD. Don't think I will ever be goddess-like but feels sort of good. Feel like I could do whole thing again at end so maybe I'm doing something wrong!?!

12.30 Lunch served. Child C eats watching TV.

Occurs to me that haven't had to take the potty to Child C once today. He's gone to the toilet each time instead. Probably speaking too soon, but we do seem to be making progress. Little by little he is becoming ever so slightly less totally horribly vile. Will take some time to get back to normal standards, since he started off so vile in the first place. Tell a lie, he was ok for the first twenty-four hours of his life (apart from the bit when he got stuck and wouldn't come out), then got worse after that. Oh, maybe it was the getting stuck trauma that led to all these anger issues. Google it. Apparently "Children who have had traumatic births are more likely to be anxious or aggressive than their easy-birth counterparts". We're doomed.

13.00 Potter. Clear up from breakfast. Deliver fancy dress pirate costume to neighbour. Post letter. Child C enjoys scooting down the road. And falling off scooter on purpose. Whiles away twenty mins or so.

Play board games. Lovely that he's reaching that age.

Child C plays in the sandpit outside making cakes and pies.

14.45 Go to collect Child A and B. Child A thrilled to bits that a tooth has fallen out, and super proud of the special envelope that the school office gave him to put it in.

16.00 Serve dinner to stop Child A and B eating everything in the house. Child C picks things off his plate with "that make me sick". Eventually convinced to eat a yorkshire pudding for the first time (have tried before and failed), and some potatoes (after a toy monkey pretends to eat them). Even a tiny teeny bit of meat. Strategy working very very slowly. Starting to eat some of the bits on his plate when faced with no other alternative.

Wash up. Hear all three children playing board games we played earlier together. Breaks out into a fight approx. every three mins, but with regular refereeing, they are actually playing a proper game. Whoopeeee.

17.15 Child B asks for some popcorn. Put it on. Pull up chairs so that they can all see it popping in the microwave.

Remind Child A that he has a yoghurt in kitchen. Won't eat yoghurt in kitchen. Wants to eat it in the lounge. Not allowed to eat it in there. Says he won't bother. Wants strawberries. Can't have strawberries. Wants strawberries. Can have them if he eats his yoghurt. Won't. Repeat for forty-five mins. In which time he refuses to have a bath, and is banned from cricket practice, Beavers and a cricket match on Sunday. One tooth fallen out and he's gained the attitude of a grumpy teenager.

19.00 Husband calls to say on his way home but sat on M25. Read chapter of book to Child A (calmer now) and B.

19.23 Go to get wine from the garage. Hear Child A and B. Remind them it's not an optional bedtime. Apparently Child B is waiting for Child A to get his riddle. Tell them to guess it and then go to bed. Pronto.

19.30 Remind them that it really is bedtime. "Why?" asks Child A. Grrrrrrr.

21.10 Crisis. Realise that Child A went to bed with a note for the tooth fairy asking for a "yourow". Haven't got one. Husband hasn't got one. Got two euro piece, but that won't be any good. Options are:

1. Give two euros, and say that one is in advance.

2. Give him £1 instead and say the tooth fairy had run out.

3. Launch desperate Facebook appeal.

Opt for option three. Within minutes local friend has come to my aid. Thank goodness for Facebook at crucial moments like this.

Diet Cokes: 3.

Chocolate: 2 bags of buttons.

Glasses of wine: 2. 1 before tooth fairy incident. 1 when I got home from the currency exchange.

Day Twenty-Seven
(Saturday)

6.00 Distinctive sound of ping pong ball on plastic. Investigate. Cricket being played in Child A's bedroom. Cross face and tell them to play something quiet.

Hope that everyone will go to sleep til Morning Time (6.45). No one does. Child C starts calling out. Convince him to come into our bed. Enter Child B. Complains that Child A doesn't understand the rules of *Animal Top Trumps* (can it be that hard?). Gets into the bed. Child C gets cross about the lack of duvet. Enter Child A. Exit Mummy.

8.05 Undecided about whether to go and watch Child A and B play football today. Noisy game of cricket in the hall follows. Child C getting stressed about everything and with everyone.

8.10 Decide that staying at home is a better option. Pack bags. Make drinks. Draw map of where to go so that they are in time for 8.40 departure, as estimated by Husband. Child B disappointed that I'm not going, as last time he scored when I went to the match. Perform a good luck dance for him to bring him good fortune – cross between the Hakka, a rain dance, and the American Smooth.

8.50 Still not left.

8.52 Leave in a mad rush. Both children upset about various things. Husband stressed at Child A and B not listening. Do they ever?

8.53 Peace. Just me, Child C and an episode of *Dora The Explorer*.

8.56 Pack up the car and Child C for trip to Lidl. Out of fruit and veg and figure that Lidl will make a change and save money. Got to be quiet at this time and most sane people only just getting going. Right?

9.05 Wrong. Queue for the car park. Evidently all savvy shoppers come before 9.00. Child C refuses to get out of the car til the story CD has finished. Won't sit in the buggy in the shop, and runs round like a crazy person on an Easter treasure hunt set in a supermarket. While I look for yoghurts, he runs from aisle to aisle shouting "Look Mum. A baby chick", "over here a blue egg" and other such seasonal comments. Lidl shoppers are not amused. Can't find everything I need (no french beans, no spinach) but can't face going to another shop so abort mission and pay. Exchange pleasantries with checkout assistant about boys / men and shopping.

Child C insists on pushing the buggy all the way back to the car, endangering his own life, that of others and narrowly avoiding ruining the paintwork of a number of cars in the car park. I am weighed down with bags, so not really in the best position to negotiate. No one killed and no cars damaged so all's well that ends well.

Return home feeling suitably thrifty.

Receive goal updates from Husband via text. All doing well. Good news.

Child C and I read books, tidy the playroom, he throws books at my head, he gets told off and we get toys out of the shed.

11.15 Husband calls to say that they are en route but popping into town to get some things for Mother's Day.

11.50 All home. Lunch nearly ready.

12.10 Call Child A and B in from the garden for lunch. No sign of anyone coming in. Call again. Gather it's "next goal wins". I keep the lunch warm until they are in with washed hands. Tempted, sometimes, just to serve it up and let it sit there and see if they notice or ask why it is stone cold. Or maybe just let them cook one day and when they let me know it is ready just sit and do something else for five mins.

Conscious that lots of homework this weekend so clear up from lunch and get everything ready for Child A and B to make a start on it all. Determined not to leave it all til Sunday teatime this week ... start good habits now and all that. But at the same time, they are only seven.

Child A and Child B read well. Both delight in noticing where Roald Dahl has started sentences with "and" and "but", and complain that "you're not allowed to do that". Explain that they are right. You're not allowed. But in his style of writing (oh, and here too) you sort of are. Not sure that covers it.

Child A and B play in the garden. Child C insists on watering the waterlogged plants. And the pot plant he potted at preschool for me, already sitting in a tub of water. And then playing with the hose. And then getting every ball out of the shed. Then tipping the pot plant and water all over the kitchen floor.

15.00 Sort stuff inside. Fetch and carry. Child B smashes Husband's pint glass with a football. Fetch dustpan and brush. Child C walks mud through the house. Vacuum it up. Child A is thirsty. Carry him a drink. Put out two lots of washing.

17.10 Tea for kiddies. Sarnies all round. Child C informs me that it's my birthday tomorrow and that "there are lots and lots of teddy bears" for me. Husband gives him death stare. Had better practice surprised face in time for Mothers' Day tomorrow.

Child C insists on watching an entire episode of *Balamory* on the potty. Child A and B watch sport on TV with Husband.

17.45 Bath for Child C. Encourage Husband to tidy garden with Child A and B. No action. Encourage again. Ultimately they do a fab job. Apart from Child A kicking a Croc over the fence into neighbours' (who are on holiday) garden. Erect complex series of ladders and Husband, Child A, Child B and I take it in turns to hunt the shoe. Eventually found and ladders retrieved. Harder to do that than I'd imagined. Pleased that we found the Croc and that we didn't make the fence fall down.

Shower for Child B. Bath for Child A, who soaks entire bathroom shooting water out of a snorkel pipe. He is delighted that he has perfected his technique. Mummy less so.

Bedtime chaotic but all in bed with story read by 19.00. Clocks change tonight. So an hour less to endure tomorrow.

Squeeze in Pilates DVD. Husband shattered so opts out of a workout. Feel much better for it. Think am fast becoming a Pilates bore. Google "can Pilates make you lose weight?". Seems that it can't. Shame. Guess I might have to also do some exercise that involves getting hot.

20.30 Dinner and watch TV. Husband falls asleep on sofa. No chance of waking him.

Diet Cokes: 4.

Chocolate: ¾ bag of chocolate buttons, 1 chocolate cornflake cake, 1 mini Bounty, 3 teaspoons of Nutella, half a bag of sharing Minstrels.

Glasses of wine: 0.

Day Twenty-Eight
(Sunday)

My Grandma always used to say that she didn't believe in Mother's Day as you should be nice to your mother all year round. She had a point.

6.09 Vaguely aware of Child A and B coming in wanting to give presents. Pillow is over my head.

6.20 Husband takes the children downstairs to make breakfast. Child C screams. Hushed to a whisper with talks of "make Mummy breakfast".

6.23 More screaming.

6.24 Sense it might all go horribly wrong. Go downstairs to assist. Change Child C out of wet nappy and give him something to eat. Husband unaware of the "hungry toddler who hardly eats any tea gets more mad the longer he is left unfed even if he doesn't seem like he wants to eat" philosophy. Am informed that screaming was due to Child C wanting to run off with Child A's hand-crafted Mother's Day card.

Sit in lounge while magic is worked in the kitchen. Child A and B bring me water and juice. Child A brings me toast and marmalade as he remembers I "used to like eating it".

Spaghetti drops out of kitchen cupboard onto Husband's head. Hear Child B crying in the kitchen because he wants to cook a boiled egg. Can hear them busy making cereal. Point out that I can only eat so much, and to hold the cereal. Turns out no one knows how to cook a boiled egg. I cook four boiled eggs.

Child C still going nuts, but the rage lifts as food is absorbed.

Child A, B and C bring in presents. Teddy bears of varying sizes, from medium to humungous. Child C assumes they are all his. Fight breaks out from all sides as to who gets to hold the biggest teddy bear.

Go for shower. Shave legs. Been so long since I put plug in sink that it seizes and I can't empty sink at all.

Child A and B want to work on their stories on Powerpoint. Introduce them to clipart. Delight coupled with screams of "this computer is rubbish". Welcome to computing, kids.

Nag Child A and B to put their socks on, put their shoes on and clean their teeth. Manage to get plug out of sink with the help of a rubber glove and a knife.

10.00 Child A and B go to cricket. Child C plays on shuffle "play with me", "come with me", "sit with me" and "Grandma and Grandpa play with me". Do puzzles, read books, play chase and repeat. For an hour.

Cook spaghetti and meatballs for lunch. Child C eats nothing. Child A only eats meatballs. Child B eats most of his plateful. No one offers to wash up.

Child A and B keen to plant seeds they were given for their birthday. Ask them to wait. They don't. Child C wants to join in. Child B kindly gives him one of his sets, on proviso that I replace it.

12.45 Husband, Child A and B go and play football in the garden. Husband suggests going for a walk. I clear up and get normal Sunday bits sorted.

14.30 Head out for a country walk. Car park packed. Eventually find space. Right next to an ice cream van. Child A wants an ice cream. Tell him he can't have one. Tears and screams of "why not?". I list the reasons:

1. Didn't eat all of his lunch.

2. We have loads of ice cream at home.

3. I don't have any money with me (not strictly true – Husband has some).

4. He doesn't need one.

Both Child A and B insist that they need ice cream as soon as they get home then. Insist that it has to be after tea. Both cry. Child B says that he will just help himself. Stomp through the forest with crying children telling them that this is exactly my point about why there is no point saying nice things in cards and then acting horribly. Reach semi-compromise when I say that after tea they can have so much ice cream that they can eat it until it comes out of their noses. No more tears after that. Just grumpy faces.

Cheer up when trees to climb, branches to carry and sticks to collect.

17.00 Home in time for tea. Made by Mum. Sandwiches, crisps etc. all round.

Ukulele practice, baths for all muddy children and bed. Child B shares a room with Child A and asks Husband to read them their children's bible before bed. There is some hope then.

19.30 Husband and I embark on exercise DVDs.

20.30 Curry and TV. And Minstrels. There goes all the benefit of the DVD.

Source shoe box lid x 2 for making Easter garden at school, and money for Easter egg hunt.

Diet Cokes: 4.

Chocolate: 2 bags of buttons, half a bag of Minstrels, spoon of Nutella.

Glasses of wine: 0.

Day Twenty-Nine
(Monday)

4.44 "Weeeeee weeeee Mummy". Shoot out of bed, grab potty and Child C. Though it takes me a while so am sure that some of it goes in the nappy before I get there.

4.52 "Sticker book Mummy".

5.30 "Uh oh Mummy".

6.10 Alarm goes off.

Up for shower. Child C still quiet. Child A and B still asleep.

Child A makes an appearance at 6.50. Asks where Child B is. Appears he went to bed in Child A's room, but isn't there. On further investigation he's in his own room – fast asleep.

7.15 Child B appears. General consensus is that he must have sleep walked. Or is it slept walked? No. Sleep walked.

Child A eats loads. Child B not fussed and asks for porridge. Find some, previously used for reindeer food, at the back of the cupboard (pre-glitter, obviously) and knock up a bowl. Think he eats more jam than porridge, but at least some food in his tummy.

Child A and B get dressed into school shorts for the first time in this school year. New ones – look v smart. Growing up. Child B says it feels weird so promise he can go back to trousers tomorrow if he prefers. Child C bites my leg while pretending to be a tiger. Banished to naughty step. Hope the whole biting thing isn't going to start again, and that he was just "in character". Note to self to warn preschool.

9.15 Do a few emails. Ignore washing up. Go for run and take post to postbox, and prescription request to doctor. Feel super efficient. Home and energised, do ten mins Pilates. Wash up from breakfast.

11.43 Eat left over curry. Had better brush teeth before collect Child C from preschool.

Collect Child C without incident. Other than him taking an age to get in the car. "This chair too hard, this chair too soft" scenario acted out until he finds a car seat which takes his fancy.

TV, lunch, games and stories. Manages to not go for a wee the whole time from pick up to when I make him sit on the potty just before we leave for the school run. Am wondering whether my comments of "ooh that's as big as Daddy's wee wees" have sent a message that you should hold on til you do a huuuuuuge wee. Seems to be going that way. Backed up by him sticking his head in the potty when he goes go and saying "what's that wee wee?" until we decide how big it is on the scale. Not sure how to reverse that.

14.45 Scoot to school. Turn my back on Child C to lock front door. Turn back. He has crossed the road and is scooting off into the distance. Call out to him. He abandons scooter and dives into nearest garden vegetation to hide from being told off. Track him down. Tell him off. Threaten that next time he'll be strapped in the buggy. Not sure he gets it or is that bothered.

School run horrid. In the course of fifteen minutes Child C:

- Refuses to leave school gates open (crushing mothers trying to get to school).

- Gets pulled along path to school by gripping my leg and shouting "stoooppppppp".

- Refuses to hang up scooter at school gates, where they have to be left.

- Limbos under the Do Not Enter tape surrounding unsafe trees singing "limbo limbo limbo ... I did it" again and again.

- Tussles with six other children in one go, all of whom want to shut the windows on the playhouse, which he is inside – intent on opening the windows.

- Forces me to walk a hundred yards sideways, again gripping my leg, so that I can make progress through the playground. Mothers ask if I have invented a new crab walk.

- Scoots round a corner, straight into Child B, who accidentally knocks him off and scoots over his fingers causing Child C to sustain a blood injury.

Another mum / childminder comments midway through the above that "it's boys" and intimates that not all children are like that. Really? Do some come when you call? Do some not throw a tantrum every other time they speak? Are some eager to please? Perhaps it's all to do with the gene pool. Or drinking too much Diet Coke / eating too much broccoli in pregnancy.

Strops continue through teatime (as does Child C's bladder control). Serve up pasta with bolognaise. Child C refuses it three times and takes it back to the sink each time. Finally (after much repetition of "that's all you're having", "try and beat your brothers", and "I'll do a funny dance") he gives in and eats half a bowl. Result. Child A and B eat well, talk about football (might as well be Swahili) and are back on the computer within twenty mins. Do reading, bath and all to bed.

Clocks changed last night so much lighter than we're all used to. Had forgotten how much of a difference it makes at bedtime. No one (apart from me) is convinced that it is bedtime.

19.00 Plan for right now and evening: Pilates, wine and a burger. Best known cure for the common cold as devised by me right now.

Pilates – Clears airways.
Wine – Little of what you fancy does you good. And I deserve it.
Burger – As per wine. Iron or something in red meat. Done in the George Foreman so healthy option. Will have salad – that's good for me.

19.30 Workout complete. Interrupted only by Child A who picked his nose and started a nose bleed. Bleeding stopped. Workout completed. Don't actually feel like I have done much, but everything hurt while I was doing it, so that counts. Wine in hand.

19.45 Husband calls. Says I sound so full of cold he can feel himself getting ill and that one of us will have to sleep in the spare room. Finish call. Drink rest of wine so that can't be in trouble for boozing with a cold. Put furniture back so also doesn't know I've been exercising with a cold.

Diet Cokes: 3.

Chocolate: 2 bags of buttons.

Glasses of wine: 1.

Day Thirty (Tuesday)

Master plan didn't work. Up at 3.00 with fever and really really really sore throat. Lie there for a bit, then figure I'd better get something for it. Would give anything for someone else to go downstairs and get it for me but Husband asleep in spare room. Probably just as well. Paracetamol and throat sweet later, a bit more human and back to sleep.

6.20 Alarm goes off. Take shower. Attend to Child C who is calling out. Say good morning to Child A and B. Go to wake Husband. Child C finds some paperclips and insists on me showing him how to use them. Then he brings seven Care Bears, twenty-five paper clips, six small boxes and two little teddies on teeny bikes down from the spare room before I am allowed to go anywhere.

Make breakfast. Point out that don't feel well so need everyone to be nice today. Child A immediately throws strop about there being no forest fruit yoghurts.

Foggy school run. Child C gets knocked down by a tyre being rolled by another child in the playground, then caught in the crossfire of a play fight, and knocked down again. Then disappears. Say goodbye to Child A and B. Find Child C waiting by his scooter. At least he's waiting I guess. Car and preschool.

Home and back to bed, just to try and feel a bit better. Wake up two hours later. Breakfast stuff still on the table, naff all achieved, and could really do with not collecting Child C. There really should be a national drop off service, or help service or just a pause button, or a wild card which makes your kids angelic for the day while you are poorly.

Spend remainder of day like the person from the cold relief medicine ads. Comatose, surrounded by tissues, wishing I was under a duvet. Waiting for bedtime. Ask children to be nice to me at pickup. Child B is pretty good. Child A throws tantrum about me not bringing scooter. Then not being allowed ice cream before dinner. Then about fact I am cooking broccoli – apparently he had that for lunch.

Cook tea. All head out to garden. Child A and B run round the garden (very surprised they don't vomit) "training for Trainer Trek" later in the week. Child C amuses himself with the croquet set. Toys everywhere. Mud all over the carpet. Past caring. Roll on 18.30.

No bath, just bed. All kids dispatched. Husband home. Cook tea. Would much rather have someone to cook it for me. Eat. In bed by 20.00. Husband retires to different room so he doesn't catch my lurgy and asks me to set my alarm for 4.58 so I can make sure he is up for his flight. Leave all washing up for tomorrow. Just want to be in bed. Being ill and a mum sucks.

Diet Cokes: 2.

Chocolate: 1 bag of buttons, 1 triangle of Toblerone.

Glasses of wine: 0.

Day Thirty-One
(Wednesday)

4.58 Alarm goes off.

5.00 Go to check that Husband is up for flight.

5.01 Back to bed.

5.39 Hear Child A shutting his door.

6.02 Can hear Child C. Only a matter of time before he starts calling, so get up. Feel bit better. Not 100% but bit better. Weigh in pre-shower on the basis that being ill will have made me lose weight. Theory disproved. Now one kg heavier than I was. Based on recent exercise and fever, this seems totally unfair.

Have to find footie kit x 2, yoghurt pot x 1, mufti x 1 and all other school stuff for today. Child A annoyed about there being no "cosy socks". Oh, and wash up all the pots and pans and plates that I didn't feel like touching last night. House looks like we have been burgled.

8.12 Scaffolding people and builders arrive to look at leaking roof.

8.15 Leave for school.

Get to school in good time, for a change. Top parking spot which means no roads to cross on return to car which means that Child C has less chance of killing himself. Another mum asks if we can take her child in. As soon as she is gone child says that he wants to be taken in by a different mum as he'd rather go in with her son. Child C trips in playground. Knocks head on large wooden train. Big blue bump on head. It's ok when the bump shows isn't it? I'm sure it's when there is no bump it's time to worry.

Child A and B kissed goodbye. Preschool run. Admire tadpoles in fish tank in the playground. Note request on tank for more pond weed. Gather from preschool leader that last year they didn't have enough to eat and ate each other. Eugh.

Write in accident book about bump on head. Notice that one of his mates has an accident logged in the book for a bruise to the face at local National Trust toilets. At least Child C isn't the only one. Feel reassured further when mother of aforementioned child recounts how he locked himself and the keys in the car this morning. Husband had to be called back from work to free him. Maybe my day hasn't started so badly.

9.17 Home. Make tea for brickies. And biscuits.

Spend morning sorting out paperwork and finances. Takes ages and feel like I've achieved nothing. Google "secrets of tidy people" and waste time reading how the tidy folk live.

11.45 Make more tea. More biscuits.

12.00 Collect Child C. Throws strop about wanting to bring home picture. Ask teacher. Apparently it was part of a collage that is going on the wall. Try to explain. He doesn't get it. Explain again. And again. Not making progress. Use distraction and move onto something else.

12.30 More tea and biscuits. Entire pack of biscuits gone now. How can they drink that much tea and not need to use the toilet? Hope they are not going in the bushes.

Lunch for Child C.

14.00 Might as well get out of the house and Child C needs a haircut, so he scoots to the hairdresser and I jog to keep up. Hairdresser looks bored, watching a violent action film on the huge TV on the wall. Makes no attempt to change the channel and wonders why Child C won't keep his head still. Mutters something about "Not changing it to CBeebies" and "Gonna cut your ear off if you don't stay in one place". Zero out of ten for customer service.

Child C opts to walk / jog home so that he can eat the lolly he got at the hairdressers.

Do some puzzles, get some online clothes bits we need while being shouted at by Child C for not doing more puzzles.

16.15 Collect Child A and B from football. Snacky tea. Child A and B bicker non-stop about the game of cricket they are playing in the hall. Tell them not to play with each other. Carry on playing with each other. Carry on bickering. Something about them that's reminiscent of really strong magnets. Pulled together uncontrollably sometimes, and then other times, have that repelling force between them that means that they can't settle next to each other in any way.

17.15 Start the bath process.

18.30 Bath process ends. All three children are clean (as much as muddy bath water allows). Husband arrives home early. Child A, B and C delighted. Chaos ensues. Hot, excited children finally settle later than planned.

20.00 Dinner for us. Early night out the window, as Husband wants to go through paperwork and finances. Inwardly groan.

Know that we have to do it, and important and all that but not my ideal way of spending the evening.

22.00 Bed. Hurrah.

Diet Cokes: 3.

Chocolate: 1 line of Dairy Milk, 1 packet of buttons.

Glasses of wine: 1.

Day Thirty-Two
(Thursday)

3.33 (I think, though not sure if the clock I was reading has been changed to summer time yet) Child C calls out. Ignore him. Calls louder. Wants teddy. Retrieve teddy. Wrong teddy. Retrieve another one. Sorted. Back to bed.

6.20 Alarm goes off. Put on doze.

6.22 Child C calls "wee weeeeeeee" at full volume. Peg it but there too late. Sheets and PJs all wet. Up and changed. Not interested in waiting in cot while I have shower, so plonk in bed with Husband and stack of books.

Get all family members fed and ready for the day. Child C utterly vile on school run … leg clinging, wailing, the full repertoire. Hope beyond hope that this all stops some time soon. Feel like never get a proper chance to speak to Child A and B. While I wait in the playground he runs approx. two hundred metres back to the school field. At what point will he realise that he is not invincible?

Dad's Day and Trainer Trek at school today. Husband unable to make it, much to his disappointment and that of Child A and B. Explain to teachers at drop off. Say that they'll look out for Child A and B. Gladly drop Child C at preschool. Only today and tomorrow then I've got two whole weeks of him being a giant pain in the backside.

Change out of summer cropped trousers and back into jeans. Sun not come out and getting cold. Wishful thinking on my part.

Try on few bits that I had ordered last week and which I hadn't had the chance to try as yet. Pair of cropped trousers in brown not as flattering as the black ones so package up to send back. Feel suitably virtuous at getting money back. Hope that the parcel will fit in standard postbox rather than have to suffer the pain of queuing in the post office. Way too many tempting toys at perfect eye level for young children. Too alluring to not touch, but guaranteed to incur the wrath of the lady who works there if you do. None of which is helped by my tendency to get followed in shops anyway. Possibly due to wearing a rucksack. Or having noisy children. Or a buggy full of stuff. But extremely off putting to be glared at for a crime which has never been committed. My children and I have never committed an act of shoplifting … oh, apart from a packet of Boursin once in Tesco, hidden under a re-useable bag, which I didn't see on unpacking and didn't see til we got to the car.

9.50 Do some emails and paperwork bits. Try to get everything in order. Mammoth job. Book up tickets for Day Out With Thomas. Now to teach Child C to sit still for long enough to ride on a train so that Husband is not proved right in saying that he is too young.

11.18 Must put sheets on to wash.

Strip cot, grab other washing. Armful of wet washing still in machine from yesterday. Nose blocked so can't tell if it smells damp. Wash again or tumble dry? Bit of space so will wash again. One day I will be organised, and tidy, and run a house with seamless efficiency. Just not today.

11.25 Have most out-of-character overwhelming compulsion to watch rubbish daytime TV before picking up Child C. Either very ill indeed, or stems from knowledge that kids will be at home for two weeks. Make comfort food lunch. Watch *This Morning*. Listen to piece about having breast implants removed and one about being stalked and wonder if this is really what the world has become. Realise not washed up from breakfast, or unloaded dishwasher. Arrgh.

12.15 Arrive home from preschool run. Need to head out again in twenty mins in time to get to school for Child A and B's Trainer Trek. Make quick packed lunch for Child C. Put him on the potty, then in the car, grab mini deckchair, lunch, drink, bag and go. Have to park so far away that might as well have walked. Child C in buggy, with some negotiation. Load up buggy with selection of paraphernalia and set off at quick tempo.

13.00 Trainer Trek begins. Child A and B alternate between sprinting like their lives depend on it and a walk. Lots of very hot children. Lots of very pink-faced girls walking and chatting. That would have been me when I was seven. Child C happy sitting in deckchair eating sarnies for a while. Then decides to run the course. I follow in hot pursuit. Child C and friend opt to play in the car park (while I cheer on Child A) then in the nettles (while I cheer on Child B). Child C and friend then set off round the running course in the opposite direction to eighty-five children. I follow. Numerous accidents narrowly avoided, while children shout out to me "Did you know your little boy is running the wrong way?" I smile through gritted teeth, and answer "Yes, thank you very much", as I pant after him.

Trainer Trek comes to an end. Collect Child A and B from their classrooms. Child C wants to eat all their Easter eggs. Strop follows. Child A and B cross that car parked so far away. Child C claims that Child B pushed him over in the car. Child B claims that Child A hit him. So begins the holiday.

14.30 Home. All three children want to eat chocolate and play on electronic devices. End up with Child A on phone, Child B on laptop and Child C randomly tapping iPad. In the space of fifteen minutes we have become the family I said we'd never be. Point out loudly that it will not be like this every day in the holidays. Today is an exception.

Child A and B start banging on about "How many ticks have we got on our reward chart?", and "When will we get Match Attax?" "I'll see" is the response. The holiday pestering has commenced.

Start thinking of things we might be able to do in the holidays, in order to provide wholesome low cost days out. Suggest to kids that we go on a train tomorrow afternoon. Child C says he will only go if he can drive the train. He might be disappointed.

16.45 Tea for all. Child B throws tantrum about not having an ice cream when he got in from school. He had asked. But at school. Nearly three hours ago. Point out that he should have asked when he got in. Tears. Shouting and attitude. Tick removed from reward chart. More tears. Wails about the injustice of not earning Match Attax. Child C rejects dinner and takes it to the sink. Twice. Then hears mention of ice cream. Point out that he has to eat tea. Makes a stab at it, but more on floor than in his stomach. Eating improves once he rearranges chairs to make a bus, which I have to drive. Soon loses interest. Bowl drops on floor.

Child A and B eventually given ice cream after meal eaten. Tears stop.

17.20 Bath for Child C. Mixture of snot, PVA glue (I think), chocolate spread and God-knows-what-else on his face. A good bath should sort that out. Go to put sheets back on my bed. In that time fills the bath up to his shoulders with cold water. Refuses to turn the tap off. Puts on goggles and attempts swimming. Remove Child C from bath.

PJs for Child A and B. Up to bed. Fight follows over Child B wearing Child A's pyjama top by mistake. Match Attax banned for everyone. Bed.

21.55 Should be in bed. Instead, printing off a load of mazes, puzzles and other printables to keep children away from computer for more than five minutes tomorrow.

Diet Cokes: 4.

Chocolate: 3 bags of buttons, 1 line of Fruit and Nut … make that 2.

Glasses of wine: 0. Tempted by the bottle of pink fizz in the fridge but body says "no", and I figure I should probably listen to that. Besides, all the calories from chocolate probably add up to a glass (or 5) of wine, and need to offset it somehow.

PART TWO: PREPARED FOR THE WORST

"I've learned that you can tell a lot about a person by the way (s)he handles these three things: a rainy day, lost luggage, and tangled Christmas tree lights."

Day Thirty-Three
(Friday)

3.33 Up with Child C. The Easter holidays start here.

4.45 Up with Child C. Again.

5.30 Child C needs a wee.

5.39 Hear the door of Child A or B closing. What did I say to them about getting up when the time starts with a six?

6.10 Child C wants to get up. Check on Child A and B and see that they have completed nearly all the puzzles I printed off in less time than it took me to find and print them.

Decide that holiday harmony will come from clear boundaries from the outset. Announce to Child A and B that there will, henceforth, be a limit on computer time of forty-five mins per day with the possibility of rolling it over to the next day if not all used up. Can see Child A and B's brains whirring to tot up how many forty-five mins they would need to generate an entire day in front on the computer.

7.12 Drowning in an enthusiastic barrage of ideas, questions and suggestions: "Can we watch this?", "Can I have that?", "Can I eat this?", "Can I have a drink?", "Where's my (insert item here)?" There is an urban myth that some mothers exist who actually love the school holidays ... lie ins, days spent in PJs, relaxed children enjoying lazy duvet days, or playing happily with their toys or perhaps engaging in gentle craft activities. I live in hope. Til then it feels like being pecked to death by chickens.

9.20 Boden catalogue drops through the door with £15 voucher. Am sure the more I spend there, the more our kids will become thoughtful, grateful, fun loving, sun kissed delightful children, rather than the wild kangaroos they are doing their best to be this morning.

10.00 In attempt to start the holidays on a positive note, bundle children in the car, for a trip to the garden centre café. They will, of course, appreciate my generosity, and kind gesture, and reciprocate by behaving beautifully for the rest of the hols. Child A and B choose a banana, pineapple and coconut smoothie at vast expense of £3.25 each. Neither like it. I drink my own drink, theirs, and try to stop Child C from touching expensive looking ornaments.

10.45 Return home. Child A refuses to go back and shut the car door. Request that he does so several times. He refuses. Child B gets fed up of the ensuing standoff and does it.

11.00 Suggest that we play *Chinese Checkers*. Child C "helps" me, by moving all my pieces at the wrong time and to the wrong holes. Other than that, the game proceeds well until, in moment of exasperation, Child B yells out, "For fuck's sake". Send him to his room. Ask him where he has heard that. Claims it is me. It isn't. He thinks it is hilarious. Tell him sternly that it isn't. Mid-lecture about how using swear words actually shows a very poor command of the English language (and that, incidentally, footballers are a perfect example of that, by the way), Nanny calls to say that she is coming to stay.

11.50 Child A and B continue to wage a war of vileness, while Child C watches TV. Cancel planned trip to Epsom on the train, citing poor behaviour. Really want to go, and promised it to all of them, but if I give in on this at the start of the holiday, then what kind of message am I giving? Child B declares that he's "not having much fun, and would prefer to be at school". Mad now. And sad. And beginning to think that Husband telling me they are spoilt may have some truth in it.

Kids play with Playmobil while I make up spare bed. Find some old cassettes. Children intrigued. Put on cassette of *Fantastic Mr. Fox*, the sleeve of which bills it as a "babysitter you can call on day or night". Not sure you could print things like that these days, but Child A and B seem to enjoy it. Child C only partially terrorised. On the plus side, I do manage to clean the bathroom and hang a picture.

15.00 Children play upstairs while I clear up a bit downstairs. Not sure if the whoops I can hear are those of enjoyment or pain. Not sure I want to find out. At least Child C is marginally easier to entertain with Child A and B around. Even if they are not exactly playing together. And slightly worried about the thump noises. Perhaps that is Child A and B pushing Child C off the bed repeatedly …

15.37 They are still alive. Checked. Thumping noise is handles of table football banging against the wall. Sort that. Child B asks if I can distract Child C with the TV as he keeps changing the score. Remind him that he was just as annoying when he was three.

15.38 Receive email from Tesco Wine with half price offer. Coincidence or can they feel my pain?

15.49 Children have now broken all records for time spent playing without an adult needed to intervene / referee / attend to an injury or injustice. Is that what other people's children do? Is that what happens when you take away enforced fun, and leave them to find their own entertainment?

16.52. Tears now. Spoke too soon. Peace shattered. Serve early tea in attempt to improve tempers.

Suggest that the children while away some time drawing on people's faces in some old newspapers. Demonstrate with moustaches and glasses. Then realise that was a really bad idea. Forced to impose ban on drawing on anyone who is missing, is seriously unwell or who has died, out of respect and to find some quick answers about gay marriage, abortion and class A drugs.

19.00 In-laws arrive. Kids excited and on good form, having used up all their bad behaviour on me all day long. Husband home. Kids to bed.

Diet Cokes: 2.

Chocolate: 1 large chocolate brownie, 1 hot chocolate, 2 choc truffles.

Glasses of wine: 2.

Day Thirty-Four
(Saturday)

5.00 Child C awake. Evidently 5.00 is the new 6.00.

Up and get Child A and B ready and out for swimming. Grandpa comes with us. Swimming goes fine. Last lesson of term so mainly fun stuff anyway.

9.15 Feels like 16.00. Husband gets up. Been asleep all this time. Asks whether I'm in a mood. Explain that I'm painfully tired. Poorly in the week and not enough sleep has left me shattered. Mother-in-law suggests I go back to bed for a bit. Heaven. Pop in the earplugs, set alarm for an hour and a half and I'm off. Best. Present. Ever.

11.45 Emerge refreshed. Postman has been. Tickets have arrived for Day Out With Thomas. Child C wants to go now. Asks for suitcase. Starts to pack and asks if he can take all his "fings" with him. He seems to think that it involves going on holiday. Does not bode well.

Nanny has been to the charity shop while I was asleep. Two Action Men, Playmobil hen house, *Simpsons Top Trumps* and a "guess the name stuck to your head" game. Oh, and book for Child C. Child A and B delighted that they have emptied the shop.

12.30 Random lunch consisting of pizza, egg and cress sandwiches (Nanny grew cress in egg shells for Child A and B, much to their delight), onion ring crisps, salad and cold chicken. Choc spread sarnies for Child C.

14.00 Nanny suggests we take the kids to the swings. Child C throws tantrum and says he wants to go to the zoo. Or the swimming pool. Nanny persuades him otherwise. Lovely to have fun on the swings with Child A and B while Nanny and Grandpa push Child C backwards and forwards. Play for about an hour. Then Child C has funny turn. Wants to lie down, goes green and wants a blanket. Drop Child A and B home. Drive on round the block with Child C who falls asleep.

16.00 Try and wake Child C. Sleepiest ever. Figure it must be motion sickness, or that he might have dislodged his brain somehow. Wants to lie down and keeps closing eyes. Produce cookies and miraculous recovery commences. Phew.

Three cookies later, Child C is back to his normal self.

17.15 Tea and then mayhem getting all bathed and into bed. No one wants to get in the bath first, no one seems even mildly interested in cleaning their teeth, and I seem to be tag team ranting at each child, while galloping up and down the stairs to get all the stuff I need for the process to end. Not helped my Child C weeing in the bath.

20.30 Takeaway curry. Can't smell or taste anything. Yum anyway.

Watch Saturday night TV. Husband falls asleep. All in bed by 23.30. Feel sick from too much curry. Living the dream.

Diet Cokes: 4.

Chocolate: 2 bags of buttons, 1 mini Bounty.

Glasses of wine: 3.

Day Thirty-Five
(Sunday)

5.09 Call of "wee wee".

5.14 Called in to look at Child C's pictures.

6.00 Called in because Child C wants to get up.

6.01 Child C in our bed, with his singing *Thomas And Friends* book.

6.10 *Thomas* book abandoned. Remember that iPad is upstairs. Grab that. Stick *Dora The Explorer* on YouTube. Two episodes should buy us forty minutes of semi-peace. Try to forget it is Morning Time for a bit longer.

6.48 Child A and B storm in with Action Men.

7.01 Downstairs with Child C. Breakfast. Wet morning. Had meant to put weed and feed on the lawn before the rain came to revitalise it. Now just looks like a cow field. Figure if I do it in the rain now, it will still get watered in and do the trick. Better late than never. Child C throws a wobbly. On returning inside, declares that I'm his friend and he wanted to help water the garden. It's going to be one of those days.

7.30 Child B is "bored". Tell him to use his imagination.

8.00 Do sticker book with Child C.

9.45 In-laws leave amongst noise and chaos of indoor cricket match between Husband, Child A and Child B.

Child B finds art set he was given for his birthday and embarks on art project. Child A starts a project on pandas. Asks me if I know anything about bamboo. I don't.

10.30 Wonder if at any point in the next two weeks I will get any time at all to do anything at all that I need to do. Doesn't seem like it. Mountains of washing. Mountains of clean clothes. Paper everywhere. Toys everywhere. Can't find anything. Requests fired at me every ten seconds. Cleaners coming in the morning.

Child C realises others are drawing and wants to join in. Grabs permanent markers from the set (why do they ever put pens like that in any kids' set?). Get him his own crayons, paper and some very washable pens. Then wants glue. Glue has run out. All children want more glue. When can I get ANYTHING done? At what point in their lives will they realise that I am not a robot and only have two hands.

11.07 Child B soliloquies about his computer time. "if I save fifteen minutes today then I'll have an hour tomorrow. That would be quite good wouldn't it? But it might not be worth doing, would it? What do you think?". At same moment, Child C appears covered in pen, all over his hands, T-shirt and mouth. Also wielding scissors saying repeatedly "scissors are sharp". Feeling suffocated by Child C. Like being pursued by a very small, persistent, angry, disagreeable stalker. Can get nothing done AT ALL.

Child B wants to watch me. Ask him to just leave me alone for five minutes. Eat chocolate in an attempt to make it all better.

11.23 Child A and B have got the message and play a game together. Child C up to his neck in pens and Pritt Stick. If "we're not making mess, we're making memories", as the saying goes, then we're making very colourful, sticky memories which are going to take an age to dry and clear up.

12.00 Husband saves me from certain mental breakdown by convincing Child C to go to get a loaf of bread and wraps for lunch. They set off on a walk in the rain.

Child A and B decide that shopping is boring once they work out there is nothing in it for them (except lunch) and make shakers from Pringle tubes. Mad dash to tidy up Child C's toys, while he's out of the picture and isn't around to notice that they've been put away.

12.17 Child A lunges at Child B for using a shoe box that he wants to use. Child A sent to bedroom.

Afternoon rolls on with a huge fight over bubbles, bubble wands, bubble mixture, bubble blower and various other bubble related items.

15.12 Lock myself in toilet. Enter in such a rush don't manage to switch the light on. Sit in dark. Child C comes running. "Light on Mummy?" and switches on light. Shouts and shouts at door. Wonder how long I can stay in there. Read news headlines on my phone then emerge.

Child C spends afternoon with pants twisted inside out and back to front because he won't be told otherwise.

18.00 Bedtime creeps closer. Hurrah. Do physio stretches with Child B in moment's guilt at not having done them in ages, and possibly being the cause for him entering future old age still standing on tiptoes. Show him some moves from my limited Pilates repertoire while we're at it. All to bed. Child C asleep in about two seconds. Child A and B decide to share a room tonight. Child B asks me to show him my Karate moves. Confused. Turns out he thought I knew about Karate. Point out that its Pilates. Read a few pages of story.

19.58 Calls of "Muuum. We need you". Apparently Child B been punched in stomach by Child A. Child A says unable to get to sleep due to Child B. "Do you want to hear why?" they ask. "No" I reply. He tells me anyway. Something about a hand slapping game and being rolled over by each other. GO TO SLEEP.

21.10 Ironing, and remember not fixed hole on Husband's jumper. Stitch it up.

Diet Cokes: 3.

Chocolate: 2 bags buttons, 2 lines of cheap but unsatisfactory Fruit and Nut substitute, 2 champagne truffles.

Glasses of wine: 0. But might have been a better day if I had.

Day Thirty-Six
(Monday)

Day of re-attempt at train journey.

5.10 My alarm goes off. Switch it off.

5.10 and about three seconds. Husband's phone alarm goes off across the other side of the room. Give him a shove. He asks what the noise is. I tell him and ask him to hurry up and switch it off before the whole road wakes up.

5.10 and about thirty seconds. Husband's bedside clock alarm goes off.

Husband proceeds to get ready for his early start. Flying to Milan and coming back tomorrow. As usual have a million plans for what I will do with the time and will be lucky to achieve even one of these plans after a day with Child A, B and C.

Have asked Husband to blow his nose outside of the bathroom today, so Child C won't wake up from any possible noise. He obliges, but Child A and B awake anyway. Why, oh why, do our children resist sleep? They didn't go to sleep last night til about 20.00 so they should automatically be tired. Am owed major payback in teenage years, at which point I will wake them all with a hose.

6.20 Child C calls. Jump out of bed, as much as aching knees allow and into shower. Have decided that this might be the best way to get him to be quiet. Am guessing that if he can hear the shower, he might figure that he should give up yelling. He doesn't.

6.30 All finished in bathroom and dressed. Dry hair. Try and tidy last bits for the cleaners' arrival later this morning.

6.43 Head out onto landing. Exchange good morning greetings with Child A. Go to get Child C, who is ranting about bears in his cot.

Breakfast. Child B asks if we can paint on canvas today. Child A asks what canvas is. Explain what canvas is, and "no" we are not painting today.

7.28 Child A and B play football in PJs in the hall. Conversation as follows:

Child A: Who are you?
Child B: Stevie G … who are you? Suarez? [lets goal in through doorway]
Child A: How embarrassing for Stevie G.
Child B: That's cos Stevie G isn't a goalie.
Child A: That's why it's embarrassing. Don't you want to be that amazing one who went to Mummy and Daddy's wedding?
Child B: Yeah he turned up for no reason.
Child A: Why was that again? Got him in Match Attax. [Child B saves goal] Ooh nice save.

Explain to Child A and B that David Seaman was not a guest at our wedding, and that he just happened to be at the same hotel at the same time. Is it too early for a Diet Coke?

7.34 Leap in to keep the peace. Child B taken break from football to go to toilet. Singing "I love my brother. He is great" to the national anthem tune – at a very high pitch. Acoustics in downstairs loo make the tune reverberate at great volume. Child A asks him to stop. Tell Child A to go and watch TV so he can't hear it. Tell Child B to stop annoying Child A. Argument foiled. For now.

Debate whether to take the kids to McDonald's as part of our planned train trip today.

Advantages:
- Don't have to cook them a meal.

- Get an excuse to eat a McDonald's.

- Can feel like have done school holiday treat in manner of caring parent.

Disadvantages
- Good chance I will end up eating my own food plus three Happy Meals.

- Child C is normally not great at eating out. Runs off and is a general pain in the neck to his own family and all other families and individuals in the vicinity.

- Child C just ate his own body weight in cereal, then demanded some of mine, then demanded more. Not sure he'll be that hungry.

- Unhealthy and will have McDonald's taste for the rest of the day followed by post Maccy D's munchies.

Mention it to Child A and B. Child B excited. Child A declares he "doesn't like McDonald's" (how can that be?) and asks if he can take a sandwich. Not quite what I had planned but makes for a cheaper lunch I suppose.

9.20 Pack bag. Drinks. Snacks. Change of clothes x 2 for Child C. Remind Child A and B to get dressed (or I'm leaving without them).

9.30 Child A and B emerge wearing the same clothes. Red shorts and green T-shirts with cricket bats on. Neither notices til I point it out. Seeing their reaction makes me go cold. Both suitably stunned and quite lost for words. Maybe they do have some extra-sensory powers between them after all!? Or it was a fluke? Suggest they might like to wear different jumpers, so they don't look like I dressed them to match like I sometimes did when they were teeny tiny.

9.45 Cleaners arrive. Make tea. Ask them to not clean the dining room, but to clean the spare bathroom instead. They agree. Dump all other stuff in the dining room so house is clear-ish.

10.05 Realise that we should have left already. Call children down for shoes and coats. Remind Child A that his arms need to be in a coat for it to actually count as him wearing it. Then remind him to put hood down so as not to look like a criminal. Realise that we will have missed the train we were going for, so will catch next one.

10.30 Park car at station. Queue up to get tickets from the machine. Carry buggy up over bridge and wait on the platform.

Child B reads the arrivals display and sees that there will be eight coaches to our train. Comments that it will be a busy train and "that's why they will need eight coaches over there (gestures to car park) for all the people". Explain that it's just a long train. Child C keeps asking where the Fat Controller is.

10.51 Train arrives. Big step up and find a seat. Child C stays seated for approx. two minutes before starting his search on foot for the Fat Controller. Repeated appeals to sit down, on my part, are absolutely futile. Pole dances round a bar for a good proportion of the remaining journey time.

Head to McDonald's on arrival at Epsom. Child C a complete danger to his own life and that of others at every given turn. Standing in road when traffic coming. Stopping at every window to point out the items he wants / needs. Gets in the buggy, then drags legs when he wants to get out, but not telling anyone so feet just get trapped and dragged along until I realise what is going on. Order food. No seats downstairs. Direct kids to stairs. Carry laden tray, and folded out buggy, which is too stuffed with things (including three McDonald's balloons) to allow me to put it down. Make it to the top of the long and remarkably steep staircase without dropping anything. Then get to the top and drop a portion of chips all over the floor. Overshadowed only by Child B pouring half a bottle of water all over his trousers, chair and floor. Reminded why we don't go out for meals. As predicted, I eat the lion's share of the food, toys are of more interest than eating and whole thing totally shambolic. Child A and B seem to enjoy it. Child A comments that "McDonald's is a great place to come if you've been working all morning. To relax. And have nice food". They are all class.

Trip continues. Child C attempts to ramraid the displays in Lakeland, and rearranges ALL the girls' shoes in Clarks. All three children exit Clarks on their bottoms, as the "stairs are too steep". You'd think they were on a white knuckle ride or that we lived in a bungalow. Queue develops to get down the stairs after us.

14.20 Child C strapped into buggy. Get last thing we need – lamp for Child A's room.

Pouring with rain. Child A and B's coat hoods in car. Back to station. Child C let out. On the platform, spends as much time on the dangerous side of the yellow line as possible. Child A and B stressed at Child C's appetite for danger. Feel utterly fed up. Child C strapped back into buggy. More screams. Let out to get onto train as gap a bit big. Shattered.

15.10 Arrive back at our station. Child C refuses to get off quickly. No option but to grab him with one arm, buggy with the other and pull both off the train. More screams about wanting to do it himself. Try to remember at what age that defiance calms down a bit. Four maybe? At least the age when they understand the concept of "if you don't come now, you will get left on the train and you will never see us again". Certainly not going in yet.

Home to lovely clean house. Child A and B rush upstairs to sort their new Match Attax. Ask Child C to try for a wee. Refuses repeatedly. Wees all over newly vacuumed carpet. In three large patches. Explain that I'm cross and sad. Actually I'm fuming and pissed off and tired and have had enough.

16.45 Start tea cooking process since Child C and B complaining they are hungry. Child B moans when he learns it is pasta for tea. Loses a tick off his reward chart and gains a lecture in gratitude, or lack thereof. Claims that cleaners have stolen his "on bench players" from his Match Attax. Point out that is highly unlikely.

Child C amused by arranging teddies all over all the chairs in the lounge. None of us are allowed to sit on any of the seats. Keeps him quiet, if nothing else.

17.45 Contemplate whether it is wrong to have a glass of wine while reading a bedtime story to the children.

18.18 Bath time done for Child C. Wine allowed.

Painful bedtime for Child C. Calls me up for a wee. Sit with him while he is "waiting for poo poo". Doesn't arrive. Wants to finish building a square with his building bricks, despite having been to bed once already. Give up and leave him to it for five mins while round up Child A and B. Get all upstairs. Child C put to bed. Read to Child A and B.

20.00 Dinner and watch *Masterchef.* Plan tomorrow's assault. Weather supposed to be fine, so large open space required after today. Husband home early afternoon, so hearty walk at RHS Wisley on the agenda. Better get there early before all the people who actually know anything about plants.

23.09 Get chicken out of freezer for Child A and B to eat tomorrow. Occurs to me that Child C's temper could be as a result of poor nutrition. Had better make effort to cook at least Child A and B some unprocessed food in the course of the week. Also get out half a chocolate sponge. Can decorate half a cake (cut in half and then put on top) as "fun" activity.

23.35 Must go to bed.

Diet Cokes: 3 … or maybe 4. Yes, 4 I think. One of those days.

Chocolate: 2 bags of chocolate buttons, chocolate milkshake.

Glasses of wine: 2.

Day Thirty-Seven (Tuesday)

Up with the lark again. Up twice in the night to attend to Child C's calls and hear Child A and B trotting across the landing around 5.00.

Read last night that toddlers aren't trying to be complete pains in the neck (my words, not theirs) but are "just asserting their newly acquired decision-making and independence skills, regardless of whether their choices are good ones". And that they forget any of their tantrums very quickly. And that there are similarities between them and drunk people. I can vouch for the last of these, but will try and bear all in mind for a happier, more harmonious day today.

6.25 Up for a shower. Within about two minutes, all three children are in the bathroom. Child C wrapping up "presents" in his comfort blanket, Child A trying to sleep on one of the bath mats, and Child B flitting in and out trying to tell me things that I can't fully hear over the sound of running water.

Kids play game of Father Christmas delivering presents, instigated by Child C. Go to dry hair, and on passing, see that Child A and B have makeshift beds on floor, covered in towels, posing as blankets, and that Child C is "delivering" various presents in the role of Father Christmas. Child C is frustrated that, wrapped in his duvet in the style of a sleigh, he can't move, but gets over that when I offer to be the reindeer and get him to follow me. All before 6.35. Bet Angelina doesn't have all this to deal with.

Child A and B take bets over breakfast about what time the Tesco man will arrive. I go for 8.59. Child A goes for 8.30. Child B goes for between 8.30 and 8.45. Child C gets mad and screams at us all until we stop talking. Child B starts crying. Child A covers his ears.

7.45 Child A and B set about drawing competition entries for competition on TV. Child C decides he wants to join in but doesn't understand. I'm more concerned that he'll scribble on artwork of Child A and B and cause meltdowns all round.

8.40 Tesco delivery arrives. Remember all the things I forgot to order.

9.30 Head off for trip to Wisley. There in good time and top parking spot. Easter bunny hunt on and been ages since been there with the kids, so lovely to be back.

Fun but cold. Only dampeners are Child C throwing stones at the fish, attempting to push the buggy up a large number of steps in the Alpine Meadows single-handedly, wanting to go on a climbing frame way too big for him, negotiation with Child A about why he can't take home a large bamboo cane and a huge fight about who gets to hold the biro. Two hours of the great outdoors, treasure hunt complete, chocolate bunny for each child, cobwebs well and truly blown out and home.

12.45 Home for lunch. See on Facebook that my cousin's wife has had a baby at home. Child B pipes up with "Oh no. How did it get out?" Brief pause while brain whirs. Give short explanation about not everyone having c-sections and that most babies come out a different way. Both look blank, disinterested and not even sure that they hear a word I have said. More interested in their lunch.

155

13.35 Husband home. Rough and tumble with Child A, B and C while I stress about table corners and fireplace edges etc. Then he has to work. Child B is bored. Child A doesn't understand that he can't keep talking at Husband. Take shelter in lounge. Manage to get some ironing done. Figure that after a morning out, the afternoon's amusement has to be of the kids' own doing. Suggest they make something with Lego. Child B still bored. Husband finishes work and goes outside to play cricket with Child A and B. Child C exhausted like me, I think. Only wants to watch TV.

Print off selection of football orientated activities for their next bout of boredom ... word searches, story starters etc. Meanwhile Child C empties all of the Tupperware boxes out of the kitchen cupboard. Feel like I'm getting a cold on top of a cold. Read books to Child C. Not interested in most of them as "too scare scare for me".

16.00 Husband leaves for dentist. Child A and B now happy with playing in the garden. Wonder at what age they just start thinking of things to do themselves, without needing a "push" from a grown-up.

16.15 Shattered. And after just a few days of the holiday. Going to need to get in training for the summer holidays. Exhausting stuff, being "fun" and a referee and thinking of what to serve up for the children three times a day.

Sadly only one glass of wine left in the fridge. If that. Saw something last night about shops having to stock up on eggs each pancake day. Wonder if the same applies to wine and the school holidays.

16.44 Put tea on. Go to tell Child A and B that they are getting a tick on their reward chart for playing so nicely. Child A and B practice tennis on the patio. Hear them talking:

Child B [to Child A]: Would the big chest of drawers look nice in your house?

Me: Are you deciding what furniture you're having?

Child B and Child A: Yes, when you're dead.

Nice.

16.55 Quick noodles for tea. Probably extremely bad for them but they all like it. Child C stresses about the noodles sticking all over his fingers, but he eats some before going nuts, so that'll do.

17.30 Husband home from dentist. In pain. Bath time for children. Put laundry away while Child C in bath. Weird thumping noise coming from bathroom. Turns out that Child C has emptied all the warm water and filled it a foot and a half of cold. Comments that Child A and Child B "no like that – hee hee". A mastermind criminal in the making. Empty bath and refill. Child A soaks the bathroom blowing water out of a snorkel pipe. Child B fills the bath to nearly overflowing and soaks the place all over again with the shower attachment. And I wonder why the water bill seems so high.

19.00 All in bed. Story time for Child A and B. One page in and call of "wee wee". Attend to that. Back to story. One and a half more pages in and call of "poo poo". No poo poo forthcoming. Child C worried about the "drag drags" (dragons) in his room. Assure him they have all gone.

Starving so tea and TV. Get some stuff ready for Child A and B for an outdoor camp day booked for tomorrow. Will be weird without them. Quieter but weird. Child C is going to wonder what is going on. And possibly drive me even more bonkers. Today was definitely made easier by thinking of Child C as a drunk who is totally hammered. All makes sense when you look at it like that. Makes even more sense if I think of him as a drunk for whom English is not his first language.

21.22 Get ready for bed. Is it really only day two of the holidays? (if you don't count the day when Child C was at preschool, or the weekend). Will be a getting-things-done whirlwind when they do all go back to school. Productivity will be at a record high as I zip around relishing the ability to do anything I need or want to do without any requests. At same time, weird to think that the next big hols will be the summer and then Child A and B have finished infant school. And then they will be all grown up. And then my little ones will be gone. I'm such a hypocrite.

Diet Cokes: 4.

Chocolate: 3 bags of chocolate buttons.

Glasses of wine: ¾ of a glass – all that was left in the bottle.

Day Thirty-Eight
(Wednesday)

It's official. School holidays are bad for your health. Have put on more weight and still look and feel full of cold.

7.00 Pack bags. You'd think that Child A and B were going into the wilderness forever.

Child C creates mountain of thirty-six teddies of varying sizes, and two blankets and keeps calling me in with sense of urgency only to say "snug bug".

9.10 Between that, and Child B throwing wobbly over a Lego amphibious vehicle he has built which keeps breaking, and Child A wanting me to watch *Masterchef*, it has taken me two hours to get ready for the day. And haven't even cleared up from breakfast yet.

9.11 Child C wants to play shops. Can't even get past the discarded toys to reach the cupboard where the play food is. Does no one get the concept of "Mummy needs to wash up from breakfast"?

Child B mopes around asking what time we are leaving. Beginning to think he is totally incapable of amusing himself. Perhaps he's nervous about today. Not sure. Either way, seems to have lost the ability to think of things to do.

Dress Child A and B for the arctic. Feels mild outside but better to be safe than sorry.

9.50 Arrive in good time and meet their friend. Quick wave goodbye and off to the farm with Child C.

10.30 Farm is heaving. Have to queue to pay and already concerned about how many other children Child C is going to barge or push or manhandle. Luckily preschool seems to have taught him how to take turns (hurrah) and he is great on all the playground equipment, tractors etc. Very expensive to get in so determined to make the most of stay.

Beautifully sunny day so very hot. Thoughts turn to Child A and B who will have melted by now.

Go to see the newborn lambs. Child C throws animal food at them and their unsuspecting mothers. Then at the pig. Then see the notice which says "Do not give animal feed to the pigs". Oops.

11.15 Wait for animal handling. Room is swarming with people but we get the last sitting spot. Get to touch a baby chick, baby duck – both only two weeks old – a rabbit and a guinea pig. Child C an absolute gem throughout the whole thing. If you ignore him prodding the baby chick and stroking the rabbit the wrong way.

On days like this, could actually get used to this school holiday lark. Granted I'm minus two kids, but the sun is shining, and I'm having fun and not thinking about chores. If eldest come back full of Bear Grylls' enthusiasm may convince them to go and live in the wilderness for a bit to try out new found skills. Then we'll all be happy.

Trampolining, more animals, indoor soft play. Child C like a different person for the most part. Guess that's what happens when we're doing everything he wants to do and he has Mummy for himself. No competing with Child A and B, no being taken to places for functional activities, and no being told that "Mummy has lots of jobs to do". Only reverts to type whilst waiting for pig race. Decides he wants to take part. Long explanation that it's a race for pigs, you don't actually ride them, but he's not convinced. Mass of distraction techniques employed during the ten minute wait.

12.50 Short pig race complete, back to the sandpit. Build lots and lots of sandcastles, which is somehow better than when you do it on the beach. Café and toilets just a stone's throw away. Loads of buckets and spades which live there and you don't have to wash down after. No nasty sea breeze. No wet knees or bum. Climbing frames right next to you for when you're done. Yep, think this beats the great British seaside.

13.20 Hungry now. And tired. And conscious that if I want to get Child C out of here before unreasonable tiredness strikes then now might be a good time. Start the process. Attempt to tempt him back to entrance with myriad of attractions … "let's go and check on the rabbits", "let's buy birthday cards for your cousins" and "there's something really interesting in here".

Make it out and back to car by 13.45. Despite Child C insisting on pushing laden buggy up a steep incline to the car. Agrees to do a wee before we set off, then wants to carry the potty bag full of wee whilst in the car. Explain that it will split. Eventually he gets it and delays getting in the car by listing everything in the boot that will get covered with wee if the bag does leak.

14.00 Home. TV on. Lunch for me. And relax. Catch up on a few emails and calls and sort out dinner for tonight. Then sit on the sofa and move as little as possible. And then draw an elephant and provide a selection of collage materials and a glue stick for Child C who has got it in his head that he wants to make a picture, with very precise specifications.

15.30 Set off to get Child A and B. Child C wants to walk. He's doing his best to undo my good mood. Screams at me about wanting to hold the keys for the car, whilst I am driving, almost the whole journey (explain that isn't possible if we want to move) then falls asleep two hundred metres from pick up point. Ten minutes' peace in the car. Bliss.

16.00 Child A and B emerge full of chat and covered in mud and charcoal. Both speaking so quickly and over each other, that have to impose a turn taking policy after each bit of information has been imparted just so I can understand what they are saying. Have had "best day" using saws, making charcoal in a fire, making paint, making bow and arrows, peeling sticks with potato peelers and all the kind of stuff that makes boys boys. Child B has sawed his knuckles but other than no injuries that I can see at this stage. Other than chronic fatigue.

Child C sleeps all the way home. And then all the way through the confusion about where Child B left his jumper (in the boot, it transpires). And then through the ensuing fight about whose sticks are the ones in the hall, and how "it's not fair" and how "we've got to go back there tomorrow to get more sticks".

16.35 Wake Child C, whip up tea and get all fed.

Child A embarks on using his computer time on the Build-A-Bear website, planning what bear he'd like. Point out that, under no circumstances, is he having one.

Child B lies on sofa. Exhausted. Child C covers him in a mountain of teddies.

17.30 Clear up and run bath. Get Child C in bath and aim for bed ASAP.

All in bed by 19.00. Child C the last one to bed.

19.02 Pour wine. Go to check emails. Child B emerges wanting a hug. Grant hug and send him off to bed.

19.12 Called upstairs by Child C. Here begins multiple call up session. Child A and B fast asleep. Out of earshot, mutter expletive phrase under my breath. Oh. Same expletive phrase that Child B shouted out in *Chinese Checkers* the other day. Alarmed at the fact that maybe Child B *did* get it from me.

19.15 Child C seeking reassurance. "Me a bit scared of drag drags and cows. No ... cows my friend. And pigs. And sheep. One cow". The ramblings of a mad man. Asks me to roar to scare the "drag drags". I acquiesce and leave the room. "Ma maaaaa. You hear me? No work. Me scared of drag drags".

Sort a few bits. Husband calls. Put the dinner on.

Eat. Mention chocolate cake to Husband. He accepts. Ice it. Eat. Now legs of jeans feel even tighter.

21.09 Feels like 2.00. Don't want to clear up manky lunch boxes. Just want bed. And a lie in in the morning. Wash up and clear up interspersed with checking Facebook to ease the monotony.

21.45 Should have been in bed ages ago as Husband off to somewhere early in the morning. Bother. Child C asked at bedtime for me to bring up a drawing of a cow and three baskets / bags of plastic food. Get drawing. Only taking up one basket of plastic food, or it'll be carnage in the morning as he tips it all out of his cot.

163

Diet Cokes: 4.

Chocolate: 1 bag of buttons, 1 hot chocolate, 1 slice of chocolate cake.

Glasses of wine: 2.

Day Thirty-Nine
(Thursday)

5.00 My alarm goes off. Followed by Husband's alarm. Followed by me poking him repeatedly in the shoulder to get up. Followed be me saying "you have been warned" and rolling over.

Husband gets up. Child C calls out. Swear he has supersonic hearing. Or must be in a really light sleep at this ungodly hour. Go in to see him twice in ten mins. First time he tells me he doesn't want the basket of play food in his cot. Second to tell me that he doesn't like the cow picture I drew. Remove both items.

Child C drifts off. Hear Child A get up.

5.57 Husband leaves.

6.10 Child C calls to get up. Really don't want him to wake Child B who is tired beyond all measure, so bring him into my room. Hope he'll watch *Dora The Explorer* on YouTube again. Holds his interest for about seven mins then becomes wiggly. Get in shower. He does something to iPad which, by the sounds of it, requires my immediate attention. Out of shower. Soaking wet. Amend screen size. Back in shower. Water on. More screams. Out of shower. Dry hands. Unpause iPad. Back in shower. Child C disappears with iPad. Child B emerges.

Child C reappears and won't let anyone else look at the iPad. Screams at everyone. Take Child A and B downstairs and put on TV. Child B sits down. Child A insists that he wanted to sit in that spot and refuses to move off Child B's head. Deduct computer time in five minute increments out loud until he moves. Fifteen minutes lost.

And to add insult to injury, either the scales are broken but am now two kgs more than I was about six weeks ago.

Go back up and dry hair. Come back down and give each child a brioche. Child B reads fantastic acrostic poem he has written from a print out sheet I gave them both – with each line starting with a letter from the word "Football". Child A works on his, which doesn't make any sense whatsoever. Then gets cross that we don't get it.

9.20 Leave to take Child A and B to church holiday club for the morning. Allow plenty of extra time for Child C to disrupt proceedings. Rightly so. Insists on pushing the buggy once we get about half way there, which slows things down and endangers the ankles of many. Strap him into buggy, so he screams "let me ouuuuuuuuuuuuuut" the rest of the way, and through the church reception attracting a mixture of disapproving and understanding looks from passers-by. A disapproving glance and tut administered to me, from caregiver of boy whose head I knock with my laden rucksack. Can't see behind me, place swarming, and rucksack filled with wipes, travel potty, changes of clothes for Child C, emergency stuff (tissues, plasters, lip balm etc.), and probably about twenty used plastic bags, old receipts and crumbled biscuits.

One mum in the queue mentions that her girls (aged six and nine, I think) have just started bickering, and that she's "never had that before". Like, really? Is it the case that no one else's children bicker, and it's just ours? How come we got three of the bickering variety?

Stop to chat to two other mums outside. Child C proceeds with "Ma maaaaa. Talk to meeeeeeee" in an attempt to drown out anything I want to say. Other mums succeed in making me feel better by revealing their children (now older) were just as bad. Not just me then.

Let Child C out. Quick trip to chemist and then to greengrocers. Child C pushes buggy slowly. Luckily no injuries, Child C has a banana and sits beautifully in the buggy while eating it. At least a little bit of respite.

10.15 Home. Child C wants to read books so we do. Struggle to keep my eyes open. Need to make sandwiches for picnic later.

11.23 Child C wants another banana. It splits as I get it out of the skin. Give it to him. Meltdown over the fact it isn't a whole banana. Explain what happened. He yells some more. Serve up another banana. I'm not in the mood to try and explain, or to "fix it" with an elastic band, as has been known in the past.

12.00 Collect Child A and B. Arrive home at the same time as the delivery man with my John Lewis and Boden deliveries. The day just got better.

12.15 Put lunch in the oven. Child A and B hot and tired but not fighting. That's a start. Maybe some of the gospel rubbed off on them. Have the song lyrics "There is only one river, there is only one stream" from *Airplane* running through my head. Sing it as I cook.

Lunch (roast lamb) wolfed down by Child A and B. Wonder if it was because I pre-warned them this morning what it was going to be and, under no circumstances, to groan when I serve it up. Fish fingers and mini potato waffles tolerated by Child C. No bowls in the cupboard due to Child C's teddy bear picnic in the lounge, so have to use cups for strawberries / cake dessert. Not worth facing the wrath of Child C.

13.00 Child A and B kick a ball around the house. Give brief lecture about it being a sunny day and playing outside and find them their shoes. They take the bait. Hurrah. Child C follows and attempts to dig up the patio. Interspersed with "mama, me no need you anymore" as the back door is slammed. Repeatedly.

14.15 Picnic made, bag packed, footballs in the car, sandpit stuff. We're off.

14.46 Child B reminds me we're late by one minute, so far. Child C sleeps in the car. Probably from all his screaming in the buggy this morning. Park car and meet friends in park. Lovely and sunny. Child A and B rush off to play footie. Leave Child C to doze for a bit.

15.15 Wake up Child C. He's not convinced and lies limp in my arms. Eventually revive him with genius trick of dripping water from his water bottle on his legs. He is duly angry that he has woken up wet, but hey, he's awake.

Lovely afternoon. Kids eat too many crisps, biscuits and cake. I don't care. Child C has minor altercation in the sandpit with some mean kids who tease him for the way he speaks, and who then proceed to dig right where he is digging. Go over and tell them that isn't nice. Cautious that their mother(s) may be lurking nearby and that they might be really mean and scary. Child C and I escape unscathed. Though in all the fun of digging Child C does manage to bury and lose a spade and a toy car. Dispatch Child A, B and their friend to find the lost items, but come back empty handed.

17.15 Leave to come home. Bath for Child C who is totally grubby. Also for Child B, who suffers cold bath that Child C has caused, and who is still in the bath, wanting to share it with Child B. Child B gets out first. Cold. Child A in next. Child C still there.

Chuckling at the cold temperature. Child A out. Child C takes ages rearranging his foam shapes on the bathroom tiles.

All of us are shattered. Apart from, perhaps, Child C. All to bed ASAP. Read chapter of book to Child A and B after argument about whose turn it is to have the book read in their room. Interrupted by Child C who needs me to save him from dragons and cows again.

Child B redeems himself by saying "thank you for taking us out today". Admittedly, shortly after talking to him and Child A about how I haven't actually done anything for me this week. Not totally true, but close enough. Come to think of it, Child C did say something along the lines of "that was fun mama" earlier, but that could have been the Pringles and cookies talking.

18.56 Repeated calls of "save meeeeeee" from Child C. Go up once, to warn him that I'm not coming up again.

19.17 Child C finally gives up. About bloody time.

Was meant to be doing workout DVD tonight. Just can't. This school holidays business is hard core. Throat feels a bit sore again, so crisp cold white wine is the only answer. Body beautiful will have to wait til the holidays are over. Can't be Supermum and have a flat stomach. Clearly the two are mutually exclusive.

20.50 Just can't get warm and Husband due to be home late so run a bath. A rare luxury. Run it too hot. Boil. Can only stay in for ten mins. Then back to clearing up.

Clear up eighteen bowls, twelve plates and two blankets from lounge floor. Almost looks like the lounge again.

22.04 Husband calls on way home from airport. Exchange news from the day. Tell him about the "God is good, God is great, Oh yeah God he is my mate" song (or words to that effect) that the boys learnt this morning. Sing it then instantly get cut off. He calls back and hadn't lost reception. Freaky.

23.10 Eventually to bed. Start afresh tomorrow.

Diet Cokes: 4.

Chocolate: 2 bags of buttons, 1 slice of chocolate cake.

Glasses of wine: 2.

Day Forty (Friday)

6.00 Woken up, wondering whether *every* mother wakes up thinking about bedtime. Can't remember the last time I didn't.

Child A and B playing nicely in bedroom. Child C needs a wee and is highly vociferous about coming into our room. Warn him that he needs to sit / lie nicely and not wiggle about. And that he isn't playing on the iPad. Agrees. Gets in the bed. Gets out to fetch teddies. Then starts trampolining.

Jump in shower. Husband gives him iPad and goes to get ready too. Child C has what he came for and is happy.

Get dressed. Child B comes in distressed. Highly upset that we posted his entry to the colouring competition on TV, yesterday, without it being finished. This is despite him not touching it for days, being with me when I prepared the envelope, and physically posting it himself. Despite all this, he seems to think I am to blame. Obviously. Sulk develops. Do feel slightly guilty as do vaguely remember something about him wanting to colour something blue, but can't remember everything.

Child A and B come down for breakfast. Both are shattered. When will they ever learn to sleep in beyond 5.00? Kids ... realise that more sleep = more fun.

Breakfast, then Child A and B embark on using their computer time, while Child C relinquishes the iPad and has brekkie himself. Eighty-five of the ninety mins gone by 9.15. Make chocolate muffins to take to friend's house this afternoon.

While Child A and B are on the computer, encourage Child C to play with his toys. Even he is fed up of the TV and agrees to me switching it off. Suggest he plays with his Duplo. Proceeds to make a series of "dog bones" from the bricks. Keeps him happy. Child A and B entertain him too by playing with cars together. Then a fight breaks out, and it all goes a bit wrong. They need to make car mats big enough for a whole bunch of kids. Maybe we should rip out the lounge carpet and replace it with one massive car mat. That might just sort it.

9.45 Drop off Child A, B and two of their friends at the church club. Head to the greengrocers to stock up again on strawberries. Child C eats a banana on the way home while stopping to stare at the "baby chicks" in the Easter window displays. Stop to get some margarine. Child C attempts to get me to buy him pretty much everything at his level at the cash register. Try and convince him that it all tastes of socks. He doesn't believe me.

10.07 Car park ticket runs out any minute so try and hurry Child C along, impeded by Child C's complete lack of urgency. Tell Child C that if we don't hurry I'll go to prison and he'll never see me again. Still not bothered.

Luckily make it in time, on this occasion.

10.15 Home. Child C super needy. "Play with meeeee, watch meeeee". Feel bad, but have to get some jobs done.

Play a bit. Put out fictitious fires, and get soaked with fictitious hoses. Fetch Child A and Child B. Arrive at church in time to hear the song and dance routine. Child C does his best Beyoncé bum wiggling at the back of the church. Not sure that's quite the routine that was envisaged when the song was conceived. Gather all children, all bits of paper, craft, hats and bits and wend our way.

12.20 Lovely and sunny, so Child A and B go out to play footie. Child C does his best to join in. Gets his feet caught in the football goal netting at every opportunity.

Lunch wolfed down by Child A and B, and picked at by Child C. Bit more play then off to see a friend, via the house of a local mum who has posted on local Facebook group that she has a Boden free £10 voucher going begging. Have snapped it up. Now I've no excuse to not get the top in the lovely colour which I adore – but need to wait eleven weeks for, apparently. Will be worth the wait. Now just to find the occasion to wear it. Bring on long summer with balmly evenings. And obviously children who do not have sticky ice cream fingers, or sun cream on them anywhere.

BEST afternoon at friend's house. Her kids are as mad as mine, and all take it in turns to be on the receiving end of a parent yelling "(insert name), NO". Lots of trampolining, climbing on the climbing frame, feeding the chickens and the muddiest walk in a loop around the common. Highlight of which includes crossing a railway line (via a footbridge, and pretending to run along the roof of the carriages as they pass), following footprints (for Child C), paddling in the river in wellies (all children), having a cut grass fight (Child A and B), and running around like savages. Love wide open spaces. Best place for boys. No better place in fact. No one can hear them. They can't fight over sticks. Though can fight with them. And perfect for burning off lots of noise and energy. Long may the weather stay dry. In fact, how did we manage through the cold and wet of winter? Maybe that's why they have so much pent up energy to release. They have kept it all bottled up for six long months.

17.15. Pizza and chips and chocolate cake. All children on a food fuelled high. Friend's child sent to naughty spot. Mine telling unfunny knock knock jokes in ad nauseam. Child C attempts to start a screaming competition.

18.00 Ten minute warning for Child A, B and C. Child C insistent on going on the trampoline. Give strong warnings about eating a meal and trampolining. Couldn't care less. Bounces to his heart's content. All happy for five mins until blood curdling scream from Child B. Been hit in eye by Nerf gun bullet. Luckily, I suppose, fired by Child A.

Friend extremely used to incidences such as these. Fetches frozen peas. Watches Child A and C while first aid administered. Child B suffering from sore eye, but no permanent damage. More upset that I won't let him go back on the trampoline. Take that as a full recovery and continue packing up.

18.10 Head home. Very happy, very tired children. Good, honest, and only slightly painful, fun. Hopefully not too much clearing up for friend. Hard to stay behind to tidy. Gets to stage when you just need to get out before it becomes impossible to shift the children. End up getting one ready, while the other two go off and go something. Once you've got them all by the front door you've gotta go.

Reprimand Child A for aiming Nerf gun at Child B's face. Insists he was aiming for his stomach. Reprimand him for being a rubbish aim.

18.30 Husband calls to say he's on his way home. Point out that priority is kids in bed ASAP. Encourage Child A and B to race into their PJs before Husband gets home. Go with it, and beat him. Two children down, one to go ... and then teeth, and water, and kisses and cuddles.

Bedtime process seems to take ages and ages. Eventually all in bed by 19.30, after:

- All children annoy Husband by wanting his attention all at the same time, while he's just trying to send "one final work email".

- Put away football goal from garden so the foxes don't chew through the net.

- Child B almost, or maybe does, fall asleep on the lounge floor. When wakes complains that his eye is stingy and that "one side of the room is blurry".

- Child C shows Husband his entire collection of Duplo dog bones. Seventeen of varying sizes.

- Child C encourages / forces Husband to read *The Three Little Pigs* and a *Look and Find* book twice.

- Child C rejects giving Husband a cuddle or a kiss. Says he'll do it on what could either be "Friday", or "five days". None of us is sure. And when we try to get to the bottom of it, we're none the wiser and he just laughs. Haven't a clue. But he's quite insistent.

- Husband tickles my waist (during the above exchange), makes me jump and I accidentally knock him in the mouth, right where he has had dental work this week. Collapses on the spare bed in Child C's room to the extent that Child C repeats "get Daddy out. Don't want him in here" until he goes.

- Child B tells Husband that he loves me more than him. Suspect Husband asked him the question, in which case he was silly to do so. Point that out.

- Child A gets up to go to the toilet, and won't get off til he has completed a *Match of the Day Annual* word search.

- Child C has drunk three beakers of water.

- Child C refuses to go to sleep until he has given a "big cuddle and big mwah" to Child A and B. Which involves Child B being woken up in the process.

Cook dinner. Serve up at 20.15. Right on time, Tesco delivery arrives. Eat and chill.

21.57 Family day out tomorrow and keep thinking that must make sarnies. Just finish watching film. Shopping still in the hall. Wish putting it away was part of the delivery.

22.36 Shopping still in hall.

23.46 Go to bed. Look six months pregnant. Why does food automatically go straight to the void left by pregnancy, however long ago? Where did it all go before I had kids, or was it just held in more effectively?

Diet Cokes: 4.

Chocolate: 1 chocolate muffin, 2 lines of Dairy Milk.

Glasses of wine: 3 I think ... but they weren't really full ones.

Day Forty-One
(Saturday)

Oh my. A family day out. A stark reminder as to why we don't do that very often. And a reminder of the many and varied ways that Child C can be a total pain.

Wake up from dream where I had nits. Takes a few mins to realise it was a dream. Phew.

5.36 Child C up and ready for the day. Go in five times to reassure him about dragons, explain why Father Christmas has not come, tell him that he had better get more rest or he can't go to see Thomas the Tank Engine, tell him he is waking everyone up. Then just ignore him for a bit. Doze through his calls, with a pricked up ear in case he calls for a wee.

6.45 Child A comes in for a cuddle.

6.50 Child C yells "uppppp tiiiiimmme" as his clock changes to day. Now the day may officially begin.

Shower, and breakfast and sort out picnic for the day out. Husband keen to relax after hard week. Kids wanting to know when we're leaving. Tread the tight rope between keeping the kids happy and not asking Husband to hurry up. Make sandwiches, wash up from breakfast, put car seats in the other car, dress kids, get them to brush their teeth, do a wee and put their shoes on, pack cool bag, pack my bag. All just to get out for the day.

9.18 Haven't gone yet. Child A and B happy using computer. Child C a bit confused about the whole thing anyway. Hope it's not too busy.

10.30 Family departs. Husband puts on his music. Child C requests that we listen to *Old MacDonald*. All deteriorates from there. Child A and C want to listen to *Eye of the Tiger* repeatedly. Child B wants a different song. Husband cross that they are all shouting. Threatens to not let Child C come with us at all. Mutter to Husband that that's highly impractical. Satnav tells us which way to go but Husband can't hear it over the noise. Child A pipes up. Husband shouts at him stop yelling. I explain that Husband meant to say "please be quiet". Turn round to see Child A and C both in tears. Great. Perfect start to family day out.

11.30 Arrive. Husband wonders why we've got so much stuff. Not "thanks for making such a varied and nutritious picnic". Wishing I'd brought a coat. Day proceeds. Child C more vile than can ever be imagined. Am building up an emotional tolerance to Child C. He may annoy me immensely, but the last week has taught me to try and let it just float over me like a wave. Switch off the bit of me that he winds up and I can be much more objective and calm about him acting like every child I have ever seen on *Three Day Nanny* all rolled into one. Even despite today's Areas For Improvement:

- Fights with other children in the toy train track area.

- Insists on getting on and off every steam train single handed. Huge steps up and down. Causes huge traffic jams, so have to lift him off, causing ginormous meltdown every time we get on or off a train. Erratic running near hazards. Edge of train platforms a particular favourite.

- Insists on queuing for large inflatable bouncy castle style slide. Way too big for him. Involves climbing up twenty foot high inflatable thing, sitting inside a sack, and then sliding down steep drop. Even Child A and B find it hard. Child C can't even climb the ladder, and tries to get in the sack at the bottom, before even climbing. Causes a danger to all other children trying to enjoy themselves. Take him away, with force. Attempt to put shoes on, while he is wedged between my crossed legs. Child C, still kicking and screaming, shouts "wee wee" and proceeds to create a small river, then lake heading towards the bouncy castle. Get potty out to use as a chair. With no trousers or pants on Child C makes a break for it, and wants to go and see Husband. First interest he has shown in him all day. Pull him back, put trousers on, and Husband takes him off. I follow with bags, Child A and B.

- Sits beautifully to have face painted, as a cat, with silver and black face paint. Then ruins the whole bloody lot by throwing a tantrum, wiping snot and tears across his face and ends up looking like a robot.

- Won't have photo taken with anyone.

- Annoyed that Gordon isn't there. Looks for him everywhere.

- Only wants to eat Twixes for lunch.

- Won't get off the spinning tea cups.

- Buries his head from the Fat Controller, after weeks of looking forward to meeting him.

15.00 Have had enough. Time to go home. Child C decides he's hungry on the way back to the car park. Sets up picnic in the middle of the car park, as I go to reach him a drink, refusing point blank to move out of the way of on-coming vehicles. Husband, Child A and B drive to get us. Thankfully Child C asleep within five mins of getting in the car.

Survived the day out. Husband thinks it was expensive. Don't think it was that bad, and we could have made more of it, if Child C wasn't so awful. Even Child B says that it makes him think "it would be better if we hadn't had" Child C. Explain that you can still love someone and think they are a total pain. Will look back on it, in years to come, as a good day out. Probably. Just need to make the raw wounds heal.

Arrive home at 16.00. Wake up Child C at 16.30. Tries to sleep on the lounge carpet. Revive with cheese savouries. And put tea on, pronto.

Chaos at bath time, as I reveal to Child C that face paint will need to come off. Long negotiation, which I only win by pointing out that if he washes off this face paint, then next time he can choose to be something else. He insists on "helping" Child A and B wash theirs off too. Thankfully, they oblige.

All children de-facepainted (seemed like a good idea at the time) and ready for bed. Child A and B play on computer / watch Husband do intense workout DVD. Child C chooses to watch *Peppa Pig* on the iPad. In Spanish.

19.00 Child A and B happy to be in bed. Child C not interested in the slightest. Damn you daytime sleep.

19.41 Finally convince Child C to go to sleep by saying that in the morning, maybe the conkers that he has left outside the door will have become banana trees (a discussion we started this morning when I was sorting out the car seats). Parting words of "Mama you go get sunshine". So cruel that he is a total pain all day and *still* now, when the other children are asleep. Beating a person down is one thing, but to just keep beating is so wearing.

19.43 Oh. He's not asleep. Still calling "Mama. Save meeeee". Ignore and pour another glass of wine.

19.46 Still not asleep. Write email to friend with whom I was meant to be doing major day out on Monday, to suggest we do something more low key. Can't take another day of being ground down like today.

19.59 Start serving up dinner.

20.10 Child C still going strong. Husband and I decide to get him up. Half watches an hour or so of *Britain's Got Talent*, whilst rearranging teddy bears on sofas and chairs.

21.15 Insist that it is time for bed. Throws a wobbly that all teddies need to now be lying down. Assist as much as I can. Then get mean. He yells. Encourage him to help me close the curtains upstairs by way of incentive.

21.17 Child C needs a wee wee.

21.23 Yelling really loudly now. Go up. Put him into the big bed in his room and settle next to him. Starts ranting about dragons, bears, what is behind the curtain and which one is the front garden. I get the giggles. He gets the giggles. Both shake with uncontrollable laughter. Manage to act asleep by biting my lip and thinking sad thoughts. Child C does fake snoring.

21.45 Child C finally gives in. Hallelujah.

Diet Cokes: 4.

Chocolate: 2 Twix fingers, 2 bags of buttons.

Glasses of wine: 3. In the wise words of the Eagles, "Some drink to remember, some drink to forget".

Day Forty-Two (Sunday)

6.09 That child is bionic. Disappointed, but not surprised, that such a late night for Child C has made absolutely no difference to his sleep. Go in and explain not morning yet. Back to bed. Pull Child A and B's door closed. Hear them chatting but soon go quiet. Husband has incentivised them with a packet of Match Attax if they stay in bed til 8.00. It might just work.

6.39 More calling. Louder this time. Tell Child C it is just ten more minutes and to read a story to his teddy bears. Child A and B not making a sound.

6.50 "Up tiiiiiiiiiiiimmmmmme". Tell Husband I'm taking Child C downstairs and ask if I can go back to bed for an hour later. He agrees. Makes all the yelling and broken sleep more bearable.

Breakfast for me and Child C. Then TV on and Child C half watches while half playing and I half sleep.

Not a peep out of Child A and B until just after 8.00. Amazing what incentives can do. That's not to say that they have been asleep all that time. Quite the contrary I imagine, but at least it gives them the idea of physically staying in bed which is pretty alien to them. Both come downstairs, having already run in and woken Husband who had planned on sleeping for longer. Dish out brekkie and give pile of Match Attax packets to take upstairs so that Husband can give them out as their reward. He does so. Wails and tears follow.

Transpires that Child A only got two he needed in the pack. Rest are swaps. Also reckons that he has less than Child B. I do mass round up of all the left behind ones that I put together from around the house. Husband does master feat of fairness and negotiation, but Child A still feels super hard done by and throws major wobbly. Husband sends him to his room. Stays there for ages sulking under the bed.

7.45 Try and have a shower. Child C comes in once I'm out of the water, holding a packet of window crayons, wanting to draw on the windows. Figure, what's the harm, but not with the windows – can draw on the shower glass. Proceeds to scribble in red, blue, and green all over the shower. Keeps him happy. Looks terrible.

10.45 Sit down to watch start of the marathon which had been paused while Husband got dressed etc. Child C wants Child A to go and look at his artwork. I try and pause the TV. Accidentally do something which means we can't watch anything we were watching and the whole thing is lost. Husband gets cross. Manage to get it on catch up so Husband and kids watch it on that, while I keep Child C out of the way.

11.15 Lunch on. Husband takes Child A and B to register at local cricket club. Child C builds huge train track through the house, endangering all of us. 12.45 Roast beef and yorkshire puds. Child C eats nothing having eaten two fruit strings this morning.

Clear up while others play in the garden. Husband keeps Child A and B busy playing footie and cricket. Write thank you notes for Child C's birthday, three weeks ago.

Decide I'll try and enjoy the sunshine. Change into shorts. Not a pretty sight, but not going to get rid of pallor in trousers. Really not worth me sitting down. Calls for assistance at least every thirty seconds. Food, drink, sunglasses, potty, login for computer, ball, spade, wipe bottom, find toy, change trousers, find missing teddy, break up argument. Child C has huge strop about finding hats for a large collection of teddies and none of them being the right size. Husband and I both try and find hats, adjust hats and balance hats on teddies of varying sizes for well over an hour. Husband gets suntan. I get fed up of the children. Child C is possibly clinically insane.

17.00 Operation Early Bedtime starts with on-time tea. Fish fingers and chips all round. All eat up and have ice cream for pud. Child A desperate to talk to me about his Fantasy Football team. Try my hardest to be really interested.

17.30 Run bath water for Child C. Gets in and proceeds to fill the rest of the bath with cold water. Instruct him not to many many times. Then can't be bothered. If he is that foolish to want to sit in a bath of cold water then so be it.

17.49 Indeed he really is that foolish. Bath up to the very top with freezing cold water. Choosing my battles today, and not choosing this one.

All upstairs and in PJs by 18.15. All in bed by 18.30. Child C straight to sleep, thank goodness. Could not have taken another evening of constant calling. Child A and B can't sleep as it's "too light". Shut as many doors and curtain as poss, and tell them about all the fun things they need energy for tomorrow.

Catch the last of the sunlight in the garden with Husband. Feels like the first time we've really spoken all day.

Workout DVD each then dinner.

Wash up. Find choc button in the bottom of a packet I thought was empty. Must be a good omen!

Only one hundred and ninety-two hours til the kids go back to school.

Diet Cokes: 3.

Chocolate: 2 bags of buttons.

Glasses of wine: 0 … open in the fridge but managed to resist.

Day Forty-Three (Monday)

4.00 "Save meeeeeeeee. Mama. Save meeeeee". Attend to Child C who, I can only presume is dreaming of dragons and bears. Fall asleep in the big bed in his room by way of protecting him from dragons and bears. Doesn't tell me to "go away" as per normal, so either he is really scared or half asleep.

6.15 Child A comes in looking for Match Attax. Tell him that they are not there and that we'll look in the morning.

6.17 Call of "Found them".

6.20 Alarm goes off. Child C asleep. Why does he do this on a day when we are all getting up, and gets up when I'd rather not on a Sunday? Quick shower, then make the most of Child C being asleep to lie in bed again. At which point, Child C immediately wakes up.

Say good morning to Child A and B. Assistance needed with spider. Gather it has been trapped but that two legs have been chopped off while Child A was trying to trap it (standing on two bean bags on top of the bed). Spider thrown out of window. Normality restored. Get Child C up. He's cross again that Father Christmas hasn't been (in April) and is vile to everyone so take him downstairs for breakfast. Have a falling out over what he's trying to say. We eat breakfast pretty much in silence.

Child A and B upstairs talking about football with Husband. Make an appearance. Still talking about football. Request that they change the subject over breakfast, and ask how they'd feel if I talked about pink shoes all day long. They get the hint, though not sure they really understand why I don't want to hear about it all day.

Child A and B use up computer time. Child C watches TV and rushes out to kitchen to get me every time an advert shows something he'd vaguely like. Asks that Father Christmas brings it to him. Given up trying to explain, and just go with a "yes".

Activity for today is a trip to a local forest. Looks fab and have heard great reports. Set about making picnic, and unpacking bags and repacking them from the last day out. Spare clothes. Water. Money. All present and correct. One day I might be able to leave the house without a complete survival kit. All I'm missing is one of those tin foil blankets and a distress flare and I'd have the lot.

9.15 Bags packed, and just the final child stages to complete. Pop upstairs to put in contact lenses. Request that, in that time, Child A and B clean their teeth, put on their socks and shoes and go for a wee, and that Child A puts in his hearing aid. Return downstairs to find that none of that have been done. Both lose a tick from their reward chart. Both wail at the injustice. Remind them that good listening is important. And, incidentally, why don't they get that at least teeth, socks and shoes and hearing aid need to be done before we go out anywhere. Every day. Can it really be that hard to grasp?

9.40 Leave late for our day out. Meant to leave at 9.30. Five mins in and Child B asks if we are nearly there, Child A says he feels sick and Child C has screamed that he doesn't want any CDs, and then screamed that he wants to listen to *Old MacDonald*.

9.46 Have listened to *Old MacDonald* three times. Take bets from Child A and B as to how many times we're going to listen to it on the journey. I go for fifteen. Child B mid-guessing when Child C screams that he doesn't like that CD. All bets are off.

10.30 Arrive. Call friend we are meeting and she is nearly there, so get everything out of the car and load up buggy. Not sure how I'll carry everything when we don't need a buggy anymore. Pop to loos. Child C runs off into the gents and won't come out. Eventually does so when I mention food. Wants to go to the toilet, but refuses to go in a cubicle. Instead have to erect travel potty in the middle of the toilet – between the two opposite rows of cubicles. Totally in the way. Runs off when finished leaving me clutching bag of wee, surrounded by people wanting to use the toilets. Great start.

Lovely to be out in the fresh air. Loads for the kids to climb and run around. Child C not so great, arguing with other children, refusing most of his lunch, running off with the football, complaining that ice cream is too cold, lagging behind, lying down in random places, adamant that he wants to push the roundabout and then causes a Grand National style tumbling episode as he falls, and five children fall over him in succession, insisting on filling the entire buggy seat with pine cones and large stones used to construct the pathways and car park (I did put the stones back). True to form asleep within ten mins of leaving the car park. Deep breath. And relax.

Feel a bit bad that didn't get to help Child A and B on the climbing equipment as much as I would have liked but think they had a good time.

14.10 Pack up car to come home. Child A reveals that some children said something and did something mean to him in the shelter bit on one of the climbing frames. Won't tell me what it is until we get home. Worried, so ask if he'll tell me if I pull over. He agrees. Pull into garden centre, and he whispers that they told him that he couldn't be in there and threw bark at him. Meanies. Explain that that just shows that he is a better person than them, and that that is a perfect example of what mean bullies are like. Reiterate that meanies never win. Ever.

Lighten the mood with tongue twisters. Especially amusing since Child A and B missing front teeth. "Fred says thank you for the thatched cottage" turns out to be a particularly good one.

15.00 Arrive home. Shattered. Child A and B awarded bonus computer time for good behaviour on our day out. Also largely because I am exhausted and want peace and quiet. Wake Child C, and he watches TV. Outdoor stimulation complete for the day, for now.

Child C hungry (because he didn't eat lunch) so demands food. Refuse anything from the biscuit cupboard, where he is lingering with intent. Eventually settles for cheese and raisins. At least that is sort of healthy.

16.00 Serve up early tea, since they had early lunch. All done within twenty mins, so encourage Child A and B to enjoy the last of the sunshine outside. They play beautifully for an hour, until the ball gets kicked over the fence.

Start the bath (and hair wash) process at 17.00. Somehow lasts an hour and a half for all three of them. Largely due to Child C "putting out dragon fires" with cold water in a child's bowl on the wall mirror, and in Child A and B's baths. Lots of water all over the place but everyone happy.

Child A and B on good form, and tired – in a good way (rather than the grumpy way). Get ready for bed, and put Child C to bed. Several calls back. Remain patient and see to his needs. Read two chapters of book to Child A and B, and tuck them in. Child C screams variety of "save me" / "mama need you" / "can you hear meeee" throughout. Then begins a series of call backs to Child C which would test the patience of a the saintliest saint. All along the same lines of dragons, bears, and giving hugs. On the ninth call back which I respond to (circa 19.30, and ignoring all the ones I have not responded to), pushed over the edge by request for a new lamp, and that I roar loudly three times to scare the dragons away. Fling open curtains. Point out that there are no dragons or bears anywhere, ever, anywhere near us. Shout that he is making me cross and sad. States he doesn't like cows. Fling open curtains again with a call of "Cows? Cows? Nope they've all gone". Remind him (as have threatened in the eighth call up) that if I am called in again then I'm taking his toys. Forty-five mins and a very stressed Mummy later, he relents.

20.30 Want wine. Must do some exercise. Do exercise DVD, then recover with wine.

Sort dinner.

21.15 Now to clear up. Husband out for dinner but will be home soonish I imagine.

Diet Cokes: 4.

Chocolate: 3 bags of chocolate buttons.

Glasses of wine: 1.

Day Forty-Four
(Tuesday)

Child C awake at 6ish. Go in to check on his "need you" cries. Doesn't need me. Tell him to go back to bed, or read a book. "Me no want read book. Me go your bed" is his response. "No" is my response. Ignore him until alarm goes off.

Get in shower at 6.22. Tesco man coming between 7.00 and 8.00 so don't want to be wrapped in a towel for his arrival. Husband catching train to work but we don't need to give him a lift (phew). Hope Tesco man doesn't block his car in and add time to get-out-of-house-urgency.

Start the breakfast process, with promise of more to come from the delivery man.

7.45 Child B asks how long til the delivery man comes. Tell him in the next fifteen mins. "Yay" he exclaims.

7.50 Oh. Bother. Remember that booked delivery for between 8.00 and 9.00. Not between 7.00 and 8.00. Remember now that the earlier slot got filled up in the time it took me to decide to change it. Children groan at delay to chocolate brioches.

8.30 Delivery arrives. Child A and C "help" to unload the shopping faster than I can keep track. Before long Easter eggs all over the kitchen floor, whilst I am still signing the electronic thing. Child C does not get that they are not to be eaten just yet, and yells. A lot. To compensate, Child C embarks on eating mission and eats three yoghurts and a bowl of strawberries. Just pleased he's eating.

Can't find the six Kinder Eggs I ordered anywhere. Call customer services, incensed. As go through options and finally reach operator, see them lurking at the bottom of a bag with twelve cans of beer. What silly person thought to put one of the most fragile, and important-to-not-break-or-child-will-cry, items under that? Apologise to the man, who I think thought I was totally insane, and hide the eggs, before Child C wants to eat them too.

8.43 Child C sent to his cot for stamping on Child A's ankles and prior to that, switching the TV off that Child A was watching, screaming at me, banning everyone from the sofa and generally being totally vile.

8.50 Get him out. Seems a bit nicer now, and happy to play rather than cause a fight with everyone.

9.45 Head out for our walk, via next door to get our ball back. Kind neighbour offers to throw it back.

Lovely walk, apart from four of the six kids who hide in the stinging nettles, getting stung, and Child C trailing behind, lying down in fields and not willing to sit nicely in the buggy. Come home with more sticks, and lumps of chalk than I thought it possible to carry. Child A and B tell me that they are going to "make paint". Marvellous.

11.30 Go to look for a child's birthday card in the shop. Poor selection. Buy some frisbees from the shop for Child A, B and C – figure they might be fun for the beach, when we go away to visit the grandparents. Return home via garden centre to look for card. Equally poor selection. Sorely tempted to get one with "nephew", "grandson" or similar on it, just to avoid having to go to proper shops with all three children. Find a passable one with age six on it. Get it. Then wonder if the birthday boy is actually turning six.

Beans on toast for lunch. Child C refuses it. Probably stuffed from breakfast. Child A and B devour his portion. Stopping only to argue over who was the recipient of the most gooey toast.

Listen to answerphone messages. Cousins have chicken pox and Nanny has a chest infection so we're not going away as planned. Guess we'll use the frisbees in the garden.

Child A sends frisbee over the fence. One down. Two left.

Child C spends thirty mins on potty. Then decides he is hungry. "Me no like that" to anything I suggest, apart from strawberries and raisins. Returns to potty soon after. Probably the strawberries and raisins.

Child A and B fab this afternoon. Combo of making perfume, playing *Masterchef*, making paint and clearing the patio. Child A informs me he is making "Vanish powder" as he grinds chalk down into teeny weeny pieces. Might need more than Vanish to get it all out of their clothes. And a bit of football. Another ball over. Three hours of almost loveliness from them. More of that please.

Child C pootles between TV, playing at his sand table, and playing a little with his toys.

Feel shattered.

16.30 Body Low has developed into a full-on Can't Be Bothered To Do Anything. Refuel with three heavily laden teaspoons of Nutella. Fatigue momentarily eased.

16.45 Nutella has worn off. Back to where I was before. But with guilt for eating Nutella from the jar.

Run bath for Child C. See tally chart, on a piece of paper in the bathroom, with about thirty-five markings on it. Child B explains that it is his, and it was to show how many times he thought about food this morning, while waiting for Morning Time. Who says boys only think about their stomachs?!

Bath for Child C. PJs for Child A and B. Thank goodness Child C goes off without a peep. Story for Child A and B. So light, hard for them to sleep. Both complain of a range of ailments to delay actually having to go to sleep.

Start workout DVD. Interrupted by Child B. Claims he's had a bad dream about crocodiles in his bed, after only having been in bed for six minutes. Child A pops out, to join in the conversation. Tell them both to go to sleep, and if everyone feels ill tomorrow we won't see Grandma and Grandpa.

Finish DVD. Children sleep. Husband on way home. Dinner on.

Attempt to clear patio. Playing with mud and chalk has made a bit more of a mess than I'd realised. Let's hope for a rain storm.

Diet Cokes: 3.

Chocolate: 2 bags of buttons, half a bag of mini eggs meant for the kids, 3 tsp of Nutella.

Glasses of wine: 1.

Day Forty-Five (Wednesday)

2.00 Wake up call. Full search of cot required to check for spiders. Twice. Sleep in spare bed to reassure Child C. All pillows and teddies need to be lifted for full cot check. Wakes again. Murmur something reassuring.

6.15 Normal start to the morning. Apart from we're up earlier as Husband has to leave at 7.15. Not such a bad thing as I have stuff to get ready for our day out. Meeting Grandma and Grandpa at Brooklands Museum. Child C thinks we're going to the museum from *Peppa Pig*. Or Grandma and Grandpa's house. Will have to tackle that when we get there.

7.45 Really hoping that muscle weighs more than fat. Google it. It doesn't. As my research points out one kg is one kg, whether it is lead or feathers. Oh damn. Exercise not working. How can that be? Probably more active than when the kids are at school and not eating that much more chocolate than normal. So unfair.

Kids amused with TV and computer while I get the usual kit and caboodle ready. Picnic, money, spare clothes, coats for every season. Frost this morning, but forecast says it will be hot hot hot, so dress for both.

9.15 Depart. Planned to leave at 9.00 which isn't necessary, but figure that, based on experience, it always takes us fifteen mins more than planned to leave the house. Pop via post office. Leave kids outside in car and hope that queue will be short. It isn't. All killing each other by the time I get back.

9.45 Arrive. Grandma and Grandpa not yet there as stuck on the M25. Child A and B watch cars on the skid pan, through the fence. Child C throws stones at cars in the car park. Until I stop him. Then he just contents himself with putting large stones in the middle of the car park roadways.

Grandma and Grandpa arrive ten mins later. Head inside. Fantastic day. Child C his normal uncooperative self, but easier to manage with a greater adult / child ratio. Lovely to be able to ask someone to watch him while I read something or speak to someone. Plus novelty factor of Grandma and Grandpa being there is a bonus. Sun is shining, Child A and B totally enthralled by it all, and everyone happy. We get to ride in race cars, on an old London bus, and even sit on Concorde. Joy lessened only a little by Child C, shouting to Grandpa "You're wee wee. You're poo poo" repeatedly on the Concorde tour. Locate sugary snack and ram in his fist quickly before he can repeat it any more times. Followed shortly afterwards on the plane by exclaiming "Me no like planes. Take me home". Think he is a bit confused at boarding planes and not going anywhere.

16.00 Decide to head home. Child C decides that that is the moment he'd like to learn to wipe him own bottom. And test all the cold taps in the ladies' loos.

Major mission to keep Child C awake. Tiny nap and we'll all be doomed at bedtime.

16.30 Needn't have worried. Child C stays awake the whole time. Largely thanks to the toy bus that Grandma and Grandpa bought for him. Thank goodness for that. Tell boys that I think it was the best day out ever. They agree. Though they suggest that it is joint

196

first with hot chocolate and cake at the garden centre. Ah, the mind of a seven year old!

Put tea on super quick. Husband home early as been to dentist. Child C adamant he wants to play in the front garden. Leave him to do so while put the pasta on. Husband shuts front door. Point out that Child C is out there. Opens it to find Child C driving toy bus down the bonnet of Husband's new-ish car. Child C brought inside.

17.00 Tea served. Child A and B eat like they've never been fed. Child C eats one piece of pasta. Probably because of the three bags of biscuits, three fruit strings, four sandwiches, yoghurt, few strawberries and half tub of chocolate ice cream that he had earlier. Decides after tea that he'd like a bag of crisps. Request denied.

Feel shattered after the day out. Bath time for Child C who looks like a chimney sweep. Surprised the bath water doesn't turn black. Child A and B do research for their Fantasy Football teams with Husband.

18.00 Child C refuses to get out of the bath. Too busy covering himself in foam and pretending to be "Ho Ho" (Father Christmas). Probably caused by him looking at all the precious mementoes in the display cabinets at the museum, demanding he plays with them, and me flippantly saying that he can ask Father Christmas for them. Possibly not my wisest move.

18.01 Child A refuses to get changed for bed, claiming he was just about to go outside and play football. Child B happy to get changed. Husband suggests five mins of football. Child B teary. Relent.

18.10 Child C finally gets out of bath after – I think – thinking that I have abandoned him, while I clear a few bits. Get out nail scissors. He freaks. Will leave that for another day.

18.15 Mission is bedtime ASAP. Call Husband, Child A and Child B in. Point out that they have had fifteen mins. Not five.

18.20 Call them again. With angry voice.

Changed and all into bed by 18.30. Child A and B desperate for next instalment of bedtime story. Child C calling out. Refuse to read bedtime story. Then relent. It's so light and warm anyway that it's not like they will go straight to sleep. Read then say goodnight. Child C still screaming. Check on him. Same old "drag drags and cows and bears" thing. Looks knackered. Make the right sounds – including a roar to scare them away – then bid farewell.

19.00 Wine. Husband on work calls. Even warm wine feels ok this evening.

19.45 Check emails. One through about school admissions. Child A and B will be moving onto junior school really soon … end of an era. Broken from reverie as remember that washing still out. Damn.

Diet Cokes: 4.

Chocolate: 2 small bags of buttons, outside of a Creme Egg, 1 large bag buttons, 3 spoonfuls of ice cream.

Glasses of wine: 1.

Day Forty-Six
(Thursday)

Up twice in the night for Child C who seemed to be reliving our day out. Spent two periods of the night sleeping in his room, as easier to attend to the murmurs, chat and wails of "Where's my bus?", "No food. Want snack", "Me go in car" etc.

6.36 Child B comes in. Some argument or other with his brother. "Shush" him nicely and remind him that Child C is asleep, and that we'll all be happier if it stays that way. Tell him to go and play in his own room and will sort out argument when everyone is up.

6.37 Child A comes in. His version is along the lines of Child B hitting him repeatedly in the knees. Hard to imagine based on Child B's lack of physical strength vs Child A, but possible. Send Child A back to his room, and will discuss in the morning.

6.38 Call of "Up time Maaaaaa Meeeeeee". Child C has, it seems, been awake a while as he has all his teddies lined up in height order. At least that kept him really quiet while he was doing it.

All up. Child A takes one look at me (now with the lights on) and asks if I am tired. Say that I am and ask how he can tell. He replies that "sometimes people just have that impression". Husband agrees that I look "shocking" and suggests I look in the mirror. They are right. Probably a combo of disturbed sleep, in two different beds and putting on a triple helping of anti-wrinkle / plumping moisturiser last night. Think it might have left me over plumped, though certainly not wrinkle free. Am hoping shower later will deflate me.

Head downstairs with Child C for breakfast. Chaos breaks out upstairs as Husband gets cross with kids being feral, when he is still on work mode, and hasn't yet switched off for the weekend. Child A and B come down for breakfast too. Brekkie done, TV on, jigsaws out for Child C, computer on for Child A and B.

8.00 Husband down and in charge while I take a shower. Shower takes longer than normal as have to clean off Child C's window crayon artwork from the shower glass. So nice to have a shower in peace, that I don't mind cleaning the glass ... adds a couple of minutes on to some quiet time.

Back downstairs by 8.30. Wash on, wash up from breakfast, dress kids, respond to calls of this and that, keep the peace, and wrap a birthday present with the "help" of Child C. Insists on putting sticky tape in totally random locations, so that it looks like the paper has been used already. Might have to put a note in with the present to explain. Husband asks Child A and B what they'd like to do today. They mention mini golf. They get planning.

11.00 Don't know where the rest of the morning has gone ... Leave Husband in charge while I pop to post office to send present. Give instruction to "all get along". Soooo nice to pop out without children in tow. Nip in. Nip out. And not one cry of "I neeeeed this".

11.30 Early lunch, so that Husband can take Child A and B to mini golf. Which leaves me and Child C facing Tesco trip. No point going to mini golf, as Child C would be a total nightmare, based on previous mini golf episodes. Not sure he'll be much better in the supermarket, but at least no water features or hard balls and sticks there.

Fish fingers and chips for the kids for lunch. Child C eats one mouthful of fish finger. Declares that he doesn't like "dip dip" or fish fingers. There goes my fall back staple. Plan B required.

12.45 Husband heads out with Child A and B. Get Child C ready and head to Tesco. Get parent and child space (yay) and trolley. Child C refuses to sit in trolley chair, so sits in main trolley. Variety of fruit gets rolled, kicked and squashed by him, but at least he stays put. Until aisle fifteen. Hoiks one leg over the edge while I say hello to another mum from school and from yoghurts onwards he insists on walking.

On drive home, notice that two "For Sale" boards have gone up in our road. One next door, and one three doors up on the other side. Hmmm. Two week holiday. Kids at home a lot. Lots of time in the garden. Coincidence?

Child C given the ice cream he so desperately "needed" in the supermarket once out of the car at home. Insist he eats a banana first. Then eats four cheese biscuits and half a bowl of grapes. If he would only eat at normal times like normal people. Ice cream for me too. I need it.

14.35 Unpack shopping. Oops. Realise I forgot to get anything for dinner. Will have to improvise.

Attempt to tidy the lounge a bit, with Child C. He'd rather make dog bones from Duplo. Husband arrives home with Child A and B at 15.45. All had a blast. They demolish most of what I had bought.

16.24 Hungry. Tuck into an avocado before googling "can avocado make you fat?". Seemingly it can, but is healthy at the same time!?

Kids all happy playing in the garden, so moan when say it is time for dinner. Child B and even Child C eat spaghetti with gusto.

Child A less so. Then all eat a bowl of fruit, and a yoghurt. Mentally tick off another meal.

I tidy. They play out in the garden with Husband. All happy and much more relaxed than this morning. Hurrah. Child C requests broom, witch's hat and magic wand. Improvise on the last one with a drinking straw. Spends next fifteen mins "flying" round the garden and turning all of us into frogs.

17.45 Bath time for Child C. Only a couple of accidents today, but nice to have him smelling clean again rather than of a men's urinal. Explain to him about getting to the potty or toilet in time, but think I might have to work on that a bit more next week. At least he has stopped going in the bath.

Tell Child C that Husband is meeting a friend for a beer. He asks whether they will be playing *The Shopping Game*.

While Child A in bath, Child B requests scissors, tape, blu tack and paper. Sign goes up on his door. Ask what it says. He replies: "Staff only and children under six. But don't worry Mum I'm making you a staff badge. But not one for him" (Child A). That'll go down well. Duly makes my badge and shows me how to fix it to my top. Making a pass reader is next on his list. Wear my staff badge for rest of evening.

Dry Child A and notice bruising on his knee. Tells me that it was inflicted by Child B this morning. Further questioning reveals that it was the metal leg of a bed, and a different bit (a tiny bump imperceptible to the human eye) was as a result of Child B.

19.00 All in bed. Child C has tipped out all the *Mr. Men* books all over the floor. Feel a bit bad for not reading one to him. But Child B read one to him, as did Husband, so will read one tomorrow. Child A and B busy making new passes for all staff members. Child

A is now part of the "management" and allowed to join in. Child B informs me that he will have "level 5" written on his badge, and that we'll all be "level 1" but can go to a higher level if we do something good. Child C drops off fairly quickly. Read chapter to Child A and B. Both sharing in Child B's room – in king size bed. Have shared like this before but argument tonight about who is taking up more space. Brief lecture on not behaving like an old married couple, and explain a bedding set I saw on *Dragons' Den* once where there was a line down the middle. They, like me, think it's a fab idea. Both request that I draw a line on the sheets. Not going to happen.

19.35 Husband meeting friend at the pub, so serve up early dinner. Noodles and turkey dinosaurs (bought as Child C *did* like and then instantly went off the following day, so we have to eat them up).

19.50 Husband out. Exercise DVD on. I WILL have buns of steel if it kills me. Which it may well do.

Dinner and TV. Housework can wait til tomorrow.

23.20 Husband arrives home. Ten pints or so the wiser. Demolishes two packets of crisps while watching music TV. Ironic that he falls asleep on the sofa, while the TV blasts out "I don't want to close my eyes, I don't want to fall asleep … I don't want to miss a thing".

Diet Cokes: 3.

Chocolate: 1 bag of buttons, 1 bag of Milky Bar Buttons … am sure that there was more than that, but can't remember … oh yes, mint chocolate ice cream.

Glasses of wine: 1.5. Can't help but feel that cancels out the exercise but surely doing the exercise has got to have some benefit. It still hurts, if that is of any relevance.

Day Forty-Seven
(Friday)

6.00 Wake up. Husband not there. Must still be asleep downstairs.

6.20 Calls start from Child C. Go in to convince him that he should wait until Morning Time. Go back to bed. Screaming gets louder. Figure it's not worth it. Get him up.

Child A and B come in to say hello. Child C goes to see Husband.

Husband snoozing on the sofa. Brekkie for Child C who is fascinated watching the birds landing on the lawn and eating worms. Discussion ensues as to how they know where to look for worms. Child A reckons that the peck down and take a look. Child C reckons they just keep pecking til they find one.

Cuppa, paracetamol, chocolate / banana milkshake and bacon sandwich for Husband. Everyone else fed. Escape for a shower.

7.30 Get text from neighbour whose kids are fighting over scissors. Wonders if I've got any spare she could borrow. I have. Send Husband (dressed from last night) and Child A (in PJs) down the road to deliver scissors on mercy mission. Feels like we live in Ramsay Street.

8.20 Child C comes to find me. I'm just dressed. Hair still wet. Play *The Shopping Game* twice, until Child C's cheating and rule changes render the game stupid. Go downstairs.

Kids super noisy and Child C super needy. Grabs my leg anytime I try to clear anything up. Husband and Child A and B sit on sofa doing Fantasy Football things and generally talking about things that women and children under the age of six couldn't give a stuff about. Child C screams at me. Gets dragged along the kitchen floor on my leg (albeit very very slowly). Follows me with every step. Tries to barge me repeatedly with his head. Fed up and lock myself in toilet. Child C tries to knock the door down for a bit, then backs off a little. Starts saying "Mummy, big hug" so figure he's feeling less ready for combat. Tiptoe out. Big hugs and kisses exchanged. He allows me to wash up without wearing him as an accessory.

Husband goes for shower. Get boys dressed. Start on enormous ironing pile. Child A wants to watch football. Child B wants to watch *Masterchef*. Both angry that I've not recorded a review of the Premier League season which was on yesterday, from 1993. Apparently that makes me responsible for everything bad in the world. Watch something about Liverpool, and boys interested to learn about Ian Rush, in the "olden days". Even I learn something. Didn't realise that Alan Hanson played for Liverpool. Or any team in fact. Husband horrified when I reveal that I just thought he was a footie pundit. Then we watch *Masterchef*. Child C plays with farm animals in the other room.

10.45 BBQ planned for lunch. Get all the stuff ready. Child C does a wee in the potty. Throw wee down toilet. Splashes back in my face.

11.00 Husband still in the bathroom. Get BBQ and coal out. And lighter. Mention that we need to have lunch around 12ish so that Child C doesn't eat through the cupboards while he waits and that lack of food makes children really really angry. Child C dressed as a cow. Jumps off sofa repeatedly into a large bucket tub of teddies. Fetches donkey outfit for Child B and penguin outfit for Child A. All jump off sofa in style of someone walking the plank. Chaos. Child A's back gets hurt falling out of a storage trug. Mayhem continues.

11.20 BBQ still not on.

11.30 BBQ goes on. Child C extra ratty. Figure that food might make it better. Make snacky lunch which he wolfs down, while watching the BBQ. Interested in the whole process. As are the other two who construct a barrier which they don't think anyone should go past. Remove donkey and penguin suits as figure they should not be worn near fire. One spark and we could be two less for lunch.

Normal BBQ procedure. Helpers fetch and carry loads of stuff while man makes fire. Child C contents himself with throwing loads of bread out for the birds. In big chunks.

13.00 BBQ ready. Very yummy. Husband asks for score. Child A gives ten, Child B gives nine and I give eight (due to Husband's lack of utensil preparation). Child C spends the time when the rest of us are eating looking out of the window bemoaning the fact that no birds are coming to eat the bread. No surprise with the noise he makes.

Wash up. Child A and B play footie with Husband. Child C happy watching TV.

14.30 Out to mini steam trains, which are on for the bank holiday. All have fun. Child C melts down on way home. Others play Pooh Sticks. Child C doesn't get it and just chucks stones into the stream. Great big handfuls of stones. Which look like they have been put there to fill holes. Meltdown continues. Send Husband ahead with Child A and B and keys. Rescue mission initialised. I restrain Child C while Husband brings the rescue vehicle to get us home as soon as possible.

16.20 Arrive home. All children hungry. Yoghurts all round. Then don't eat their tea. Sometimes wonder why I bother cooking at all. Too tired to care this evening. Child A and B out to play footie.

Child C up to the bath. Bread still uneaten in the garden. Please let it be the birds rather than the foxes that eat that up.

Read a book to Child C while Child A and B do more football stuff with Husband.

18.45 Bedtime for all. Leg stretches for Child B. Teeth cleaned. Wees done. No bedtime story for Child A and B as I'm just tooooo tired.

19.00 All in bed. Husband and I meant to be doing workout DVDs. Can't face it. Have dinner and veg on sofa instead. And eat chocolate.

Diet Cokes: 4.

Chocolate: 2 bags of chocolate buttons, 2 lines of Fruit and Nut.

Glasses of wine: 0. Husband has suggested that we should have an alcohol free evening. Sounds like a plan.

Day Forty-Eight (Saturday)

6.00 Child C wakes. And yells. And yells. Husband sleeps through it. How do they do that?

6.45 Get up. Do breakfast. Husband sleeps on.

Child A puts on *Smurfs 2* film. We settle down to watch. Child A and I watch the most. Child B too terrified, so spends most of the time in the other room watching a different channel. Child C flits in and out depending on what is happening in the film. Can't wait to take them to the cinema one day. Child A and B never been, but can't take them til they stop being scared of everything in every film.

9.30 Husband comes down. Asks if the volume control on the TV is broken. Explain that we couldn't hear it over Child C.

Head for a shower. Ask all to include Child C in whatever activity or conversation they embark on. Ten mins later, Child C comes to find me. Complains when I won't let him draw on the shower door.

Face all puffy and splodgy. Probably all the chocolate and not enough water and sleep. Slap on tonnes of moisturiser and hope for miracle.

Head back downstairs to wash up from breakfast. Provide fried egg sarnie for Husband. He and Child A and B all request banana / choc / strawberry milkshake. Make them and serve. Husband informs me that he's going to do his workout DVD.

10.20 Pop out to corner shop to leave parcel there to be returned. Take longer drive home just so I can listen to the radio and not have to get anything for anyone for a few mins. See friend who asks if Husband taking kids to football match this afternoon. Say I'll check. He is. Three less for later on this afternoon. Shame Child C can't go. It's him I really need a break from.

Husband does workout while I pair socks. Child C annoys me by trying to empty wash basket containing folded laundry.

Child A and B argue about whose turn it is to wear the T-shirt with the footballs on it, put up football goal and play in the garden. Child C gets cross and tries to steal all the balls.

11.30 BBQ goes on. Sunny but cold, but loads of food to cook up. Have decided no more Mr. Nice Guy with lunch for Child C today. Will make mince, mash and beans and he can eat it or nothing. We'll see how that goes.

12.45 Lovely BBQ and even Child C has a stab at eating his lunch with enough mention of chocolate eggs. Eats half a bowl. That's something. Even if his initial reaction is "Me no like that. It make me sick". Have decided to do early Easter egg hunt today as due to rain for the next two days. Kids decide that they want to go with Husband's suggestion of one child at a time.

13.15 Chaotic Easter egg hunt. Try to stop Child C revealing the location of every egg. No eggs for me, so I have Child C's Creme Eggs, since he doesn't like the middle yolky bit.

14.30 Husband, Child A and B leave for football. Wash up.

15.11 Realise that Child C has been sitting on the potty for over half an hour. Think he was done ages ago. Appears that he is just using it as an armchair. Peel him off.

15.30 Go to garden centre. Child C takes forever to get into the car, preferring to hide behind the hedge. On arrival, prize Child C away from all the stones in the car park. Find grass seed. Child C chats to birds in a cage. Child C rearranges all the large pottery animals. Several times. Narrowly misses breaking them. Grab pink pot for Husband's sick mint plants from kitchen. Child C chats to parrot at counter. Scared that parrot will peck him. Pay and leave. Child C moves bird bath. Point out to him that if he leaves it there, it will trip people up as they come out of the garden centre. Four moves later, goes back to where it was.

Plant the grass seed on the lawn. Child C pretends it is snowing and scatters it all over the place. Hose it all in. Child C gets soaked, but he's happy. Now we just need some rain and sun, and we can fix the lawn which looks more like mud than lawn. Blame Child A and B and their football playing.

Wash hands and read *Mr. Men* books. Child C appears to have a large amount of grass seed in his hair. Better sort that out or he'll have a full lawn there tomorrow. Child C has twenty-five books from the collection lined up and wants me to read them all. Read two. *Mr. Tall* and *Mr. Rude*. Hope he learns something from the second.

17.00 Husband arrives home with Child A and B. Local team lost but they had a good time, despite "colourful" language from the crowd. Deliver a short cautionary tale on not using any rude words that they might have heard.

Serve up tea that no one seems very fussed about. Fly flies out of bin while Child A tries to tell me about the Watford / Ipswich match, sparking fears of an infestation. Child B takes ages to appear. On toilet, arranging Match Attax. Give up and leave Husband and three wandering children while I go and sort laundry. Can't be bothered.

Fed up. Of talking about football. Of children who don't appreciate anything. Of children who take stuff for granted. Of serving others all day and not doing anything I want / need to do.

17.40 Run bath for Child C. Hairwash for him. Call Child A and B for bath. They have discovered Husband's really old Xbox and don't want a bath. Wait fifteen mins then give up. Again. Clear up garden and tell them to wash their own hair, and that the bath's ready.

In garden and hear that kids are in the bath, supervised by Husband. Go upstairs and see they are in bath, and have used half a bottle of bubble bath. And not washed their hair. All deny any knowledge of hair washing. Feel like crying. Boys apologise for using the bubble bath. Point out that that's not why I'm fed up. Child B asks me to stop crying as it's making him sad. Child A asks if I'm alright.

18.45 All boys in PJs. Child C reading with Husband. Give two minute warning. Pays no notice and so screams house down when two minute warning up and plopped in bed. Stalls for time by asking everyone for cuddles and kisses. Read chapter of book to Child A and B, who realise that I'm fed up. Child A and B very meek and relatively well behaved. Until I stop reading and then Child B becomes lippy all over again.

Say goodnight. Clean BBQ grill. Pilates DVD.

20.30 Don't think I've burnt off the Creme Eggs but feel suitably stretched. Dinner. Bed.

Diet Cokes: 4.

Chocolate: 2 Creme Eggs, 1 bag of buttons.

Glasses of wine: 1.5. Using up bottle.

Day Forty-Nine (Sunday)

Not getting up today until Child C's clock says Morning Time. He's safe, warm, has a drink and books and toys. Hear Child A and B. Check clock. 5.52. Child C starts calling. Check clock. 6.00. Pillow over head. Doze on and off. Child A and B come in at 6.40. Child A's clock says it is morning. That needs sorting. Tell them ten more mins.

6.45 They come back. Get in bed for cuddle. 6.50 Child C calls to tell me that it is Morning Time. Go and see him. He's happy enough. See. No harm done.

Down for breakfast. Child A makes me cry by shouting commands at me. Then immediately apologises. Think he knows he's done wrong. That's progress. All sit on sofa to watch *Peppa Pig*.

8.00 Husband comes downstairs. Ask if I can go back to bed. He's ok with it. Yay. Earplugs in. Set alarm for 9.10. Explain to Child C where I'm going and what I'm doing. Ten mins later Child C at door. Knocking and calling. Ignore. Ten mins later same again. Presume it is every time Husband's back is turned.

9.00 Child C works out how to get in to the room. Brings me *The Three Little Pigs* and "reads" it to me. By the time he's got to the stick house Husband realises he's not around and comes to find him.

Lie in over. Child C and I read four books, then go downstairs. Diet Coke needed to kick in wake up process. Have shower. Child C climbs in and out of the wash basket. Scatters washing everywhere. Child A and B busy playing on Husband's Xbox downstairs. Don't like them playing on the computer that much, but it's almost the last day of the holidays, Husband is home, we're off to grandparents later, I need to tidy up for the cleaners, so just for today, I don't care. Oh and it's raining. Hurray for the grass seed.

10.15 Clear kitchen, put lunch on and set Child C up with Playdoh. Three tubs all end up mixed into one. But he's happy and not clinging off my trousers. So I'm prepared to overlook the Playdoh mixing.

Sneak medicinal bag of chocolate buttons. Incidentally, weigh 0.7kg less today than yesterday. How does that work? Stuffed my face with chocolate, drank wine and lost weight. Don't think it was the Pilates workout. Must eat more chocolate and drink more wine. Genius.

12.10 Alternative Easter lunch. Jacket potatoes. Apart from Child A and Child C who don't like them. Fish fingers for them. Will there ever be a day where I cook one meal and we all eat the same? Small amount of potato sneaked onto Child C's plate, spat all over table. Tears from Child A and B that they can't eat their pudding before Child C has finished. Child A and B won't stop talking about football. Add to that last question – Will mealtimes ever stop being chaotic? Seems like someone is getting up or down every five seconds. And Grandma wonders why we don't have roasts more often. Spend all morning cooking. Eat in five mins. Spend afternoon clearing up.

13.00 Child A and B go off with Husband to play computer games. Again. Child C wants to watch *Dora The Explorer* on the iPad. Peace in the kitchen. TV junkie children aside, it feels like there is hope. Possibly due to a lie in. Or having some time to sort the house out this morning and being able to now see part of the floor. Or because there is only one more full day of the holidays. Or, most likely, a combination of all three.

13.40 Start the packing process. Only going to be away at Grandma and Grandpa's for less than twenty-four hours. How can it involve so much energy, and take so much time? I conclude that it's a mixture of the following ...

1. The British weather. Despite checking the weather, it could be sunny, it could be rainy, it could be cold. It could be all three. Various outfits required to allow for costume changes.

2. Children spill stuff (could be on their top, could be on their trousers. In the case of Child C, could spill stuff three times or more).

3. Children like going out in the garden. Requires wellies, change of clothes (in addition to the spilling something change of clothes).

4. Children get ill. Don't want to be washing clothes in the middle of the night should child come down with attack of vile vomiting bug or similar at short notice.

5. Want them to sleep as much as possible. Thus need to take range of teddies and home comforts to make this more likely. Child C has five teddies, a singing sea horse and Gro-Clock packed. Expect Child A and B to make further selections once I announce we are going.

6. As a mother I am expected to have whatever is needed, and will be blamed by other family members if I do not. Capol, spare socks, that cereal they really like – the responsibility rests with me.

Based on all of that, we need as much for one night as we do for three or four, as always.

Gather bags in hall. Child C wants to wash his hands. Wets himself. Point proved. Change of clothes required before we even leave the house. Children over-excited and want to go.

14.36 Put bins out. Still raining. Will expect to come home tomorrow to a forest of new grass. Find coats, find wellies. Change car seats into Husband's car. Clean children's teeth. Waaay later than should have.

15.30 Set off. Remember haven't put out garden bins. Text neighbour to ask her if she could do it. Child C leans on Child B. The latter screams. More leaning. More screaming. I make fake cancellation calls to Grandma and Grandpa. Repeatedly. Eventually Child C gives up.

Really really rainy. Motorway horrible. Glad I'm not driving. Can hardly see a thing.

16.16 Arrive. Children rush inside. Pleased to see everyone and all the toys they haven't seen in ages. Play and chat.

My uncle gives children Easter eggs. Eat smarties and told to leave egg til after tea. Cook tea. Grandma and Grandpa take my uncle to the train station. Kids eat good tea. Serve up eggs.

17.10 Eggageddon. All eggs are exactly the same. Had marked Child B's with a sticker and thought I knew whose was whose on the others. Turns out I don't. Accidentally give Child B's to Child C. Don't see sticker. Then Child A and B fight over the two remaining eggs. Tears. Tantrums. Child A refuses to eat any chocolate egg at all. Point out again and again that it is the same thing. Doesn't cut it. Grandma and Grandpa arrive home to a scene of mayhem, screaming and upset. Only dies down when Grandma points out that they won't have any eggs from them if they don't calm down.

Child A and B watch end of Man U match. They lose interest when Man U start losing. Child C plays shops.

18.10 Get Child C into jimjams. Says he wants a bath. Try to convince him otherwise. Doesn't work. Such is the allure of different bath toys. Run bath.

All in bed by 19.00. Sit down for dips and fizz. Perfect.

Lovely to catch up and all in bed by 22.30ish.

Diet Cokes: 3.

Chocolate: 2 bags of buttons.

Glasses of wine: 4.

Day Fifty (Monday)

Sleep badly. Child C sleeping downstairs at Grandma and Grandpa's, so am worried that I might not hear him. As if. Conscious that Child A and B are in bunkbeds and that one might fall to his doom.

5.47 Hear Child A say to his brother "Are you awake? I've been awake since 5.32 and it's now 5.47". Can hear them starting to play *Old Maid*. Go and remind them to whisper. Carry on talking just as loudly as before. Don't actually think that Child A can whisper, and it's nothing to do with his hearing loss. Remind them again. Might as well have not bothered.

6.04 Child C starts calling. Not fair to leave him calling in a room which isn't his. Go down to see him. Child A and B follow. Work out how to switch the heating on. All fed and two of them dressed by 6.45. Child A asks to use the iPad. Answer is no. Way too early.

7.00 Grandma suggests I go back to bed. Husband still asleep. Go back and doze. Soooooo nice. Don't sleep very well but savour every minute.

8.10 Not asleep now and feel guilty about Grandma and Grandpa having to look after the kids. Husband awake too, so suggest we go downstairs.

Make an appearance. Take a shower. Interrrupted by Child C banging on the door. Apparently he keeps trying to lick everyone and is upset that no one wants to be licked. Take charge of Child C and get dressed.

Spend morning playing in the garden. Grandpa has new No Footie Rule, to protect flower beds, so kids forced to play with other toys. Bean bags, badminton, bubbles, hula hoop, slide, inflatable dinosaur, stomper rocket and ping pong catcher all out within the space of forty mins. And Child B still says he doesn't know what to play with. Think he's too used to Child A coming up with all the ideas.

Husband goes for a jog round the block. Seems surprised that I didn't pack exercise gear. Didn't even cross my mind.

Lovely roast lamb lunch. So nice to eat someone else's food. Child A and B eat like ravenous animals. Child B puts on particularly astounding show of eating roast lamb dinner, extra lamb, mini ice cream, jelly, mince pie (not exactly Eastery), lemon meringue pie, strawberries and raspberries. Surprised he doesn't go pop. Child C throws huge tantrum after he is served up grapes ("Yuk. That make me sick"), bread ("Want choc choc sandwich"), strawberries (which he does eat) and some spuds with gravy. This is all part of No More Mr. Nice Guy Approach. Standoff for the entire meal. Disrupts everything. Screams throughout the meal. However, constant reminders of "no potato no pudding" pays dividends and he *finally* eats them. First time in a long time that he has eaten roast spuds. Or any spuds. Do celebratory dance and let him eat cake and ice cream. Hoping that the whole Easter egg chocolate thing will give me leverage to help get him to eat a bit more normal food. Might even try omelette tomorrow. Start with something that takes no time to cook then I won't feel cheated if he rejects it.

14.59 Arrive home. Child B wins the bet on what time we'll make it home. No prize. Just the glory of being right. Child C asleep. Wait ten mins then wake him. Grumpy. Half wish I hadn't bothered.

Husband works – preparing for tomorrow. Child A and B play on the Xbox (plan to, somehow, stamp that out a bit once back

219

at school). Child C happy making shapes from Playdoh. Finally something which absorbs him and which doesn't involve a TV. I do short jobs in between being called to take shapes out of cutters. Thirty-five times.

16.50 Make early tea. Very light tea. Figure that so much chocolate has been consumed that no one can possibly want to eat anything much. Child C throws strop about his half piece of toast being cut into squares rather than a rectangle. Provide a rectangle. Throws a strop about the crusts being on. Cut them off. Puts them to one side "for the birds". No chance of our highly expensive grass seed growing if he is intent on inviting every bird in the vicinity into our garden.

Early baths planned all round. Get the impression that no one is looking forward to returning to normality tomorrow. Apart from me. Secretly counting the hours. Love them all dearly, but just three hours when I don't need to make a drink / meal for anyone else, wipe a bottom, break up a fight, negotiate over a toy. Bliss.

17.58 Announce five minute warning on the computer gaming.

Child A and B draw up "Xbox charts". Both with ideas of how the reward system should work. Child A goes to the trouble of sticking it up in the kitchen, with accompanying pencil, stuck to cupboard door with sticky tape folded and made into double sided sticky tape. Explain that Husband and I will have a chat and work out the rules of the reward.

19.30 Put dinner on. Sort out car seats. Put scooters in car. See neighbour who is selling his house. Mention to him that I'm very happy to keep the kids in if he lets me know when they have a viewing. He seems rather pleased. With an aside of "*I* don't mind, of course, but …".

Dinner. Help Husband with some work emails. Google "slapped cheek syndrome" as Child C been looking very red. Hope he hasn't got it, as just looking forward to some child-free time. Conclude he hasn't.

21.24 Wash up. Think about tomorrow. Have a tonne of work and chores to do tomorrow, but sod it. The first thing I do will be something for me. The other things can come next. Think I've deserved it.

Diet Cokes: 2.

Chocolate: Entire chocolate bunny and a few of the small bunnies which came with it. Feel sick.

Glasses of wine: 0. Too full of chocolate.

PART THREE: UNSURPRISED BY ANYTHING IN BETWEEN

"My mission in life is not merely to survive, but to thrive; and to do so with some passion, some compassion, some humor, and some style".

Day Fifty-One
(Tuesday)

Back to school.

3.45 Child C calls out. Go to see what's up. Needs a wee. Insists on using the "big toilet". Creep through and don't switch any lights on so as not to wake anyone up. Back to bed. Child C sings *The Grand Old Duke of York* and chunters to himself.

4.10 Child C still not asleep. Speech therapy later today. Not going to be great if he is exhausted. Remind him he needs sleep to go to school and I settle down in the big bed in his room, with the incentive of racing me to sleep. Plays with teddies and sings. At least he's not screaming about dragons or cows.

5.00 Wake up. Child C asleep. Creep back to my bed.

6.10 Husband's alarm goes off. Child C still asleep.

More organised this morning than on most school mornings. Think it's because I've had the holidays to get it all ready. Ask Child C to help choose his piece of sharing fruit to take to school. He chooses a lemon.

All set to go by 8.10. Apart from Child C who insists on wearing his rucksack before he's got his coat on. Does wee, put socks on, rucksack off, coat on, rucksack on again, into car.

All dropped off with no problems. Child C doesn't push anyone but does pick a lot of greenery and leaves it "for the giraffes and elephants" on the wooden train in the playground. Anticipating a Polite Reminder To All Parents note from the school office later.

Child A and B receive party invites. Clashes with another party. Child A looks teary and asks he if can choose which to go to. Explain that I have already replied to the other, so he can't. He cries.

9.10 Home. Ahhhh. The lovely peace of a child-free house. Laptop mine again, can tidy up without wails of "that's miiiiiiine", no one asking for a drink / snack / pair of socks, no fighting, no football talk. What's not to like?

Had planned on doing some exercise as have eaten way too much and scales either broken or I have put on weight. However, cleaners coming at 10.30 so can't start exercise regime just yet. Not only do I need to tidy up, but also doing exercise may give them the impression that I am far too important to do housework but do have time to do a workout DVD, which just feels wrong. More embarrassed than normal about the mess with which they will be confronted today. Wipe a few surfaces, to show that I care. But not using enough elbow grease to make their visit surplus to requirements.

10.45 Cleaners still not here. Could have done that exercise after all.

10.54 Really hungry. Not sure I can justify eating just yet.

10.58 Put chips in the oven.

Do a few work emails and enjoy my chips. Not healthy but I don't care. I don't have to share with ANYONE.

12.00 Pick up Child C. Full of beans. Cleaners just finishing off. Child C eats lunch in the playroom, wedged between three large boxes, two laundry baskets, two sports bags, two pairs of wellies and a pile of paperwork, all of which have been moved in there to make the house easier to clean.

Embark on making fish pie for tea for Husband and me. Child C wants to "help". Floor still wet from being mopped. Child C invents game of holding a potato over each eye and running round on a wet floor. Then falling down and dropping potatoes. Stupid game. He loves it. Gives me time to put the mash on.

13.45 Speech therapist arrives at home. This is addition to the NHS one, and is a desperate attempt to help Child C get a move on with his communication and eradicate all the other unwelcome behaviours that have accompanied his speech delay. Starts well. Gets worse. Child C in silly mood. She tries to teach him that "monkey", for example, is "mon-key". He normally says "monk monk". He does well with saying "mon-key" a few times, then applies the same rule to everything, just to be silly. So tiger becomes "ti-key", then he jumps around the room, pointing at the speech therapist saying "you're a ti-key, you're a ti-key". Hides behind the sofa. Climbs over my head. And doesn't use the equipment in the way he's meant to. I get the giggles. Shouldn't as not funny. Everything so farcical that can't help it.

Speech therapist comments "what a lot of energy he has!" Is that code for ADHD?

14.35 Speech therapist leaves. Has given me some pointers about taking a few words each day and working on them. Hard to do with such a stroppy child. Suggests we meet again in a month. Let's hope for miracles before then.

14.40 Time to collect Child A and B. Child C decides to play hide and seek. In his pants. Then needs a wee. Bits not pointing the right way so carpet gets soaked. Clean up. Coax him to put on socks (removed in wet floor potato game) and shoes, and coat and get scooters.

14.45 Set off. Late. Scoot after Child C. Arrive in time and pick up Child A and B. Both have had good day and are talking about football again. Have brought yoghurts as after-school snack. Child C ends up wearing his.

Kids play with their friends down the road, in their front garden til 16.00ish. Child C upsets friends by breaking their "favourite sticks".

Tears from Child A and B on arrival home. Transpires that they have now been invited to three birthday parties on the same day at the same time. Both wail at the injustice of it. Point out that it's not my fault. That doesn't seem to help. Put tea on pronto. Omelette, waffles and beans. Am expecting three responses of "I don't like it".

16.15 Pleasantly surprised. Child A eats it all. Child B eats about half of it. Child C eats two small mouthfuls of omelette. Albeit I did have to repeat the mantra of "no omelette no chocolate" throughout the whole episode. At least he is trying something new. Progress.

Clear up. Reading for Child A and B. Child A moans until I say maybe the Xbox minutes will reflect reading pages. Then super keen to read a whole book. Bath for Child C, who is totally shattered with a mood to match.

18.00 Call Child A and B to get ready for bed. Find them on the *Pick Me Up* magazine website entering competitions, after googling "easy competitions to win". Both hoping to win a laptop.

18.35 Final bits then bed. Child C falls asleep in two seconds flat. Chapter of story for Child A and B. Child B demands more. Tell him not to be mean and that I won't let him have the laptop (if he wins it) if he treats me like a slave.

19.03 Child A and B go to bed hoping to win a trip to Paris, a pair of Lelli Kelly shoes, a set of Palace Pets and a home entertainment system, as well as the computers they reckon they have a "really good chance of winning".

Diet Cokes: 3.

Chocolate: 1 line of Fruit and Nut. 4 chocolates that came with my Easter bunny.

Glasses of wine: 0. Despite the fact that I quite fancy a glass.

Day Fifty-Two
(Wednesday)

5.43 Can hear Child A and B talking loudly. Leave them to see if they quieten down. They don't. Tiptoe across landing and see them in the dark, in the bathroom. Chatting while looking in the mirror. Child B debating whether he could, potentially, commit a crime and pin it on Child A. Child B duly saddened by me telling him that I don't think their fingerprints would be totally identical and that his bank robbery or similar would not be a successful one. And that crime doesn't pay. Whisper for them to go back to bed and tiptoe back to bed in haste.

Too late. Child C woken by criminal mastermind chatter. Yells "get me uuuuppppppp" for the next forty minutes.

Husband off to Spain tonight, so fold shirts for his case while Child A, B and C run around the landing and from bedroom to bedroom like crazy people.

Breakfast, make sandwiches for Husband, check Husband has packed everything he needs in wash bag. Say goodbye to Husband. Child C refuses, as per usual. Get kids dressed. Beavers uniform for Child A and B, for special celebrations at school.

8.00 Ask Child A and B to put on shoes and clean teeth. Child B obliges. Child A takes a total of six further reminders and loses a tick from his reward chart for lack of doing what I ask him the first time.

8.20 School run. Every other child wearing their neck woggles. Had left ours at home as figured it was one less thing to lose. Child B sad and wants me to go back home to get them. Decline. Am deemed "worst mummy ever".

Child C yells all the way to preschool that he wants to listen to *Bananas In Pyjamas* on the CD player. Have never owned it. Update preschool teachers on speech therapist appointment from yesterday and head home.

9.10 Have great intentions today. Will drop kids off, return home, do workout, take in Tesco shop, and then do some work. Super-organised and effortlessly efficient.

9.35 Intentions not panning out as intended. Clean up old double buggy which a local mum is interested in buying. Bit of mould and lots of old grubbiness removed. Strange sense of melancholy about selling the buggy. Feels weird to see it all ready to go in the hall. So many memories. Happy ones. And those involving wrestling young children into the straps and leaving places with people staring at two screaming children.

9.55 Conscious that I was meant to finish some work this morning and haven't. Will do DVD later. Work emails.

10.10 Tesco man comes. Asks if I remember him (I don't but say I do), and asks to use the toilet. I say "that's fine" but he seems to take rather a long time, and I start to worry that he might have installed hidden cameras.

10.14 More work emails. Then someone presses the fast forward button and it's 11.45. Where does that time go? The minutes just zap away. Always thought would have SO much more time when Child C at preschool, then when more sessions, then when all week. But the time just gets sucked up. Maybe the children make more mess and washing as they get older so the extra hours go into handling that.

12.00 Pick up. Child C happy. Not bothered about leaving particularly quickly. Happy pottering in the playground.

Try Something New To Eat Programme, as introduced by me, continues at lunchtime. Sarnies served up – ham, cheese and marmite. Asks for "choc choc". Tell Child C we've run out. Refuses the ham but eats the bread and ALL the rest. I can handle him not wanting the ham. Keep thinking of those episodes of *Supernanny* with the bad eaters. Have her ringing in my head saying "he's only eating custard creams all day because you let him". Have to take control. Have to be strong. Will get him eating food like normal people.

13.30 Coax Child C into car to come to the shops with me. Child C yells that he wants to watch the Xbox game *Ridge Race*r on the TV. Doesn't articulate it quite like that, but that's the general thrust of his shouting and pointing. Point out clearly that it's not a TV programme but he doesn't get it. Make vague mix of "later" / "we'll see" noises, at which point he relents and gets in the car. Assisted by suggestion that he takes his cuddly cat "to see the shops".

13.42 Remember why I don't go into town very often with Child C. Child C intent on "driving" the Noddy car outside the supermarket. Don't put any money in. Never have. Figure that if I never do, then the children won't know any differently. Eventually, and after counting to three, remove Child C from Noddy car and strap him into buggy. Great strength required to match Child C's superhuman force and will to get out of the buggy and get back in Noddy car. Screams around the supermarket. Lots of disdainful glances at terrible mother.

Let him out after he calms down. Allowed five more mins on Noddy car. Seems to have got the message when I say it's time to leave this time. Proof that staying calm and being firm is working. Ha!

Child C amused by headless mannequins in shop windows, by throwing his comfort blanket to try and make it fly, and by running up and down the aisles of Boots speaking into a banana and holding a packet of batteries, that we are not buying. I am amused by the first, and not by the other two. Glad I'm not in a hurry.

14.50 Now in a hurry. Can't remember what time the car park time runs out. Hurry Child C along.

14.51 Child C finds bouncy ball in his pocket, releases it, and it bounces under the shelving units in Boots. Scrabble on hands and knees to find it (very dusty under there for a shop which promotes health and well-being), while Child C wails inconsolably.

14.58 Fortunately security guard appears with a stick long enough to retrieve it and we are on our way.

15.15 Return home. Check on grass seed. Not sure if some of it was there before or if it is new grass. Think the birds have eaten about half of it. Give it a couple more days before I cast judgement. Hope it was worth it. Could have bought several pairs of shoes for the same price.

15.50 Put macaroni cheese in the oven, so that it's ready for return.

16.15 Collect Child A and B from football. Child C even less keen to get in the car this time. Must be annoying being carted here there and everywhere. Try and distract and encourage along the way, but I'm tired too now. Child A and B both happy as both scored a goal today.

16.20 Realise that we don't have Child A's bag, containing his shoes and clothes. All trail back into school. Swears that it's not in his classroom. Send him to his classroom. Finds it on his peg.

16.45 Arrive home. Macaroni cheese dry and horrible. Serve up fish pie and macaroni cheese. Child A hates macaroni. Child B hates fish pie. Child C hates both. Child C wanders off and decides to not bother. Child A does valiant effort. Child B looks like he has a bad smell up his nose. Teach him how to eat something you don't like, in case he ever needs to, by encouraging him to hold his nose and have a drink with the rest. Easter egg allowed for Child A and B for their efforts.

17.30 Bath for Child C. Reading for Child A and B. Child C does best to disrupt reading. Just find this time of the day so hard. Need to do homework with Child A and B. Child C tired and doesn't want to be left to amuse himself. All the rest of us tired too. Bath for Child A and B too. Child A complains of stinging boys' bits. Hard to ascertain if it sounds like an infection or not. Will reassess in the morning.

Child C and B play a game involving throwing wooden blocks for each other before the other one goes to collect it one all fours, in their mouth like a dog. Did I find that kind of thing fun when I was young? Perhaps me thinking that it is daft, and possibly dangerous is just an adult's perspective on a bit of fun. Still tell them to stop.

18.40 Child C in bed. Several "goodnight"s before he settles.

18.50 Bedtime story for Child A and B. Both opt for a recipe instead of a story this evening. Frozen Fruit Ripple for Child B. Jambalaya for Child A. Both sound yummy. Kids happy. Bed by 19.20.

19.22 Decisions, decisions. Eat dinner and either get work project off my desk, which was meant to be done earlier today or delay it by another day and do some exercise. Opt to get the work sorted.

22.43 Finish work. Was meant to blitz the washing pile tonight but that hasn't happened either. Need a clone. Perhaps a more effective one.

23.38 Ready for bed. Not sure the kids have all the clean clothes they need but will sort that in the morning. Hide clean laundry pile so Child C doesn't jump in it in the morning, with a face covered in Weetabix. Feel about nine months pregnant. Blame the mini eggs.

Diet Cokes: 3.

Chocolate: 2 lines of Fruit and Nut. Half my (ever increasing) body weight in mini eggs.

Glasses of wine: 2.

Day Fifty-Three
(Thursday)

3.43 Woken by Child C having a nightmare. New approach now. Just grab pillow, plonk myself in the big bed in his room and make calming noises like "ssssh" every time he mutters or sits up. Means I can maintain a sleepy state whilst also making sure that he's not dying. Fall asleep and then wake up and go back to my bed. Totally disrupts the night's sleep but involves minimum effort, whilst also putting my mind at rest.

Pop to toilet and, on return to bed, notice that under cabinet lighting isn't working. In fact, isn't there at all. Presume cleaners have vacuumed it up, since it was hanging off on the floor. Can't get back to sleep as fretting about the email of complaint I will need to write.

5.48 Hear Child A and B up.

6.00 Hot water comes on and sounds like Niagara Falls in the bathroom. Make mental note to bleed radiators.

6.20 Alarm goes off.

6.25 Goes off again. Call Husband as had promised to, to make sure he is up. He is. I am, barely. Rant about cleaners. He has seen the lights in a basket under the sink. Feel bad for mentally wrongly accusing cleaners.

Child C awake but leave him to it while have a shower.

Child A complaining of sore back, leg, neck and tummy. Doesn't eat all of his breakfast, but neither does Child B, so put it down to a large dinner last night. Both still going on about entering more competitions.

8.15 All off to school. Take sewing club forms to office. Coax Child C out of reception class area where no children are allowed to go before school, and where he is intent on playing. Kiss Child A and B goodbye. Tempt Child C out of what used to be a big sand pit and is now just a big mud pit, where he has been making "sandcastles". Hands and trousers coated in mud. Back to car. Child C falls over handlebars of scooter. Twice. Pink knees but no other damage.

Drop Child C at preschool. Dash back for hairdresser.

9.54 Hair nearly done. Phone rings. Ignore on basis that probably call centre or Grandma (who I can call back later).

9.55 Mobile rings.

9.57 Hair finished. Check phone. School. Child A feels ill, keeps going hot and pale, and can I come and get him? Day three of the term. Day three and illness is back. That serves me right for relishing child-free time. Pleased I blitzed most of my work deadlines last night.

Pay hairdresser and dash off to get Child A. Looks a bit peaky and off colour.

10.05 Arrive home. First words of "ill" child are "Can I use the iPad?" Must be really, really ill then. Answer is "no". Let him watch Sky Sports while I sort the laundry. No temperature, but does seem a bit under the weather.

11.50 Go to collect Child C. He's delighted that Child A is home. Both eat good lunch. In fact, "ill" child eats massive lunch, and wonders whether he can ride his scooter and eat his Easter egg. Then builds a train track with his younger brother.

Child C eats well too. Figure maybe he was bored with the same old food that I was serving up. Not that he's massively changed his dietary habits, but perhaps me being more chilled, and also more of an Eat It Or Nothing Approach might have helped a bit. Think he enjoyed making bits of breaded turkey (probably not the healthiest but it is meat of a sort) walk the plank into the ketchup.

14.00 NHS speech therapy for Child C. Child A, who I had beginning to think was faking the illness thing, comes over a bit funny in the reception area. Wonder if keeping this appointment was such a good idea. Session starts well, then Child C gets tired / shy and isn't particularly interested. Covers his eyes, and I spend a lot of time reminding him that he can eat biscuits if he cooperates. Speech therapist determines that progress is being made. Back to car. Child A cries. Says his neck and under his jaw hurts. So, maybe he isn't very well. Oh bother. Child C falls asleep almost the second we leave the car park. Quiet journey home.

Settle Child A under duvet on sofa. Wake Child C (too dangerous to let him sleep past 15.00) and undertake quick weed and feed of unfed bits of lawn, to get rid of stripes I have encouraged with my haphazard lawncare.

15.45 Leave to collect Child B. Child A totally perky again. Weird.

Child B shattered. Child C annoying everyone, and upsetting Child A and B with his shouting, since both are unusually tearful.

Child B tries to eat through the house while I cook, despite my protests. Then, at dinner time, can only manage one slice of pizza and then gets mad when I enforce the No Dinner, No Pudding Rule. Throws a few bits of paper, and pushes stuff across the table, in manner of disgruntled teenager.

17.15 Wash up. Run bath. Children play some version of *The Three Little Pigs*, combined with bundling off the sofa onto the floor, entangled in duvet. Child A just wants to rest. Child C intent on mischief. Child B follows me around a lot. Seems super clingy.

Can't be doing with reading tonight. Just too much else going on.

All in bed by 18.30. Child A and B asleep by 18.40. Guess with Child A he feels poorly, and with Child B the first three days back at school have finally caught up with him. And of course, getting up before 6.00 every day doesn't exactly help.

Child C calls me in at 19.00 claiming he needs a "wee wee and a poo poo". Latter doesn't materialise and former has already been done in his nappy I think.

19.15 Don't feel like exercising. At all. If I don't do it tonight though, I never will. No excuse. Do DVD and really enjoy it. As much as you can enjoy that kind of thing.

20.00 Eat huuuuge dinner. Official portion size should probably be half. Do work emails.

22.44 How did it get so late again?

Bleed radiator. Doesn't seem to be any air in it so just get covered in water. Go to loft to check water pressure. Top it up. Scared to death by Child B standing hauntingly on landing, wanting more water. Says he doesn't feel well. Not another one. Pllleeeeeeaaaase.

Diet Cokes: 3.

Chocolate: 2 lines of Dairy Milk, 3 handfuls of mini eggs.

Glasses of wine: 0.

Day Fifty-Four
(Friday)

6.20 Alarm goes off. Just. Too. Tired. Switch radio on to stop me falling back to sleep. Child A and B up. Wonder how they are doing today, or whether they have any new ailments.

6.36 Shower.

Child A still feels "ill" but symptoms non-descript.

Don't know whether to send him in or not. Figure, do brekkie first and re-evaluate. All three children play game which seems to mainly involve wrecking my duvet. No one realises what a hassle fixing the two duvets back together and then putting it back in the cover really is.

Mention to Child C that he will be having lunch at preschool today. He's been going on about it for weeks. A big "NOOOO. Me not have lunch at school". Today's plans going rapidly downhill.

Breakfast for all. Child C eats while wearing the large white cricket hat he has taken to calling "Daddy's cowboy hat". Child A eats a brioche and drinks a glass of Nesquik, but only eats a tiny bit of cereal. Hmmm. Good sign? Bad sign? Don't want repeat of him puking over fellow classmates but he seems a bit too keen to stay at home and watch TV for my liking.

7.30 Sod it. They can all go to school. Will explain to teacher when I get there to call me if ANY problems at all. Child A not impressed. Takes refuge on sofa, in style of someone with not long to live.

Point out to Child A and B that they just have to get through today and then it is the weekend again. Just a few hours. Then they can come home and play on the computer til their eyes go square for all I care. Just make it through today.

Child C helps me make his lunch. Figure that that will help him buy in to the concept of staying and eating it. Marmite sandwiches, cheese sandwiches, strawberries, a few crisps, a yoghurt and a small chocolate biscuit. He may still be eating it when I pick him up.

All children fine on way to school. Child A and B scoot from car. Child C has brought one of my dolls and sits in the pushchair with it. Think he's had enough of scooter for now after falling off yesterday. Child A and B play football. Child C "looks after" dolly.

8.45 Tears from Child A at In Time. Just when I thought he was sort of doing ok. Apparently someone barged him on the football pitch and it hurts. Big hug, inspect that damage (though can't actually see anything) and tell him not to play football with that boy again. Speak to teaching assistant, who apologises for sending him home yesterday. Reassure that I would have done exactly the same thing. Explain random symptoms and ask to call if any problem.

9.01 Leave school to go to preschool. Bother. Have forgotten fruit. Go home to get a banana. Set off again. Child C goes in fine. Puts away lunchbox. All seems ok.

9.20 After coat, boots, wee, fruit, lunchbox and goodbye, finally get back in the car to go home. Pop to shop to get prescription for Husband. Takes ages.

10.00 On a continued mission to blitz the washing pile. Even all the random stuff that gets left at the bottom … chef's outfit, cuddly polar bear, rash vest, J cloth … by the end of today I want them all washed and gone. Fed up of fire fighting.

Do some HMRC paperwork. Terrified of them fining me some hideous amount that I don't have for doing something I don't understand and haven't done. Go online. Don't understand the website. Don't understand the options to click on. Don't understand the terms and conditions. Tick the "I understand" box anyway. Think I've sorted it. Will soon find out.

Get distracted watching YouTube videos of John Travolta and Olivia Newton John singing the old songs from *Grease*, which a friend had put on Facebook. Waste ten mins.

11.00 Start workout DVD. It claims to last "just 30 minutes", but by the time you've added in the warm up and cool down it is, disappointingly, a bit longer. Just when I think it might be time to end, the instructor shouts out "If you want results, you've got to earn them". Urgh.

11.45 Killer workout ends. Had to keep pausing it so that I didn't die. Hence why took so long. Even need a shower after it. Must have done some good if I got that hot, surely?

12.15 Wash up from breakfast, poached eggs on toast for lunch (that's healthy right?)

So lovely to have an extra hour to get things done today, while Child C has lunch at school. Took it for granted when Child C was younger and used to sleep twice a day. Or even once a day, or when went to preschool and did that and then slept. For that reason I shouldn't feel guilty about him spending longer at preschool. He used to sleep all that time anyway. And it's only one day a week.

Hope he likes it. I could get used to having a tiny bit more time to do some of those jobs which have been on my To Do List for seven years.

13.00 Collect Child C. He was fine and ate his lunch. Did wet himself, but that was because he refused to go to the toilet when asked.

Give him a mini talking-to in car about going to toilet when the teachers tell him but try to focus on the "well done you for staying for lunch".

Home and feel that I can give him extra time. That's the thing. Given the chance, and the time, I can devote quality time to the children. It's rubbish for everyone when trying to do fifty jobs at the same time as a child wants to read a book, do a puzzle etc. Read books and watch a bit of TV together.

14.30 Pick up comes around pretty fast. Pouring with rain and don't know what state Child A will be in so drive to school. Which means leaving half an hour early to ensure a car park space in the same village. Get the last good space. Child C intent on walking with an umbrella, so takes the best part of fifteen mins to get to the school from the car.

Teacher says that Child A been off colour and not himself all day. But that he did play football at lunchtime. Asked him if anything is bothering him. It isn't. Friend just gone home with similar thing. Maybe it is some kind of bug. Rushes off to play football when out of the classroom so I just don't get it. Child C stands at classroom door of Child B with hands on hips until Child B is released. Then throws paddy as birthday boy giving out sweets and Child C wants some. Gets a rice cake instead. More tears. Collect Child B. Holding post it note with "negative numbers" written on it. Check with teacher exactly what he needs to do. Apparently just know what they are. Good. No need to teach him addition of them or anything. Can't even remember how ... a minus and a minus means a plus, or was it a minus ... I forget. And he is seven. How will I cope at seventeen!?

Home and, after a fight about who gets to get through the front door first, all three happy to chill. Noodles and chicken nuggets for tea. All eat well. Though admittedly Child A only does so as I won't let him have a pudding unless his plate is clean. Let's hope I don't see it all again later. Into jimjams by 17.15. Starting the evening process super early.

Child C doesn't want a bath. But bath already run so has to. Quickest ever. Then back to watch iPlayer that I have set up on the Wii ... can't believe it has taken me this long to realise that you could. Kids totally taken with it and spend next hour watching back issues of all the programmes they missed while at school. Goodbye arguments. Well, some of them.

18.04 Nanny phones to say hello. Child C screams "get off the phone" for the entire duration. Hides inside trug bucket, with box on his head pretending to be a baby chick hatching. Repeats approx. fifty times. Each time observer enthusiasm required to be at the same levels as at the seventy million previous baby chick hatchings. Bedtime now, pleeeeease.

18.25 Child C in bed. Goes down fairly quickly. Should be shattered. A longer day at preschool, and all that hatching has got to tire him out til morning.

Read to Child A and B, who are niggling. Book too exciting to put down, so read an extra chapter. Child B keeps not understanding what is going on, and Child A keeps doing gymnastics while listening. Try and catch him out and ask him to explain the passage just read to Child B. Annoyingly gets it right each time.

18.54 Reading all done.

19.15 Making up for lost time on the exercise front so do thirty mins Pilates. Feels easy after workout this morning. Though that probably means I'm not doing it right. Some of the balance bits mean I can't do those bits anyway. How do you even get to be that flexy? Child A and B chatting, but quietens down after ten mins or so. Yay. Evening is here.

20.19 Mobile blips to say Husband has landed. Sort my dinner. Random "whatever curry is in those small boxes in the freezer" dinner for me. Backside aches from workout. Drinking wine so probably cancels out all the goodness of my efforts today.

Diet Cokes: 4.

Chocolate: 3 … or was it 4 … lines of Fruit and Nut, before 9.30.

Glasses of wine: 2.

Day Fifty-Five
(Saturday)

2.20 Up to get Child B a drink.

3.15 Child C calls out needing a wee.

5.23 Morning comes and it feels like night time never really happened. Go back to my bed from Child C's room. Don't remember how long I was sleeping there.

5.30 Start hearing noise from Child A's room where both he and Child B are sleeping. Loud laughter and noise of thudding on floor. Don't even want to know what they are up to. Don't suppose Child C will sleep through that.

6.33 Child C now yelling. Get up for shower.

Child B comes in after my shower. Was planning on leaving Husband to sleep a bit, but not sure that will be possible since all kids up and LOUD. All awake now. Ask about the source of such riotous laughter. Game involved climbing inside the duvet cover with the duvet and falling off the bed. With both of them, and the duvet inside the cover. And this is a game apparently devised by a child who doesn't feel well. I am mystified.

Breakfast. Child A and B busy catching up with Husband on football and all that kind of thing. Tea for Husband. And fruit salad. Call others down and sort their breakfast too. Make two cups of tea for Child A and B that won't get drunk, because they are "too hot". Child A only picks at cereal again.

8.00 Get kids dressed and ready for swimming. Both now in later class, starting at 8.45 so we get to leave half an hour later – hurrah. All ready to go out of the door by 8.17, when Child A bursts into tears again and says he "just doesn't feel well". Instruct Husband to give him lots to drink, collect wee in a cup, and I'll take him to the out of hours doctor later.

Swimming goes fine. Quite nice to have just one child to look after. Catch up with friend while Child B swims.

9.25 Return home. No wee collected, so sort that and call doctor. Put it in fridge so no one drinks it. Get out of hours appointment at hospital for 13.30. That's today's entertainment sorted then. Concerned that the doctor will think we are totally wasting his time. Can't win either way.

Wash up, empty bins, fetch and carry. Normal Saturday morning. Pleasant change that footie match season over so no more rushing out to stand in a field for an hour or so.

Lunch on. Children temporarily entertained. I should just relax but feel like I should be motoring on with jobs. Not used to just sitting.

12.00 Child C Eating Programme continues. Actually eats normal non-processed chicken. Requires me to dance round the kitchen in the style of a chicken, but he eats at least one small strip. That is something.

13.00 Take Child A to the hospital for 13.30 appointment. Husband phones to check I have urine sample and to let me know that Child

C has just weed all over his clothes. Waiting room full on arrival. Overhear receptionist saying that they are running an hour late.

One and a half hours later we get seen. Probably caught more in there than we had in the first place. No urine infection. Probably viral. Go home, via Tesco to pick up flowers and chocolates for host this evening. At least now know that Child A hasn't got anything nasty.

Arrive home to a get well soon poster that the others have hung out of the window. And lots of pairs of wet pants and trousers from Child C. Child A wants to play on the Xbox. Miracle recovery. Point out that he has to do homework first. Spellings followed by ukulele done without any moaning. Fantastic.

16.30 Husband has used up all his energy with Child B and C in my absence and "needs a sleep". And a cup of tea, and half a packet of digestives, and two mini Bounties, and half a bowl of the kids' tea.

17.10 Teatime. Child C even eats homemade bolognaise sauce. Teeny weeny spoonfuls but eats it and even says "yum yum, me like this". Perhaps he was getting as bored of the bland food as I was of cooking it. Serve it on same plate and in same style as that for Child A and B. Perhaps that is helping too. Don't know. Either way, just pleased it seems to be working.

18.00 Husband watches football on TV, Child A and B want to play Xbox, Child C watches *Peppa Pig* DVD in another room. Husband agrees to play Xbox with the children in half time.

19.10 Still playing. Can't put Child C to bed as far too much whooping and cheering for him to settle. Trying to get changed so that Child C doesn't realise that we're going out, but so that I am as good as ready when babysitter arrives at 19.30.

19.15 Ready to lose it. Xbox match finishes, rush Child A and B into PJs and upstairs. Hurry Child C along as best I can and bid them all goodnight. Loud chatter from Child A and B, accompanied by calls for Husband. Child A asks why I look like I'm going to cry. Start explaining that I spend all day running round and just want five mins to get ready, and I can't even get that. Not sure they get it, though Child B does apologise. Don't start on the fact that, in instances such as these, the whole day is planned around getting them to bed early, and now it is forty-five mins later than I had planned them being in bed.

19.25 All in bed. Child C asleep. Trickiest one down. The rest don't worry me so much.

Child A and B keen to say lots of goodbyes. 19.45 cab arrives. Husband agrees that Child A and B can wave us off from landing. Only remember this when we have left our road. Hope they aren't still waiting there, with tear streamed faces, when we get back.

Lovely evening. Lovely food. Lovely to be out, and lovely to get a cab. Lovely to wear something that isn't jeans.

00.15 Get home. Not so lovely. Will regret late night in morning. Husband insisted on power napping in cab. Kept poking him to stay awake until he looked like he was getting cross. Chat to babysitter about various.

00.45 Bed. Husband asleep on sofa next to consumed packet of barbecue beef Hula Hoops. Need sleep.

Diet Cokes: 4.

Chocolate: 2 lines of Fruit and Nut, 2 mini Bounties, lots of Matchmakers.

Glasses of wine: 5?

Day Fifty-Six
(Sunday)

Hear Child A and B from 5.40. Starts with them having fun. Soon turns less fun. Ends up in verbal and physical fight.

Never before have I been more pleased that Child A and B have a four and a half hour party lined up. We hardly ever go out, but a long party would be handy after every time that we do.

6.50 Tell Child A and B that I don't care who started it and to just try and be nice to each other. Send them to different bedrooms and forbid them from talking to each other. Take Child C downstairs for brekkie. Child C still wearing hi-vis jacket he went to bed in, and desperately searching for toy hammer. Cries of "when can I come down?", "when can I come out?", "how much longer?" follow me. Remind Child A and B that the timer starts all over again until they are quiet.

6.55 Go to speak to Child A and B to explain the seriousness of their actions. Both in Child A's room, playing beautifully and looking through Match Attax. How can it be then when I'm still fuming, they are totally over it and the best of pals again? Give them a brief lecture on listening to my instructions, and if they are this friendly now, why did they bother having such a massive brawl over nothing?

Child A and B wake Husband on sofa. *Match Of The Day* goes on. Make breakfast for Child C. Eating it seems to take an age. Out

251

of chocolate brioches (damn – forgot to grab some at the shops yesterday) so make toast with chocolate spread. Doesn't want to get it on his fingers, so takes ages finding right place to hold it, then wipe off any that gets anywhere. Never realised that personal hygiene was that high on his list of priorities.

Hoping that the day ahead will be a proper Sit And Read The Sunday Papers Day. Haven't had one of those in seven years. Child A and B play on the Xbox, and Child C happy with Playdoh, so the prospects for a peaceful day are looking up.

8.30 Go to put bin out. Notice that one of the air vents is damaged. On closer inspection, a section has been bitten off. Teeth marks in the fallen off plastic and shavings of the plastic all over the floor. Damn. Could be mice, but with that determination and sharpness of teeth am thinking more like rats. Looks like even a hole been bitten through the concrete. Have visions of rats running wild through the walls and ceilings of our house. Google it, and seems that a mouse or rat can get through a hole the size of a pencil, and that rats can, indeed, chew through concrete. I blame Child C scattering his post-preschool raisins and cheesy biscuits on the driveway "for the birds". Told him it would attract the foxes, but wasn't counting on it attracting rats.

Someone coming to collect buggy this morning, so need to do last bit of making sure any grime is off it. At least the surface grime. Lady collects it at 11.00ish. End of an era. Child C screams that she has taken Child A and B's buggy. Try to explain that she has given me "shiny gold coins". He gives up.

11.45 Take Child A and B to party. Child A has been absolutely fine all day long and now is not. Gets all teary and then when we get there says that he feels sick. Asks me to stay for a bit, and then just keeps welling up. Take him home. So unlike him and so frustrating and upsetting all rolled into one. It's like he's allergic to going outside. Must be something leaving him feeling washed out, but with no temperature and no visible symptoms it's hard not to think that something is worrying him. Ask gently searching questions on way home. Nothing gleaned.

Drop him home and go to B&Q to get as many rat / mouse poison things as I can find. Browse the shelves for a bit then opt for a box with poison in it, some bait things that you have to attach to things with wire, some wire to attach them and some bait sachets. Over £43 later I feel that the war has begun on the little blighters.

13.30 Arrive home. Husband has been asking Child A if anything wrong too. No news. Put down poison and cover hole with a stone. Figure I'll get it out there as early as poss.

Do the ironing, tidy up a bit, and do some more ironing. Sort school bags. Child A and Husband fall asleep for an hour, despite Child C's best efforts to wake them up by shouting "wake up" in their faces. Hurry him upstairs to "look out of the window for mice". It works. Pootle upstairs for a bit, building towers and the like.

16.10 Go to collect Child B. He's on the trampoline when I arrive. Has had whale of a time. Climbs a bit more, collects shoes, and party bag and we head home.

Child B asks me why there isn't a party bag for Child A. Explain that he wasn't at the party. Feel sad that Child A wasn't there. He would have loved it.

Chat on the way home about Child B's favourite bits … the go karts, the pig race, the animal handling. Ask if he saw any lambs. Saw some being born. Informs me that one was born "with a number on its back". Now less convinced that he saw it actually being born and explain that lambs don't come out pre-numbered.

16.40 Home and put the tea on for Child A and C. Spaghetti with sauce, and bacon. Child C tries (and dislikes) bacon. Both eat up all the rest.

Husband shattered and feeling ill. Child B tired. Child A with aches and pains and washed out. Child C ratty. Don't know what advice to offer to anyone. End up just saying "oh dear" to any afflictions mentioned. That's about the best I can do. Don't know enough and can't fix it enough to say any different. "Oh dear" to everyone for everything.

18.30 Go online to order *Ten Days To A Less Defiant Child* and *Peaceful Parent, Happy Kids*, as well as *Overcoming Your Child's Fears And Worries*. Figure that should sort them all out.

Kids in bed by 18.45. Asleep by 19.00. Sort meatballs and spaghetti for me and Husband.

20.44 Remember that Child B saved some pictures on my computer which he wants me to print off to take in for his project on giraffes. Print them off and some facts. Print some off on pandas for Child A, though he didn't seem that bothered at the time. Wonder if this is the beginning of the whole Doing Your Children's Homework For Them thing.

Diet Cokes: 4.

Chocolate: Far too much. Due mainly to late night. Entire bag of large chocolate buttons. Read somewhere a while back that you consume an extra 6300 calories when you've been out drinking. Today I'm living proof of that.

Glasses of wine: 0. None needed. Last night was enough.

Day Fifty-Seven
(Monday)

6.20 Alarm goes off. Hit snooze. Children all seem quiet. Curse the fact that they lie in on a weekday.

6.25 Alarm goes off again. Get up. Realise that children are all awake but quiet. Does that mean that Child A has recovered?

Shower, dress and down for breakfast.

Go to check whether stone has moved and any poison gone. Stone has indeed been moved and a bit of the bait eaten. And they have been inside the box and gnawed the poison there too. Does that mean that it's more than just one, and we're being overrun with a whole pack of them? I know they say that you are never more than fifty metres away from a rat, but I'd rather they kept to public footpaths and roads (preferably in another town), and not under our house.

Plan on sending Child A to school today. But come downstairs, and he doesn't fancy breakfast, just wants to lie on the sofa and isn't right at all. Plan B. Call doctor. Get appointment for 11.20 and take children to school.

8.15 Leave the house. Realise half way down the road that haven't put the bins out. And it's black bin week. Stress about the fact that if they don't get collected then will have more rubbish in two weeks,

255

and that will have to sit in black bags which our rodent friends will probably eat through.

Child B and C scoot. Child A walks with me. Start wondering whether he has a fatigue thing.

8.30 Birthday boy from yesterday dashes about a hundred metres to us, calling Child A's name, and holding a party bag. Feel myself welling up. Really thoughtful of them, plus frustrated at the whole mystery illness thing, plus sad that Child A just isn't himself and not able to enjoy all the stuff he would normally love, plus just annoyed about the whole rat thing. Oh, and the bin thing.

Drop Child B off. Explain to Child A's teacher that he won't be in. Take Child C to preschool, via home to put the bins out. Just make it in time.

9.15 Home. Put TV on for Child A. Gets stuck into *Homes under the Hammer* and *World Diving Championship* back to back. Here begins this morning's series of phone calls:

1. Ring the builder to ask him about the house construction, i.e. should I expect rats to climb up to the roof, from entering at ground level. Apparently where they have gone in is the "void under the floor" and the cavity walls are sealed. That may be so, but am sure that they have eaten through the concrete anyway, so I only feel a little bit reassured. Also, what with all the other things that have gone wrong since moving in (leaking roof, cracked floor, dripping pipes etc.) it wouldn't surprise me if they forgot to seal one of the cavity walls anyway.

2. Ring the pest control people. They can come on Wednesday morning. Major dilemma as clashes with Boden clearance sale. Next day after that isn't until the following Tuesday. Could be zillions of them by then. Book it for Wednesday. Damn you rats for ruining

our house, for making me spend loads of money on poison, and for stopping me from making wise investment decisions at Boden sale.

3. Ring my parents to update them. They had a dozen rats living under the floor in their airing cupboard, so they know what it is like.

4. Ring the tiler, who I have been chasing for weeks, to come back and dig up and replace more tiles. Mention that we have rats so I want to get it sorted. Forget to mention that we have skirting boards off and parts of the under wall voids showing, where they might get in somehow. He thinks I am nuts.

11.20 Appointment for Child A at the doctor. Running to time, thank goodness. Checks him out and gives him a clear bill of health. Says to come back if still like this in two or three weeks. Better not take that long. He can see that we've been to the out of hours doctor at the weekend. Feel like a bit of a fraud. Didn't realise their system was all that sophisticated. At least we know that everything – even the bits not checked on Saturday – are ok. Doesn't help me get him sorted though.

Return home. Starving hungry. Make a sandwich to stop me eating every other single thing in the house.

12.00 Collect Child C. He stayed dry today and even took himself to the toilet. My pep talk must have gone in a tiny bit. Child A has a corn thin and strawberries in the car. Leave him while I collect Child C. Return to find that Child A has eaten Child C's yoghurt (brought to stop Child C turning into evil hungry child on collection) "by accident". Really cross. Just mean. And just not like him. I cry at the sheer desperation of it all. He cries because I'm crying.

Cook lunch while Child A and C watch fifty million episodes of *Peppa Pig*. Child A wants to carry on watching the programmes he was watching this morning. Child C having none of it.

After lunch (Child C tried cucumber – didn't like it) clear up, lay more poison, and break up Child C pushing Child A off sofa, and jumping on him repeatedly. Surely that's enough to make you want to go back to school? Combined with *Peppa Pig* again and again. Having not broken his brother's resolve with the jumping, Child C drinks about one and a half pints of water, belonging to Child A, in futile attempt to annoy him.

14.30 Leave to collect Child B. Starts raining. Typical. Child C refuses to try for a wee. Pack two pairs of extra trousers. Decide to let Child A scoot, by way of a back to school trial. If he is happy and has the energy to do this then he can jolly well go back to school. Scoots fine. Child C scoots into a bramble on purpose and gains two nasty scratches to the hand. Child A plays football on arrival at school. That's him sorted then.

Collect Child B, and after much calling (and in the time it takes for Child B to make a fifteen-daisy-long daisy chain) extract Child A and C from football pitch. Takes ages to get going, and then as I chat to another mum, Child A informs me that Child C has crossed a road. Give lecture on road safety again. Ignores it again. All scoot home safely from then on. Child B a gem, stopping at all the agreed waiting points where I can see him, before heading onto the next one.

Child A and B both tired and want to carry on watching diving. Interrupted only by their calls for snacks, and mine of "if you don't eat your dinner when I serve it up you will sit there all night".

16.30 Serve up early tea. Chorizo sausages (which they loved on the BBQ), a cheesy potato gratin from a packet and long beans. Chorizo sausages a "bit spicy", neither like the potato bake, and Child A picks at beans. Child C has beans on toast, but does try a tiny bit of potato which he says will "make me sick". Guess Husband and I will be eating rest of that. All eat yoghurt for pudding, with only a minor disagreement over which character they want on the lid. Try, as always, to point out that the yoghurt still tastes exactly the same and that the pot goes in the bin, but with limited success.

17.30 Bath for Child C. Other two had one last night so they can go without. Doesn't want to get in, then doesn't want to get out. Wash all the vitals then attempt to get him changed, while he role plays the part of a baby chick / lion cub and insists that he will only answer to "Baby Jake".

18.30 All children dispatched to bed. Child A looking like he will fall asleep in two seconds flat, Child B possibly not all that tired, and Child C dressed in a full flight suit, with toy compass and breathing apparatus attached. Warn him he will be hot. Stop him looking for the whistle which is meant to go as part of the set. Bed.

Feel like I've achieved almost nothing today. Not Child A's fault as didn't really sit with him all that much, in attempt to make time at home seem less interesting than school. But house a tip, hardly any work done and shopping not all unpacked from this morning.

18.44 Child B comes down asking for a hug. And that I print off the additional giraffe picture he wants for his project. Dispense hug. Get him back to bed. Promise to print picture. Child C chatting to himself. Check on Child A. Fast asleep. Can children get exhaustion?

18.46 Child C calls out. Wants more water. Has already drunk two beakers. Expect extremely wet nappy or series of yells in the night. Suggest that taking flight suit off might really be a good idea. Admits he is a bit hot and agrees to remove flight suit.

All children asleep by 19.00.

19.11 Need to get something from the garage. Bit scared to go out in case I get chased by a rat. Creep out. Stone still in place, and coast is clear, but every sound makes me jump.

Dinner and do some work. Husband calls at 21.30 to say he's on his way home.

Check on children before I get ready for bed. All fast asleep. Child C has a really wet nappy, and another empty beaker of water. Change and put back to bed. And fill up beaker. Try to wrack my brains to think what he had for tea and why he is so thirsty. Beans I guess.

Diet Cokes: 4.

Chocolate: 4 lines of Fruit and Nut, 6 of Child C's mini eggs (shhh!).

Glasses of wine: 0.

Day Fifty-Eight (Tuesday)

Wake just before 6.00. Hear Child A and B. Sounds like Child B is scampering back and forth across the landing, wearing his leg splints. Eventually hear the sound of Child A's door closing and things are a bit quieter again.

6.10 "Weeee weeee". Guess Child C drank that other beaker of water. Manage to get away with putting Child C back to bed. Phew.

6.20 Alarm goes off. Into shower. Hear Child A and B come in to talk football with Husband.

Downstairs for breakfast. Child A peaky and doesn't eat much. Child B and C just fine, apart from wobbly tooth for Child B. Didn't think that there were any more to go.

Off to school. Child B chats to Child C about what he might do at school. Suggest Child C paints a picture of him. All scoot from car.

Child A fine, then teary as soon as time to say goodbye. Explain to teacher what's what. She's lovely about it. Feel like crying all over again.

Drop Child C at preschool. Sees paint and paper, hands me his banana, and goes off to paint a pic of Child B. In orange.

9.15 Back home. Oven cleaning man coming today but can't remember what time. Eat chocolate. Sort some emails.

So much paperwork from school. Forms for swimming, forms for clubs. Too much to remember. So much to pay. Sort online payments. Write some birthday cards.

Oven man comes. Gets to work. Not one to get excited about ovens but always totally amazed by what he achieves, to the extent that I don't want to use it after he has finished.

11.50 Phone rings. Local number. School. Child A's teacher on the other end of the phone. Gives me update on Child A. Teary at school. Not 100%. Don't know whether to get him or not. Decide to leave him at school for now but ask them to call me if there is any problem at all.

Collect Child C. Attack of conscience about Child A and call back. Arrange to pick up Child A at 12.45, after he's had his lunch.

Five mins later, school calls to say Child A is just fine. Has perked right up and is totally fine. Art this afternoon so they think he will be ok. I agree. Child A stays put. Rollercoaster. Mention that I'll collect them after choir. Receptionist points out that choir starts next week. Just as well she rang or they'd have been left alone at the school gate. Mind fills with images of bedraggled children left in the rain outside the school gates, hours after school has ended.

Make lunch. Doze on sofa while Child C watches *Peppa Pig*. Woken up every time the credits roll. Sometimes wish they made feature length episodes rather than ones that last five minutes.

Wash up, unstack dishwasher. Put lamb in the oven. Child C helps me prepare the potatoes by choosing which spuds I should peel. Play shops with Child C.

14.30 Go to leave the house. Planning to drive to school. Shouldn't. Journey so short. But not sure how Child A will be feeling. See gardener is outside. Child C insists on chasing his lawn mower (which is on) while I try desperately to get the car ready.

Collect Child A and B. Child B throws wobbly about me not having brought his scooter. Get home and Child C refuses to get out of the car until the story CD has completely finished. Need keys for front door so we all sit in car to hear the end of *The Smartest Giant In Town*.

Children play in the front garden. So fantastically lovely to have Child A back to normal. Only been a few days, but such a shadow of his former self that a worry. Plays football with brother, climbs over the front wall to retrieve ball. Chatty again.

16.15 Serve up tea. Roast lamb, roast spuds, veg and gravy. Child A and B's fail safe meal – plates always clean. Continue new approach with Child C. He eats french beans, a bit of potato and a few small mouthfuls of meat. At least I didn't have to cook him a separate meal. Manages to smash a glass bowl sending glass and gravy all over the floor but even that doesn't bother me if he's eating.

Bath for all. Let Child A go first. Just as well as contents of bath always look decidedly suspect after Child C's bath. Make mental note to sterilise bath before tomorrow.

All ready for bed. Repeatedly peel Child C off Child B. Why won't he just play with toys, rather than annoy other people?

18.30 All in bed. All muttering to themselves. Couple of call backs to Child C. Child A asleep by 18.40. Maybe he's just really really shattered.

Head downstairs to tackle everything. Followed by Child B calling me up. Seems like it's his turn to grab a piece of the action:

1. To wipe his bottom.

2. To read me four short poems from his school library book.

3. To tell me all the songs that were sung at school today.

4. For a cuddle.

5. To share three facts that he has learnt:
   - You grow shorter during the day and taller again at night.
   - If you get rid of all your body hair you lose about three kilograms.
   - Bananas take forty years to decompose.

The first one is true (I googled it). I very much doubt the other two.

6. To tuck him in.

At least going up and down the stairs must be a bit of workout. He's been a real star while Child A has been under the weather. Just won't stop talking.

19.20 Workout DVD. Got to be doing some good. Right? Poss counteracted by all the chocolate. It seems to be getting easier. Will do the next level tomorrow. If I can face it. Interrupted twice by Husband on his way home. Gives me chance to get my breath back.

20.10 Finish workout. Delay due to Husband's calls. Too hot to get changed. Put dinner on. Husband arrives home. Get changed and clear up crusty green Playdoh from all over the table and floor while tea is cooking.

Eat curry. Watch TV. More work emails.

21.30 Husband shattered. Asks if ready for bed. More paperwork, find football kits, clear up.

22.09 Still not in bed.

Diet Cokes: 4. Largely due to not drinking.

Chocolate: 4 lines of Fruit and Nut, 2 heaped tsp of Nutella, 1 fun size bag of buttons.

Glasses of wine: 0.

Day Fifty-Nine
(Wednesday)

6.20 Alarm. Feel like I could sleep all day.

6.25 Get in shower. Have shower, brush hair so doesn't dry and make me look like scarecrow. Get back into bed.

6.40 Remind Husband he's meant to be getting up.

6.45 Child B comes in. Claims that Child A says that he woke him up 4.45, but that on his clock it said 5.58. Enter Child B claiming that he's so tired as Child A woke *him* up at 4.45. Have absolutely no idea who to believe. New rule, to add to the zillions of rules we have already: No going in your brother's bedroom until 6.20.

6.50 Child C calls "up time". Ironic that he's sleeping the best out of all of them. Or at least staying the quietest.

Child A eats a bit more breakfast than he has done for a few days. But then goes into decline and lies on sofa under duvet and with pillow.

7.30 Kiss goodbye to Husband. Looks tired. Try a few motivational "c'mon c'mon"s as he heads out the door, in attempt to inspire and energise him for the day.

8.15 Leave the house. Child C unhappy at his seat. Swaps with Child B. Refuses to wear his coat. Wants to hold an umbrella. It's not raining. He screams. I get umbrella. Get three doors down in the car and realise have forgotten Child A's hearing aid. Quick three point turn and race back home. Get hearing aid. Back in car. Set off again.

Still manage to get top parking spot at back of school. How does that work? Some days we are super early and all the good places are taken, and other days we're later and there is still loads of space. For some reason Child A and B don't want to scoot today. Odd. Especially after tantrum yesterday for not bringing scooters. Child C wants to scoot. And wants me to hold his umbrella. Gets bored of scooting half way there. Give umbrella to Child C. Leaves me holding two school bags, a rucksack (containing three water bottles and a travel potty), two football bags and a scooter.

Drop off Child C. Rush home to get back in time for rat man who is coming between 9.15 and 10.30. Arrives at 9.20. Delighted, as if he's quick I can make it in time for the Boden clearance sale which I thought I'd have to miss – yaaaaay!

He informs me he thinks it's mice rather than rats, checks the loft, the pipework, and only charges me the call out fee rather than the full one. Reckons we've caught them early and keep on with the poison we've got. Hurrah.

Second he leaves, jump in the car to get to the sale.

10.10 Excitement fades as I near the car park, or should I say car parks, packed full of shoppers' cars. Every mummy in the county is here, it seems. Look at the other shoppers getting out of their cars and contemplate the Boden demographic. How did I become aged thirty five plus, wearing sensible (yet stylish) clothes? Doors opened ten mins ago, but queue still stretching round the back of the building. Take my place behind an older lady and two hardcore mums with babies in slings and buggies.

Place is totally heaving. Fill basket with random objects in my size. No stuff for boys at all. Grab coat, two tops, two pairs of trousers and a dress. Once I can't find anything else I like, take them to one side. All awful. No wonder they are in the clearance. Some tables are three people deep before you can even get to the boxes of clothes. Try on two pairs of trousers. Equally bad. Leave empty handed. Feel extremely virtuous. So, a complete waste of a morning on the one hand, but would have been annoyed if I hadn't gone and would have wondered "what if?"

Drive home, make work call, make a sandwich.

11.50 Morning gone before I know it. Head off to get Child C.

Child C not wearing the clothes he wore to preschool this morning, but happy and full of chat. Sits in lounge on his deckchair, eating lunch. Cheese sandwiches, fish shapes, ketchup and strawberries.

14.04 Head out to feed the ducks. Four pieces of bread. That should cover it. Can't find many ducks. Couple of moorhens and that's about it. Maybe they heard us coming. Or don't like our brand of bread. Either way, chuck it all in anyway. Figure they can come and get it once we're gone. Plus, Child C happy whether ducks or no ducks.

Child C spots a huge muddy puddle. And another. And another. And some of that mud that makes your wellies stay in it when you try to move your foot. Whole new experience for Child C. Loves it. Decide it isn't worth fighting this battle. A tiny part of me is thinking of the washing pile. And the car seat. And the fact that in five mins he won't want to be in those wet muddy trousers, boots, T-shirt and pants anymore. But a bigger part isn't fussed. The sun is shining. Child C is happy so I'm happy. We don't have to be anywhere else. It's only mud. Though I do blame *Peppa Pig* and all her jumping in muddy puddles. She is totally to blame for putting it at the forefront of young children's mind.

Ten mins later and Child C resembles something from a washing powder ad. Mud even up his nostrils, in his ears, and boots full of water. Would be easiest if there was a Teflon coating for children in general. Just let him splash then wipe him down.

Walk a bit further. Child C runs from one puddle / squelchy mud patch to the next. Enjoys getting boots stuck. Extract him repeatedly. Screams at the sight of every dog, big or small. Several owners offer a stroke of their dogs. Runs in terror.

After a pretty impressive length of walk, Child C is fed up of quantity of water in his boots and wants to sit down. Glad I brought the buggy. Tip water out of boots, ring out socks (which used to be white and are now black) and push him back to the car. Strip off trousers and head home.

15.10 Arrive home. Straight upstairs for bubbly bath. Manage to get rid of all the mud.

All dressed, all clean, TV on for a little bit. Child C keen to play puzzles on my phone. Distract him for a bit. Then give in. Solely on the condition that he gets ready for pick up when I say so.

15.45 Leave to collect Child A and B. Child C insists on taking his deckchair, and keeps talking into his wrist, calling for "Toodles". Erects his chair on the path, right in the way of everyone. Try in vain to help another mum who has lost her keys somewhere on school grounds, but can't do much while keeping an eye on Child C.

Child A and B finish. Both in argumentative mood. Give their friend, who has tummy ache, a lift home. Child C screams and screams and takes ages to get into the car. Screams all the way home. Drop friend off. Child C carries on screaming.

Child A and B start football match. Carnage follows. Can't work out who is to blame but see Child B giving Child A a nasty kick to the leg for seemingly no reason. Confiscate the ball and deduct a point from Child B. Child B declares that Child A is a "bumhead".

Child C plays with new Playdoh. Love that smell.

17.00 Tea served. Pasta in sauce with french beans and lamb. Child C rejects the lot, despite my protests that he has eaten it before. Perhaps a bad idea to give him a banana and biscuit on return from walk. Child A eats it all up. Child B gets in a multitude of strops and keeps pushing it away in anger. I get giggles, as does Child A thus sending Child B into deeper level of strop. Sits under the table for five minutes. Like that's going to help.

Refreshing change not needing to bathe Child C. PJs for Child A and B. Child A has muddy knees from footie but can't be bothered to wash it off. Figure that some of it might rub off in the night on his pyjamas, so that he doesn't have muddy knees for school tomorrow.

18.00 Attempt to do school reading with Child A and B. Love hearing them read, but Child C seems intent on being as needy as possible at this very moment. Child A reads ok and then offers to read to Child C. Child B moans about reading and then insists on jumping (not literally) all over the book (albeit a factual book) and missing sections out. Put his awkwardness down to tiredness. Wonder why aren't children tired like adults i.e. yawn a lot and fall asleep on the sofa? Why does it manifest itself in stroppy moods and naughtiness?

18.45 All in bed. Head off in search of Child C's "Snug Snug". Child B in strop that I'm not reading to them tonight (figure it's too late bearing in mind Child A "doesn't feel well" again). Child A reveals that he might be upset because one of his teachers has changed. Not convinced by this. Think he might be searching for reasons. Though that does point to a worry-related malaise rather than a physical one, perhaps.

Remind Child A and B that they are not to go and see each other before 6.20. Under any circumstances.

19.30 Attempt level two of *Killer Buns* DVD. Have only done it once before, last week, and I have never sweated so much doing a workout DVD. Manage it, but have to style some bits out, as not quite there yet. Hope that it is doing some good. Theory is that, not only will I look like Elle Macpherson, but that also Husband will only notice my two new bikinis for all the right reasons, rather than for the drain they may have caused on family finances.

20.30 Have shower. Open wine. Husband out for drinks, but not sure if I should be putting dinner on for one, or waiting. Will wait til hunger strikes.

Empty car before it gets dark and the mice, or whatever they are, come out. Wellies (still with water inside), socks that need more water wringing out of them, coats and jumpers all come in. Normally forget, leave them all in the car and then they are too cold in the morning for anyone to want to wear. Stuff boots with newspaper, put them in the airing cupboard and hope that Child C doesn't need them in the morning.

21.06 Put dinner on. Eating at this time is probably v bad for my metabolism. Wine has filled the huger void so not even hungry. Look at oven. Think about how much I love my oven man. Go out to freezer. Somehow not quite so daunting now I know we're dealing with mice rather than rats.

Find myself doing squat motion to get plates out of cupboard, and side leg raises as I reach for something from worktop. I've changed.

21.23 Feel quite sozzled. Maybe drinking on an empty stomach wasn't such a great idea.

Diet Cokes: 4.

Chocolate: 1 line of Fruit and Nut (all that was left), 1 fun size bag of buttons, 1 tsp Nutella, do I have to count a Nutella sandwich? – surely it's nutritious if it's between 2 slices of bread!?

Glasses of wine: 3 I think.

Day Sixty (Thursday)

6.14 Child A comes in saying he still doesn't feel well. Tell him to go back to bed and that I'll see him when it's morning. Tell him I'll be up in five mins.

6.16 Child C calling for juice. Go in. Search cot. Find beaker. Back to bed.

6.20 Alarm goes off. Into shower.

6.26 Out of bathroom. Child C calling for a wee wee. Grab potty. Get him up.

Breakfast for Child C. Then Child B. Child A follows last after football chat with Husband.

TV on. Clear breakfast table. Get clothes for Child A, B and C. Child A going downhill rapidly.

Say goodbye to Husband. Hard day ahead for him.

Get Child A, B and C dressed. Sort out fruit and waters. Finalise school bags. Child C's wellies still damp. They'll do.

8.30 Get prime parking spot. No one wants to scoot. Child A because he feels ill. Child B … actually not sure why. And Child C because he wants to hold a small football and an umbrella.

Other children arrive. Child C goes off to jump in puddles, following on from yesterday's success. Kicks football in puddles. Bit like a form of sub-aqua footie. Child B plays with his friends. Child A sits / stands with me. Looks more and more tearful as the minutes pass. Other mums try to make conversation with Child A, to distract him. Just gets more and more tearful.

From there, just awful. Child A sobs uncontrollably into by my jacket. Holding back the tears myself. Just sobs and sobs and clings on to me. I just don't get why now. Teacher is fab and ushers him in asking for his help. Start crying as try and explain the teacher what's what. Take Child B to his classroom. Child B asks why I'm crying. Child C turns up saying he's been looking for us "ev ev where".

Child C runs off after a football. Another child sees it across the playground and goes for it too. Child C picks it up, narrowly pipping other child to the post. Tussle ensues, Child C loses his footing (and the ball) and falls backwards onto a metal ramp. Gather him up in my arms, and realise that my hand is covered in blood. On closer inspection, the back of his head is a mass of matted hair and blood. Quick dash to school office. Kind staff clean him up and put bandage around his head. Resembling Mr. Bump, put him back in buggy, push with one hand and call preschool with the other. Leave message to say that Child C won't be coming in. Bet they'll be delighted (though concerned obviously). Drive to hospital and sit. For. Ages.

11.45 Finally leave hospital. No stitches required, nor glue. Apparently "just" a puncture wound, and already healing nicely by the time we'd been sat there all morning long.

Head home. Sarnies for lunch. Child C moans that his sandwiches aren't "choc choc". Lie and say that we haven't got any again. Eats all his lunch, then comes for more, and more, and more. Playdoh and tidy up playroom, in anticipation of his friend popping round later.

Child C has upset tum. That probably explains his huge appetite.

12.55 Tidy up playroom. Child C plays the drums. Sort out kitchen and make chilli.

Child C makes Playdoh eggs on the toilet floor. Not terribly hygienic, but it's keeping him quiet. Phone rings. Child A's teacher on the phone. She is totally lovely and allays my fears. For now. Has asked Child A for lots of "help" today and is keen to get him involved. Mentions that she has given him a certificate for "being so helpful". Suggest that Child A goes in a tiny bit early tomorrow. Think that might help, to avoid the anticipation and wobbles.

15.30 Mention to Child C that friend will be arriving soon. Stands on the bench on the landing looking for him and asking where he is. Arrives in due course, and Child C super duper excited.

He's never really had a playdate before. Child A and B had loads. Different with Child C. He's had friends round a couple of times with their mums, but this is the first without a mum. Albeit he'll only be round for a little bit while his mum has to go to a school meeting. Child C so excited. Shows his friend all his toys.

15.50 Time to leave to get Child A and B. Have left it a bit late. Makes me smile as they chat away and reminds me of having young twins in the car again. One giggles. The other giggles. The first one giggles again. The second one says "that's not funny". And then it starts again.

16.20 All home. Child B helps take off friend's shoes. Interesting to see him interact with another child. Play with cars, paddle in the Duplo bricks all over the carpet, chat and giggle, play the drums. Friend asks Child A what "the thing" in his ear is for. I explain that Child A's ear doesn't work quite as it should and that it gives him hearing superpowers. He seems to think that is a perfectly acceptable explanation.

Child A and B play on computer, doing their online school reading thing and word searches. At least it's educational.

16.30 Friend's mum arrives. Child C and friend chuck stones in front garden. We tell them off. Wave goodbye.

Noodles and bacon for tea. Random combo, but all of them eat it all (no bacon for Child C). Then strawberries, and yoghurt, and biscuit.

18.30 Bath time for all. Child A and B in bath together for speed purposes. Wash hair, and both stand to style it in the mirror. Feel hairs on the back of my neck stand up as see Child A and B both looking in the bathroom mirror. Guess that's what is meant by mirror twins. Looking at their faces as they are normally, I can easily see their differences, but in the mirror each one looks completely and utterly like the other. Have never noticed it quite like that before. For all intents and purposes, in the mirror Child A becomes Child B and vice versa. When they speak, it gives the strangest feeling in the world that the voice of Child A is coming out of the mouth of what appears to be Child B (even though my head says it isn't). A feeling I can't quite get over. Magical and unsettling, both at the same time. Child B speaks and I have to ask him to stop, as it just feels too weird that my eyes and ears are tricking me – like some strange body swap has taken place. A bit like Tom Hanks in *Big*, or Lindsay Lohan in *Freaky Friday* – only this time it's in our bathroom with Child A and B. Husband and I had had our suspicions about them being mirror twins (one has bigger right ear, one has bigger left ear, one left handed, one right handed) but what I see in the mirror takes my breath away and I can't quite believe it. Child A and B vaguely amused and interested. But then Child B shoves Child A while he is styling his hair, and awe-inspiring moment contemplating the wonder of nature, twins and genetics is broken.

19.00 Complaints from Child A and B that no bedtime story. Need them to get their sleep.

19.20 Pilates. Getting hooked. Then dinner and chocolate and wine. Would all be going so well if I could convince myself that I didn't like chocolate and wine. Maybe I should have hypnotherapy to convince me that all chocolate tastes like vinegar or something.

Called by Child C just as going to bed. Go in. Asks me to sleep in his big bed. Lie down. He's asleep already. Go back to my bed.

Diet Cokes: 3.

Chocolate: 2 fun size bags of buttons, ¾ bar of Lidl chocolate (medicinal), 3 squares of Fruit and Nut I found in the cupboard.

Glasses of wine: 2.

Day Sixty-One
(Friday)

4.30 Child C calls out. Go in to see him. Fall asleep in big bed. 5.30 return to mine. 5.52 called again. Asks me to lie in big bed. Explain I will but have to go back to my bed soon as my alarm will be going off. Child B comes in for a kiss. Oblige. Child C tells me to go away. Leave gladly.

Various calls from Child C. Ignore them all until Morning Time. He's fine in there.

Keep looking at the clock expecting the alarm to go off. Time standing still but not long enough for me to get any sleep.

6.20 Alarm goes off. Hit snooze. 6.25 goes off again. Get up. Child C calling. Child A and B both up. Husband suggests going to get Child C and chatting to Child A and B. Reply with a "no way". Shower time is my five mins peace before I am properly on duty with everyone. Need that time just to prepare myself for the day. Get in shower. Feel bad, about "no way" response, as that's the only time Husband really gets with the kids. Let him know. He goes to chat. Exit bathroom. Child A and B are in the bed chatting about footie. Child C is in his cot, but apparently wants to stay there until Morning Time.

6.28 Call of "wee weeeee". Dash to Child C's room. Once I'm there (i.e. he has an audience), tells me which teddy he has lined up represents which member of our family. Then proceeds to throw 80% of teddies on the floor. Not sure what the reason is. And hopefully we are not represented by the ones he has savagely chucked across the room.

Down for breakfast. Take fruit up for Husband. Child A and B still in the thick of footie talk. SO hoping that Child A goes into school better today. Seems perky so far.

Eat most of my breakfast away from Child C. Then feel a bit bad about lack of interaction. Join him at the table. Insists on eating half my remaining cereal. Wish I'd stayed where I was.

7.40 Child B wants to play on the computer. Normal rule would be not until dressed for school. Since I am nowhere near ready to locate their clothes etc. I let him get on with it. Uses my laptop to find a cricket game. Calls me as screen "full of pictures". Dash at super speed to ensure he hasn't infected my computer with a deadly virus that will steal all of our identities. Just a giant pop-up this time so get rid of it and play continues.

Child C finds a glue stick in the kitchen and wants to glue. I object. He persists. Just need to get on. Relent. Pick your battles and all that. Find paper, and some cut up bits for him to stick on. He's happy. And half dressed.

Say goodbye to Husband.

7.45 Computer freezes. Point out that now isn't a great time to be playing computer games and, by the way, I'm also managing Child C's art project and trying to get three people dressed.

7.50 Call time on computer games. Get Child A and B dressed. No more computer activity until they have their shoes on and teeth cleaned. Works.

Husband calls. A3 a nightmare. Asks me to check traffic on iPad. Do so. Big accident up ahead. Asks if he should catch the train. Haven't the foggiest. Whichever choice I make is likely to be the wrong one.

Make sarnies for Child C. Try and make lunch as interesting, wholesome and yummy as possible.

8.15 Time to go. Child B begs that I leave his tab open so that he can carry on later. Agree. Must remember to do it. Though good chance he will forget if I don't.

Receive text from Husband. Just missed train. Will have to wait thirty mins for the next one. He thinks he probably should have stayed in the car.

8.26 Arrive at school. Hoping and praying that Child A is ok. Have to go to office as threw away important permission slip in smug moment of thinking I had paid for a forthcoming trip and therefore didn't need the letter. Child A and B scoot. Child C carries plastic bus with pop up characters, which sings *The Wheels On The Bus* so opts for the buggy. But mostly runs / walks / lies down.

Child A and B play football.

8.40 Take Child A to his classroom under the guise of helping the teacher. Goes in with no problem at all. Thank goodness. And great idea from the teacher.

8.45 Drop off Child B.

Head back to the car. Child C is fine going in to preschool. V excited to have his toy bus with him. Take off wellies, put on slippers. All sorted.

Pop into doctor and pick up Husband's prescription. Take to chemist. Say I'll be back in five mins. Go to shop. Realise haven't got purse. Go back to chemist to tell them I'll come back later. Queue too long so give up. Hope they don't call my name all morning. Dread prospect of going back later with Child C. Only positive is that we do tend to get served quite quickly when the children are with me, as they can't wait to get us out of the shop.

Home. Chance to catch up on bit more work. Funny what difference that extra hour makes. Seems like so much longer. Ring the bank. Wash up from breakfast. Find various kit for Child A and B ... Beavers uniform, cricket shirts etc. for tonight. Heaven forbid if I don't know where everything is at any given moment, and that all clothes aren't clean and in a good state. *Buns* DVD on. Can't do all the exercises. How did I manage to do more of it the other day? Maybe my run has caused muscle fatigue. Jeans feeling tight and thought it was meant to tone me, rather than build up muscle. Perhaps just a transition phase. Will have sleek physique by the morning.

12.45 DVD finished. Boiling hot. No time for shower. Try and not look hot and get changed. Will never understand how some people manage to exercise and not look hot. Only have to do two mins on a treadmill and look like I've done several marathons.

Collect Child C. Has had a fab time. So pleased that he enjoys it so much. Makes it all so much easier. And he is getting easier. Still a total pain at times, but easier than he was, probably even sixty-one days ago.

Off to do errands. Pick up prescription (Child C pulls out countless items of makeup from the display unit), get batteries for Hexbugs (Child C investigates bags of birdseed), put in dry cleaning (Child C knocks over tower of duvets), get strawberries (Child C knocks over stack of oranges and grapefruit sending them bouncing across the floor and under the display unit). Go to the next town to get cricket trousers. Only one pair in right size. Other pair I'm offered would fit me. Take the one pair and go to the sports shop in the next town to that. One pair in stock there too. Bit too big and way too long but that's all they've got. Shopkeepers – seriously – with twins you need to have two of the same thing available. Sort it out!

Go home. Text Husband. Informs me that cricket trousers are meant to be long. What is the point of that? No one ever warned me that motherhood required quite so much sewing.

14.40 Scoot off with Child C to pick up Child A and B. Meant to leave earlier but Child C glued to TV. Get stuff ready while he's caught in the tractor beam, then head off.

15.00 Pick up Child A. Happy. And received the Golden Certificate this week. Chuffed to pieces, and totally oblivious that he got it, in part, to counteract his wobbles. Big congratulations and hugs and praise.

Child C intent on playing with all the equipment which is being set up for after-school Fun Sports Club. Spend seven minutes trying to get him away from a yellow hula hoop. Only manage when tempt him with looking at the newly hatched baby chicks in Year R classroom. Leaves the hoop, runs off, and proceeds to terrorise the chicks by pressing his face up close to the glass.

Round up children and just get out of the playground before the gate is locked up.

15.30 Home. 16.00 Quick tea for Child A and B. Get them changed while they try to play ping pong. Child C demands food.

16.20 Take Child A and B to Beavers. Home for Child C and cook spaghetti, as per his request. Not that fussed about eating it, but tempt him to eat more by going on about being big and strong and being able to lift me up. Says he's got a "full tum tum" after a bit, and attempts to lift me.

17.30 Collect Child A and B. Child C sits colouring in doorway as twenty boys stream out. Won't move until he's finished his "treasure maps". Get changed for cricket. Head to cricket club. Child A asks if I've got the bats. I haven't. Go back. Start off again. Halfway there transpires that Child C not strapped in. Pull over, strap him in, pick up stone he stole from Beavers car park, which he had dropped and wants back. Go to cricket club.

Child C wets himself on arrival. Child A and B run off. Chat to other parents while Child C throws a tennis ball around. Mostly at the windows, people's ankles and expensive pieces of equipment. Then wets himself again. Abort mission. So lovely to chat, but can't stand by while Child C runs around (and wrestles frisbees off other children) with very wet trousers.

19.02 Arrive home. Husband home. Fetching jumper before going to watch the cricket practice. Update him on car parking and where I put the boys' water bottles. Child C hungry (should have eaten his spaghetti) so has yoghurt then to bed ASAP.

19.36 Child C finally asleep after two calls of "wee wee" (only one produced), three calls of "need to talk to you" and various other undefined calls.

Such a mountain of housework to do that I don't know where to start. Pour wine instead. And put dinner on.

20.12 Husband and Child A and B arrive home. Child A and B totally high – like they've just come out of a sugar-fuelled party. Bowl of cereal as they are "starving" and then bed.

Dinner and film. Husband falls asleep twenty mins in, so switch onto something else.

21.30 Cold. Run a bath. Plan on reading magazine. Headline on *Style* magazine (which I was given perhaps because I have none) is "Could you survive a month in flats?". Seriously? Clearly these people have no children, and don't walk more than one metre. Flick through kids' furniture catalogue instead. Don't need any of it and all looks lovely but wouldn't make our kids any tidier, or better behaved. Bin it.

Can't face doing anything much. Finish online Tesco shop and head to bed. Washing up will have to wait.

21.55 Check on Child C, who has wet through his sheets. Not sure if water or wee. Adjust pull ups, change trousers, put blanket down on top of bottom sheet.

Diet Cokes: 3.

Chocolate: 2 heaped tsp Nutella. Fruit and Nut from Lidl and a bar of crunchy chocolate.

Glasses of wine: Probably 3.

Day Sixty-Two
(Saturday)

Another disturbed night. Don't know what time Child C called out, but went to sleep in his room for a bit, and only woke when Husband came up in the middle of the night.

5.30 Child C ready to get up. Go and sleep in his bed (again). Well, not sleep. Pretend / try to sleep. Child C plays with grabber, teddies and various other items. No intention of sleeping.

5.45 Tell him I'm going back to my room and that I'll see him in the morning

6.00 Child B comes in for a hug. Says our bed is "sooooo comfy". Let him stay on the proviso that he doesn't chat.

6.18 Child B bored of not being able to chat and goes back to his own room.

6.20 Child B goes to see Child A. Child C hears him and shouts his name for the next seven minutes.

6.27 Go to get Child C up. Wants to show Child B his "surprises". Pretending it is Child B's birthday or something. Child B comes in and acts suitably surprised, thank goodness.

6:45 Call of "Mummy, something has happened to your

computer". Child B informs me that Child A clicked on something and "now it has all gone funny". Rush to computer. Word files seem to be flashing weirdly. Close everything. All seems ok. Crisis averted. Though a valuable lesson perhaps. Must back everything up.

7.30 Final preparations for swimming. Wobble from Child A. So slow to get ready then gets teary. Threaten to go without him (which doesn't really work as it is probably what he wants anyway). Get Child C to do a wee, so less likely to wet trousers while home alone with Husband. Leave at 8.25.

Child A teary again by the pool, but perks up once in the water. Beginning to think that it might be a confidence thing.

Lesson goes very quickly as chat to friend on poolside. Cold boys have hot shower and need more help getting changed than should be required by the average seven year old.

9.30 Supermarket to fill up car. Pop in to get all the things I have forgotten on the order which is coming this evening. Then spot some things for lunch too. Had promised Child A and B they could choose a cake. £25 later, we leave the supermarket. Coffee cake for Child A, decorate your own gingerbread men for Child B and a bag of chocolate cookies chosen by me, to share. Spend journey home discussing best way to share out the chocolate cookies.

Home. Husband declares he has had the worst two hours with Child C ever. Two pairs of wet pants, one pair of wet trousers and Child C shouting "me no like you" for the duration. Cake remedies things for Child A, B and C.

10.30 Mountain of laundry to sort so make a start. Put up footie goals. Give Child C outdoor crayons. He starts redesigning the patio. Thirty mins later patio has psychedelic rainbow effect.

12.15 Start making lunch. Neighbour pops head over and asks Husband if we can keep the kids in around 13.00ish, as they've got a couple of viewings by potential buyers. Slow lunch down so that it can coincide with timings. Child A and B being particularly noisy so can't blame him. Lack of sleep has left them looking for a fight.

Yummy lunch of french bread, pâté, cheese, ham, nachos, salad and houmous. Child C goes to wash hands. Doesn't come back. Call him a few times. Still no Child C. Investigate. He is washing up a selection of items (none of which need washing) in the sink in the downstairs toilet. Floor is soaked, as are all items, including an egg box. Coax him back to table. Not remotely interested in eating, having eaten half a cookie and a gingerbread man. Child C eats nothing, but makes a picture of a dinosaur (apparently) with his lunch. Child A and B eat plenty. As does Husband. I'm pretty full as stuffed my face during preparation stages.

14.00 Remind Husband that he needs to collect his dry cleaning. Launches into action and asks who wants to go with him to the swings (and to get the dry cleaning). Adds in getting diesel and going to the car wash for good measure. And wants to try and be back for 15.00 for Man U kick off. Good luck with that. After much kerfuffle, all three kids want to go. Pack water, travel potty, change of clothes. Give instructions about Child C. 14.18 leave. Predict at least two tantrums, one set of wet trousers, and several "it's not fair"s. They may or may not be speaking to each other on their return.

14.30 Argh. Must remember to wash Child C's sheets from last night.

Have two hours of lovely peace. Clear the kitchen and lounge. Catch up on emails. Buy friend's birthday pressie. Chat to neighbour and meet new neighbour. Clear old food out of fridge. Peace.

16.20 All arrive home. All really hot and really tired. Surprised that Child C hasn't fallen asleep on the way home. Child C upset that they didn't make it to the car wash. Promise him that they can do that tomorrow. Ice cream for Child A, B and C. Husband declares that they were awful, that they caused a complete commotion in the shops, and takes himself off to the garden. Think he's traumatised. Mention something along the lines of "welcome to my world", combined with a big "thank you" for keeping them out for a while. Husband mutters that they are at school most of the time. Point out that there are holidays.

Child C settles in deckchair watching *Peppa Pig Santa's Grotto*. Seems odd hearing jingle bells ringing from the TV in May. He's happy though, and on a short fuse there, so that's fine with me.

17.10 Tea time. Ask children to wash their hands. Child B obliges. Child A doesn't. Child C throws huge tantrum, is given a lecture about dog wee and germs on slides, and then promptly wets himself. Child A relents after issuing me with a range of blackmail threats. At very same moment Tesco delivery man arrives. Call Husband in as matter of urgency to oversee dinner. Take delivery of shopping. Sign machine.

Supervise tea. Clear up. Child C plays with Playdoh. Child A and B play football in the garden, and argue.

17.45 Bath time for Child C. Not interested. Standoff ensues. Eventually lets me wash him standing up in the bath but won't sit down. One down two to go. Read books to Child C.

18.10 Give Child A and B a five minute warning.

18.15 Call Child A and B in. Both boiling hot. Child C to bed. Child B wants bath. Just as well I left Child C's water in there. Quick bath for both (one at a time, as way too much fighting) then bed. Water looks like muddy pond water by the time they have finished. Quickest bedtime goodnight as can make it.

Meant to be doing workout DVD, and Husband had mentioned going for a run, but his eyes look ready to close and I can't be bothered. Don't bother. Take plan B approach and drink pink cava on sun loungers under a blanket (because it's not that sunny any more) in the garden. Nice to catch up after noisy day.

20.15 Not warm at all anymore and cava nearly gone. In for dinner and the rest of the film we fell asleep watching last night. Watch / doze through movie.

21.30 Husband asleep.

21.56 Still need to sort out the cricket trousers. Maybe I'll just take the scissors to them.

22.56 Trousers done. Bet they complain that they are too short or too long. Recounted to the kids just yesterday how one Saturday night, sixteen years ago I spent the evening dancing the night away on one leg, in a club, with a leg in plaster and on crutches, behaving as if invincible (and warned them never to do anything so silly and irresponsible). Wonder if in another sixteen years I will be telling stories of how I spent this Saturday evening, cutting, pinning and Wunderwebbing cricket trousers. How times change!

Diet Cokes: 3.

Chocolate: 1 large chocolate cookie, 3 large squares of Lidl chocolate.

Glasses of wine: 3.

Day Sixty-Three
(Sunday)

5.32 Child C begins his morning ritual with "My cow's fallen out of my cot". Ignore, attend, go back to bed.

5.35 "We going to school today?" Ignore, attend, get in his big bed. Tells me to "go away".

5.41 "Don't want this book Mama. Want that book". Worried that he will wake, or has woken, Child A and B so don't ignore this time. Stress that it is still night time. He bids me "night night."

5.50 "Is it up time?" Ignore twice, then attend. Remind him that it is not.

5.56 "Need a wee wee". Damn, he's played the trump card. Can't ignore that one. Arrive in his room with the potty and tells me "Done wee wee in my cot. Want big toilet". Ask him to stand up then so that I can lift him. Replies with a "Noooooo. Bring the big toilet here". Characteristically unrealistic and unreasonable.

Child C does his wee in the big toilet then comes into our room with books.

6.30 Child A and B come in. Want to check Fantasy Football points on the iPad. Start checking. Child B gets bored of waiting for his turn and goes downstairs to use my laptop. Child C plays jigsaw puzzles on my phone, with a bit of assistance.

6.35 Three out of the four people in the bed looking at computing equipment and a further one downstairs doing the same. Is that what the modern Sunday morning looks like? On the plus side at least it prolongs staying in bed.

7.45 Go downstairs. Croissants as a treat, in yesterday's Tesco delivery. Devoured almost as fast as I can put fillings inside them.

Get Child A and B dressed in their cricket whites. Child A's trousers are huge, so tuck everything in to keep them up. Get water bottles ready and read instructions about where they are meant to go. Read that I was meant to reply to confirm they would be there. Oops.

Go to get cardigan. Notice in mirror that my nice summery trousers have developed a split around the waistband. Not even worn them for a whole day. Are a little on the tight side, but didn't think they were that tight. Must be defective workmanship rather than too much chocolate (or muscle!?) on my part.

Fix side of cricket bats with superglue. Get too much of it on my fingers. No one seems very interested in me losing half my thumb prints.

9.30 Husband comes downstairs. Get Child A and B in car. Husband in a hurry. Wants to take their picture. Can't find any of his stuff. Cross that they aren't in the car quick enough. Shouts at Child A and B. They cry. Great start. Kiss kids goodbye and tell them I'm see them in a bit.

Get Child C dressed.

9.54 Head off. By time we're at the end of the road, Child C starts shouting that "You drive. I get out here". Again and again. Explain that's not possible. Then decide there is no point trying to explain. Find parking space and track down the cricket pitch.

Match has started. Child A and B play ok. Pretty well bearing in mind they've never played in a cricket match, or with a real cricket ball. Get out five times between them. Just as well getting out doesn't mean that you're actually out in their matches. Take call from babysitter. Wonder why he's calling. Turns out I called him without realising it, so he was calling me back. Explain that I called him with my backside – but did need to speak to him about sitting next weekend, so perhaps intuition on the part of my rear end. Amuse Child C while half watching. Play catch, chase and then mostly shops. Actually not too much of a nightmare to entertain today. Luck or entering a better phase? Wet patch on trousers indicates he needs a wee. Does wee and poo in travel potty, then realise that there is huge tear in liner and contents leaking out everywhere. Luckily have plastic bag in rucksack. See, there is a point to carrying round all that stuff. Not only did the plastic bag come in handy (though begrudge using an M&S one I had to pay for) but also found a toy train, car, pencil and range of other items for Child C's pretend shop.

11.45 Get home. Child C discovers buckets and sponges in the garage while I get BBQ out. Explain that they are for washing the car. Wants to wash the car. Not top on my list of priorities. Still not washed up from breakfast. And need to marinate chicken (which I should have done earlier). And meant to be lighting BBQ.

Child C brings the buckets etc. inside. Informs me that he wants to wash the insides of the windows. Granted, they need washing. But not by a three year old. Compromise and say he can wash the patio and plastic climbing frame. At least that will get some of yesterday's artwork off the patio. Sets to work, while I light BBQ and clear up.

12.15 Husband arrives home with Child A and B. Kids rush out to play football.

Child C munches through long lunch in run up to the rest of us eating. Should sit with us, but actually eats quite a good meal, and lunch running a bit late for his tastes today.

13.00 BBQ ready. Child B throws strop about something being unfair in football match. Child A and Husband tuck in. Child B eventually gives in, though not before sulking for at least ten mins and complaining about the injustice of Husband's referee skills. Child A sings a song about the "River Gordon".

14.00 Clear up. Child A and B play on Xbox. Realise, hearing them chat, that Child A has taken to saying "do you agree?" and "don't you think?" and "wasn't it?" and various other variations, after 80% of what he says. Incidence of this in his speech coincides with his lack of confidence / mystery bug that never really seemed to be bug. Hmmmm. Perhaps coincidence. Perhaps not. Perhaps it really was / is a wobble in his confidence.

Child C happy playing in garden. Makes "birthday cakes" with sand and sticks, helps me wash the bird poo off the slide, and gets all the croquet hoops out of the shed, and sticks them in the ground. Then in to play with Playdoh. At least he's not watching TV for a change. Or screaming at all of us.

Husband works on presentation for later in the week.

15.45 Child C wants to water the plants with a watering can. After fifteen trips backwards and forwards to the hose, I put the brakes on this operation. Recognise that he can't do everything himself, but I can't be hose operator all day. Suggest alternative game of pretending to fix the ride on cars in the garden. Pack rucksack full of tools for him, give him a cap and he's happy fixing. For five minutes. A bit of knocking with a toy hammer, then back inside again.

16.10 Child C asks to watch *Peppa Pig*. Watches two episodes from the *Santa's Grotto* DVD, then appears in the kitchen wanting to play with Playdoh again. It is a bit better now he can do a bit more. Certainly less looking for a fight today. Makes a nice change.

16.49 Take it back. Wants to play on my phone. Say he can if he uses the potty, as can see from his jigging that he needs a wee. After throwing potty across the room shouting "I don't need a wee wee", proceeds to wet himself all over the kitchen floor in spectacular style. Phone removed. Tears. Horrible mood. Rubbing eyes. Shouldn't have got up so early. Don't need this after a morning of playing with him and an afternoon of fetching everything he could possibly need. Says he needs snacks and starts rooting through the cupboard. Tell him it's beans on toast for tea. Says he hates it.

17.10 Serve up beans on toast. Child C sits down with a "me loooooovvvve beans on toast".

All eat quickly. Child C starving, Child A and B desperate to get back to the Xbox.

Run bath for Child C, while he watches *Peppa Pig*. Hair wash night. None of them like having their hair washed but can't remember the last time I did it, so figured it's time. Duration of Child C's bath is taken up with acting out *The Three Billy Goats Gruff* with five assorted plastic animals, only one of which is a goat.

Shower for Child A and B. Child A fine with it. Child B upset at losing the football game on the computer. Says he not going to have a shower. Or a bath. Or anything. Tell him he's not having any computer time tomorrow then. Gets into bed and pulls grumpy face. Tell him he'd better not go to party tomorrow as it's a computer games party and he better get used to not always winning. Fifteen mins later relents. Has shower. Grump forgotten.

Bedtime takes ages. Child C wants to construct crane Child A and B were given for birthday. Then wants to build stuff from Meccano, and spills it all over the carpet. Child B starts constructing something complicated. Child A cross that he's not allowed any more computer time. Warn him he's turning into Mike TV from *Charlie And The Chocolate Factory*. Or that one who sings "I want it now. I want it right now". And look what happened to them.

18.40 Put Child C to bed. Sit to read story to Child A and B. Two paragraphs in, Child C calls needing a wee wee. Back to bed. Sit down in Child A and B's room. Calls for another wee. Doesn't do one this time, but does insist on having his blanket, kitten, water, and a toy fireman beside him. Tell him wee wee will come in the morning and put him back to bed.

Read story, bid goodnight, tidy garden, dinner, and film.

Diet Cokes: 3.

Chocolate: half a chocolate cookie, one line of Fruit and Nut.

Glasses of wine: 1. Bottle is open. Shame not to have any.

Day Sixty-Four
(Monday)

No one should be woken up at 5.15 on a bank holiday. Ever. Unless the house is on fire. House is not on fire, but Child C very much awake and not going back to sleep until bedtime tonight. Get up and get into bed in his room. He "reads" to me from his cot. I am prompted to make the right noises of agreement / interest at the right time. Then wants to read in the bed that I'm in. Do that for a bit. Until 6.00. Then he needs a wee. Get up. Ask him to be quiet. Meet Child B on the landing. Does no one like sleep in this house? Child A awake.

Go downstairs with Child A and C. Child B stays upstairs to practice his spellings which I'd left out. May have vested interest in that he knows he can't use the Xbox until homework is done today. Remind all that no one is playing on the Xbox until at least 9.00. Lie on sofa and try to doze while kids watch TV. Child C in foul mood. Screams at everyone.

6.30 Child A says he's hungry. Fetch chocolate brioches for them all, to eat in the lounge. Try to eat my cereal in kitchen while Child C screams at me for not eating it in the lounge.

7.02 Take cup of tea, croissant and banana up to Husband. He's awake. Not surprising, based on the noise levels. Mention that I have been up for two hours, and could really do with a bit more sleep. Agrees that he'll watch the kids once he comes down.

8.10 Ask if Child A and Husband can come down so that I can sleep. They do. Yay.

Despite the fact that Child C comes in and Husband ushers him out saying I've gone out (hopefully no psychological damage done), and then comes in again looking for Husband in a game of hide and seek, still manage to get an hour's doze and a peaceful shower.

Do reading and spellings with Child A and B. Child A reads about defensive shots in cricket, and Child B reads about how to make fruit lollies. I guess it is reading, and they seem fairly enthusiastic. Don't understand much of the cricket one, and have to point out many times to all children that we are not making lollies today. Both even do their ukulele practice, albeit very quickly. Then allowed to play on the computer. Going to a computer games party today so a little concerned about overdosing. Point out that they will need to play outside at some point during the course of the day.

Clear and clear some more. Don't know if others don't see the mess or just know / think that it will get cleared for them.

12.15 Serve lunch. Pasta with cheese. Low nutitional value but everyone eats it. Child A and B desperate to get back to computer. Put limit on finishing the game they are playing. They do so. Then Husband wants a go. Child C wants to do *Peppa Pig* painting on the iPad, so all hooked up, while I sweep kitchen floor and do the bins.

13.45 Friend drops friend of Child A and B's round, so that we can give him a lift to the party.

All boys go out to play football with Husband.

14.14 Come in for drinks. Child C insists on having a pint of water like the boys four years his senior. Might as well just sellotape the potty to him for the rest of the afternoon. Trying hardest to teach him, kindly, that he needs to get to the potty before the wee goes everywhere. Large drink may not be the best move.

16.30 Five large wees, one pair of wet trousers, and a wet carpet later, am hoping that the water is out of his system. Child A and B at party with friend, while Child C and I play shops. Serve up tea as a break from shops, and keep reminding myself that mustn't forget to collect Child A and B.

17.00 Collect Child A and B from party. Both stuff faces with sweets then settle down with the Argos catalogue to start their Christmas lists, seven months early. Remind them that they had better behave themselves if they are expecting presents, and to not forget that Father Christmas is always watching them from his "cameras" (aka burglar alarm sensors).

21.30 Get ready for bed. Even Husband notices my food baby. Discuss how I look nine months pregnant. Wonders why I have a bit that sticks out. Presume it is the baby bit that has filled up with food. Either way, not a good look. Less food starts tomorrow. Soup for lunch … that's my plan.

Diet Cokes: 4.

Chocolate: Can't remember, which probably means lots.

Glasses of wine: 0.

Day Sixty-Five
(Tuesday)

Husband's alarm goes off at 5.15. Rest of the house quiet. As predicted. They only ever want to get up when we need to sleep. All part of the Wearing Down The Parents To Achieve World Domination Mind Games.

5.52 Child B has massive coughing attack. Husband goes to check on Child B. Child A comes in looking for Husband, and suggests that we give Child B some water. Tell him that I'm hoping that's what Husband has gone off to do. Husband unaware that he needs a big cup at times like this, so take my water in. Child C awake and singing.

6.00 Husband says goodbye. Asks if he should say goodbye to Child C. Say not to. Otherwise won't be able to get dressed without World War III breaking out.

Child A complains that he still doesn't feel well. Try being nice. He continues to tell me he doesn't feel well. Explain firmly that he is not ill. That there are people dying and he is not.

Child B is pleasant, albeit wanting to play on the iPad all the time. Put an end to that by 7.30, or they will be square eyed before they get to school.

Child C is the most ginormous pain the backside from breakfast through until I drop him off at preschool, as illustrated by the following key indicators:

- Not letting anyone else sing at the breakfast table apart from him.

- Not wanting to change out of his pyjama top.

- Sitting on Child B on the sofa, insisting that that part of the sofa is his cushion.

- Switching the TV off when other people are watching it.

- Stealing and hiding Child A's jumping beans that he got in a party bag and wants to take into school.

- Refusing to put his jumper and shoes on, and drawing "treasure maps" instead.

- Screaming over everyone in the car, and shouting that it is his turn to talk. It isn't.

- Scooting into the bushes on purpose.

- Climbing on the climbing frame at school, which is out of bounds before and after school (did come off when I told him there was a big dog in the shed which might bite him).

- Insisting on being carried into the playground.

- Confiscating the football that fifteen Year Ones and Year Twos were playing with.

- Crying when I gave the football back. Replaced with a yellow one, kindly, by another child.

- Screaming that he doesn't want the yellow one.

- Screaming that he does want the yellow one.

- Screaming that he wants to talk to me.

- Screaming that he doesn't want to scoot.

- Screaming that he wants me to pick him up.

- Screaming that he wants me to pick him up higher.

- Yelling that he wants his scooter back.

- Yelling that he wants to put the scooter in the car.

- Yelling that he doesn't want to take his backpack off in the car.

- Yelling that he wants to eat dog food (God knows where that came from).

- Yelling that he wants to go home.

- Yelling that he doesn't want to go to school.

- Screaming that he does want to go to school.

- Screaming that he has spilt the contents of his backpack all over the car.

- Screaming that he wants me to clear them up now (had offered to clear them up, but was planning on doing it later).

- Pouring a mixture of water and sand into the tadpole tank.

- Answering "to the moon" when I ask where he needs to go when he needs a wee at school.

Do I have to go and collect him at 12.00? Wonder if he is competing for the Worst Behaved Child In England. He has a pretty strong chance of winning.

Can't give up chocolate as part of my healthy eating after that. Scoff line of Fruit and Nut.

Do new abs DVD. Really hard. Not sure I was doing it correctly enough to burn off any calories. How do people even get that fit? Soup for lunch. Do Tesco shop and order lots more soup.

12.10 Child C home. Swans from pond up the road, in our front garden on arrival home. Child C suggests we "get a scarecrow to scare them away". When they do move on he comments that he has scared them away with his teeth. How on earth does his mind work? Eats lunch in lounge. "Helps" me get ready for Nanny and Grandpa coming to stay. He plays while I sort stuff out, but at least he is happy.

14.10 Nanny and Grandpa arrive. Child C super duper excited. Cup of tea, while Child C plays and generally shows off.

15.30 Collect Child A and B from choir. Both give cursory hello to Grandparents, and more interested in getting their snack. Scoot home in chaos. Lose Child C for five mins. Embarrassed by the lack of togetherness in our travel home process, in front of Grandparents.

16.00 Once home, Nanny takes Child A and B to the charity shop. Come back with a diabolo for Child B, which is an instant hit. Decides he is going to keep it a secret and then learn loads of tricks and surprise everyone. Landing on the floor every five seconds at the moment. Harder than it looks. Child A has chosen *Elefun* for bargain price of £1. Child C thinks it is the best game in the whole world and sets about playing it continuously.

16.30 Serve up tea. Child C requests spaghetti and eats it all up. Child A and B have (very extravagant) steak and chips. Figure red meat might do them some good. Wolf it down.

Reading and bath and bed … and argument over bedtime story for Child A and B. Have finished our other book. Child A wants *Danny Champion Of The World*, Child B says he won't listen to it. Read one chapter, which don't think either of them listen to.

19.04 Kids in bed. Child A "feels sick". Explain that you can feel sick but that it means something is bothering you, rather than being physically sick. Tell true story of some girls being mean to me when I was in top infants, because they didn't like my shoes, and how they wouldn't play with me because I didn't have long hair, and how when I grew my hair, they had theirs cut. Finds this quite amusing and seems to take his mind off things.

Drinks for all, and sort out dinner.

19.45 Husband arrives home. Tired and preoccupied. Dinner, finish Tesco shop, and bed.

Diet Cokes: 3.5.

Chocolate: 1 line of Fruit and Nut, Ben and Jerry's Chocolate Fudge Ice Cream.

Glasses of wine: 2.

Day Sixty-Six
(Wednesday)

I genuinely think that Child C has been sent here to destroy me. Up at some middle of the night ungodly hour. Spent time in his big bed. Got him up for a wee he'd already done. Ordered me to sleep in his bed again. Tried to go back to mine. It woke him. Had to stay there for longer. Eventually got back to my bed around 3.30. Must have been with him well over an hour. Then bionic child awake and raring to go at 5.30. Tell him, in no uncertain terms, that everyone is asleep and that he is waking everyone up. Makes no difference. Tell him he is making me sick, and that I need sleep. Settles down a bit, so pull the door as closed as I can without actually closing it so that he doesn't wake the whole road.

6.05 Alarm goes off. Husband catching train in today.

6.15 Go in to see Child C. He is sitting in an empty chicken noodle box in his cot with two teddies. Apparently he is going into space in it. Wish he would for a couple of hours. How can he not have much sleep, for a small person, and still wake up so perky?

Child A and B in Child A's room playing with the *Elefun* game.

Get dressed. Child B enters in state of distress. Tears, wails, the full works. He has lost one of his toy jumping beans. Declares that it is a disaster. Warn him that that's what happens when you take things to school, but that I'll help him look. More tears. Takes himself off to bed in a state of depression. Attempt to dry hair while Child C tries to buy various items from my "shop". Invests in a wet towel, a teddy and a blanket.

Go downstairs with Child C. Child A and B upstairs with Nanny and Grandpa. After rummaging through Child B's school bag, find jumping bean on the floor. Drama over. Happiness restored. Child B back to his normal self.

Child A and B keen to get on computers. I'm keen that they interact with Grandparents.

Bid farewell to Grandparents at 8.00. Call surgery to try and get appointment for Child A. Call on mobile and landline at the same time, to both surgery numbers in attempt to get through.

8.17 Get through and manage to get appointment at 17.30.

8.20 Leave house. Child C slows down our departure, by trying to skip with the diablo rope. No matter how many times I point out that it isn't a skipping rope. Lucky not to kill himself in it.

Child C only marginally less of a nightmare on the school run than yesterday. What with having a ten minute discussion on why he can't take his scooter in the playground (which is the rule of which he has been fully aware since birth), some rant about the Big Bad Wolf taking it (think I might have started that one the other week) and the full on tears, leg pulling, screaming for ten mins regarding playing in the cordoned off sand / mud pit (cordon just acting as an invitation for him to go and explore), I'm done with his morning temper tantrums. Also reckons he doesn't want to go to school as "there is a bear there". How can I possibly answer that, since "no there isn't" doesn't seem to cut it? Realise have forgotten football socks for Child A and B. Child A says "We could always wear school socks". Delighted, I say "Could you? Would that be ok?" He replies "No, not really".

Child A gets teary when I say I'm not going to go and get them. Point out that he can't just turn on the tears to get what he wants. But do relent and say I'll bring them in later.

9.20 Get home. Answer email from teacher about Child A. Catch up on a few other things, then 10.00 already. Stick workout DVD in the machine. Getting naff all work done by exercising. Get changed, then Tesco man arrives. That blows my hope that he might arrive half way through and create opportunity for a breather.

10.45 DVD just too dull. Must have got used to the pace and difficulty of the other ones. Not sure I worked anything much out.

11.05 Had better put Tesco shop away. Eat a satsuma (to cancel out chocolate from earlier). Starving. Had better put some soup on.

12.00 Collect Child C, come home and he has lunch in front of the TV.

12.45 Clear away bits from Child C's lunch. Find left over sticky toffee pudding from last night. Would be wasteful not to finish it off. Delish.

13.00 There should be a law against mental cruelty to parents by toddlers. Forced, or rather encouraged loudly, to take part acting out the story of *The Three Billy Goats Gruff* by Child C. Play role of troll. So totally tired that keep falling asleep on the carpet between Billy Goats trip trapping over the bridge. How come I am exhausted, and he just doesn't give in? Other people recount how their children have a nap still, or have a snooze on the sofa. I wish. And I'm hungry.

Pull Child C off my leg and explain clearly that I need to put away that shopping that was delivered this morning. He gets mad. I get mad. Switch on TV, put out Little People toys. Doesn't want them. Put them away. Wants them. Get them out.

Put some shopping away. Then google "how to get rid of muffin top". General consensus seems to be lots of exercise, drinking loads of horrid stuff made from veggies, and for 39% of mums you can't lose it easily anyway as your muscles have separated. Won't be fixed by the weekend then I'm guessing. Oh, also have to hold abs in the whole time to train them. Starting. From. Now. Further investigation also reveals that "a loss of sleep also triggers the release of stress hormones, causing you to retain weight in your stomach". That'll be it then. Not the chocolate. Just children not sleeping.

14.10 Chris and Pui are doing something about cows, on CBeebies. Child C decides he doesn't want a dog anymore (wanted one this morning) and now wants a cow. Keeps pulling his mouth out sideways with his fingers and saying that we wants a cow like that. Asks if we can go and see cows now. See a glimmer of opportunity. Opt to go with the cow plan, drive in general direction of some fields and hope he will fall asleep.

14.45 Plan an overwhelming success. Asleep halfway round the ring road. No cows required. He's likely to go totally mad when I wake him and there are no cows. And suspect he may wet himself as he drank half a bottle of water before getting in the car. But he needs the sleep. And I need him to be asleep. I can't take him screaming at everyone all the way until bedtime.

Leave him to sleep in the car. Get lots of useful jobs done. Balance and order restored.

15.30 Wake Child C. Plan turns out to be epic fail. Spends a full fifteen mins screaming about cows, a further five about pigs, and then decides he wants to go to the zoo (he's never even been to the zoo) that instant, and screams about monkeys and "eh eh fants". Try variety of reasons why we are not going to the cows, the farm or the zoo:

1. The cows are asleep. I spoke to the farmer and he told me they were resting so there is no point going back.

2. It's raining.

3. I don't have any money to go to the farm. It's really expensive.

4. We're going to go another day with Child A, B and Husband.

5. It's nearly tea time.

6. Child A and B are at school (counter argument is along the lines of "I know. We get them from school and we go later" – my argument goes back then to point four – to which his counterargument is "aaaaaaaaaaaaaaaaarrrrrrrrrrrrgh").

7. No.

He hasn't wet himself, so that's a bonus, and does a wee sort of in the potty with the incentive of two cookies but bits pointing the wrong way and wees mostly over the floor.

16.00 Leave to collect Child A and B. Child C vile. Decide that him riding in the car / buggy would be the best option all round. Glad to meet friend at school gates, for some sanity.

Football finishes, and take children home. Stop car once on way home to have strong words with Child C who insists on shouting over everyone. So horrible. Feel so terrible for Child A and B, who just want to chat and catch up, and Child C is intent on spoiling it, just because he's not the centre of attention. Not much better when threaten to take him out of the car. Try and explain that we take turns to speak.

16.35 Arrive home. Child A pushes past Child B in a race to see who can use the downstairs toilet first and gets told off. Demands begin.

- Where's my Snuggle?

- Can I play on the computer?

- Can I have something to eat? (having just had a snack at collection).

- When's tea?

- Can I play football in the front garden?

All set against a backdrop of Child C screaming at everyone about everything.

Lose it with them. Fed up of serving up tea that isn't eaten as they have eaten too much before tea. Offer them a corn thin or nothing. Child A relents (he had wanted Easter egg – as if!?) Child B sulks under the kitchen work top. Child C screams. Point out to them, loudly, that I'm just a human and that I have feelings too. Child C tells me to cheer up, Child A asks me to stop crying, Child B stays under the worktop.

16.45 Apologise for losing temper. Explain have had an awful afternoon with Child C and am fed up of being shouted instructions and people being mean. Nicer after that.

17.00 Child C rejects ham, cucumber and red pepper. Eats two pieces of pasta and tell me he's finished. Comes back for a little more, but gives up well before Easter egg stage. At least he's happy to admit defeat willingly. Child A wolfs it down, as does Child B a bit slower. Then both eat a whole Easter egg, six strawberries, and a whole kiwi. Perhaps they were hungry.

17.30 Arrive at the doctor's surgery. Explain Child A's strange symptoms over the past few weeks. Doctor gives Child C a check over. So, that child who had a bad throat several weeks ago, who I thought was having "issues" with separation and school and a million other things … turns out he has chronic tonsillitis. Oops. Antibiotics prescribed, and a sense of relief all round now we know that we can make it better.

17.45 Home, via chemist. Served super fast, before Child B can help himself to mascara, Child A can ask what tampons are and Child C can try on more than three pairs of sunglasses.

18.15 Run bath for Child C. Quickly try on outfit for 1980s party at the weekend. Child A and B play on computers. Feel awful for not spending enough proper time with them, due to Child C leeching all my attention. Child C continues his tantrum marathon, by insisting on sorting about thirty "pictures" he has drawn into a certain order and refusing to get in the bath. He stinks of wee so not having a bath is not an option. Even his head smells of wee.

18.30 Have tried being nice but fed up now. Advise already naked Child C that I'll count to three and if not in bath then going to bed. Naked. Doesn't get in bath. Put him in bed. I've have had enough.

Get Child A and B changed. Go back to Child C. Only because he is screaming "Potty, Mummy". Does a wee, then finally relents and gets in bath.

18.45 Child C doesn't want to get out of bath. Point out that he wasted his play time having a tantrum. Wants me to play *The Three Billy Goats Gruff* with farm animals. Say I'm too sad and tired.

Which is true. Gets out, changed and in bed by 18.53.

Finally some time with Child A and B. Child B has comprehension to complete so we do that. Used to hate comprehension and now I remember why. So easy when you're a grown-up, you can skim read, and you know what it's going on about. A seven year old has a totally different take on things. Question about "Do you think we should read stories from other countries? Why?" has him stumped. Answers "No – cos we can't understand what they are saying". Give mini talk about learning about different cultures through their stories, which goes right over his head.

Meant to be doing reading with Child A but give him a night off on account of his diagnosis. Both want to use the toenail scissors. Am surprised they have anything left to cut, such is their interest in male grooming.

19.00 Turns out Child C not asleep and wants to talk to me. Wants a wee. Says he doesn't feel like a nap. Too bad. Lists all the animals that are "probably asleep" … foxes, hedgehogs, owls. Don't like to point out that these are the animals which actually will not be having a nap.

19.30 Pilates DVD on with added incentive of wine afterwards. Pineapple Dance Studios crop top to wear on Saturday so need to do something to train stomach muscles.

20.00 Done. Wine. Catch up on emails and put dinner on. Husband late home tonight so not sure whether to cook for him or not.

Diet Cokes: 3.

Chocolate: 1 long line of Fruit and Nut – the last of the packet.

Glasses of wine: 2.

Day Sixty-Seven (Thursday)

Sleep deprivation experiment continues. Child C awake from 3.30ish and doesn't ever really go quiet again as far as I can tell. Rubbish night. Try and sleep in his room to settle him, but he's too busy singing "Happy birthday to Mummmmmmy" and pretending to wrap up half the toys in his cot. Repertoire also includes "Hump hump dump dump fat on a wall".

4.30 Fed up, tell him I'm going back to my own bed.

6.15 Child B comes in complaining about Child C's noise.

6.20 Alarm goes off. Not much point having one. Everyone up. Get Child C (who has enough energy for all of us) up.

Go to have shower. Child C winding me up. Lock bathroom door. Child C screams the bedroom down. Just need some peace in which to wake up. There is another adult in the same room as him and he has plenty to play with. He can wait.

6.26 Finish in bathroom. Unlock door. Child C rushes in screaming. Wants to sit on my lap while I dry my hair (badly).

Child A and B in bed with Husband discussing last night's football match.

Downstairs for brekkie. Husband doing work call from home, before catching train in. Child B has consultant appointment to assess his tiptoe walking, so manic morning ahead.

8.15 Leave for school. Stopped raining properly but still drizzly. When, oh when, is spring going to arrive?

Scoot back to car with Child B and C. Drop Child C off. All fine. Back home to take Husband to station. Arrive home at 9.48, in time to leave for hospital appointment. Pop in to grab snack and book for Child B in case we have a wait.

And what a wait. Can only imagine that one hundred people went into spontaneous labour last night, as the car park is totally full and operating a one in / one out system. Twenty five mins later we progress from the road just outside the car park, to a car parking space. Ten mins late for appointment.

10.30 Needn't have worried. Walk into a waiting room, totally heaving with people. Take the last two seats. Child B does some colouring, doesn't feel like reading and cries when there is no more plain paper to use. Arrrrgh.

11.15 Relief comes in the form of the refreshment trolley. Agree to buy Child B some crisps, since at this rate he might miss lunch. Join the queue. Has his heart, and stomach, set on packet of prawn cocktail crisps. Lady in front of us examines every sandwich on the trolley. Then some more. And some more at the back. Wait so long our name is called. Child B heartbroken that he misses out on crisps.

11.20 Good news from the consultant. Doesn't need to see Child B for another year. Just keep doing more of the same.

11.30 Head outside. In flash of genius inspiration remember that there is a vending machine in A&E. Thankfully has some prawn cocktail crisps. Child B's wishes are granted.

Takes another age to get out of the car park, so get to school for 11.45. Shoot home, have super fast sandwich and go to collect Child C. House a huge tip. Haven't opened curtains or washed up from breakfast. Child A and B's pants and pyjamas still strewn across the floor where they left them.

12.20 Arrive home. Make lunch. Make a few calls as fast as poss before Child C starts screaming "Get off the phone. I told you. Get. Off. The. Phone". Make last call in the back garden, with the back door locked, while Child C tries his best to yell through the door, palms flat against the glass, in a rage.

Rest of the afternoon a bit of a daze. Body Low Time. Child C keen to engage in make believe games, so we do a medley of *The Three Little Pigs, The Three Billy Goats Gruff* and shopkeepers.

14.45 Can't keep eyes open. Luckily shopkeeper game involves sleeping for a nanosecond until the customer (Child C) arrives. Can't work out whether it's the lack of sleep, or eating bread (after an article I skim read yesterday) making me so utterly sleepy. Perhaps a killer combo.

Long afternoon. Decide that now might be a good time to give Child C a wash. Smells yukky, hair needs a wash, and he'll be in a better mood now than later. Takes the bait. All clean by 15.15. Well, cleanish, as refuses to use any form or soap or wash his body. Get him dressed and dry his hair.

15.17 Child C promptly wets himself.

15.45 Leave to get Child A and B. Child C insists on taking a full size football, and kicking it all the way from the car, up a hill. That's precisely why all journeys require me to double the expected travel time.

Home, food, and showers for Child A and B. Child C does a poo in his pants while I'm giving Child B a shower. First time in weeks and weeks. Think perhaps I didn't sprint fast enough. I blame it on the fact he was insistent on me putting the potty in the dining room. That debate might have cost us. Either way, guess that's what he thinks to having a shower in the middle of the day then.

Child C in bed by 18.25. Child A and B by 19.00. Hope Child C's bedtime doesn't backfire on me in the morning. He should be bloody tired.

Don't feel like doing any exercise. Should probably get sorted and get the house tidier. However, the DVD woman's motivational words are ringing in my head so get changed, and get into it. Feel much better for it. Then drink a glass of wine and eat a huge dinner. Tastes are changing however. Could be the shock of my trousers splitting the other day (though still stand by the fact it was faulty workmanship). Or maybe the fact that I was half a kilo lighter on the scales this morning, but either way, not eating quite as much chocolate, and genuinely able to resist it some of the time.

21.29 Was determined to be in bed by 21.00. That hasn't happened so determined to be in bed by 22.00. Got delayed googling old school teachers. For no reason, other than mildly interesting. Finally give up and go to bed.

Diet Cokes: 3.5.

Chocolate: 2 fun size bags of buttons, 1 mini egg.

Glasses of wine: 1. Last of the bottle.

Day Sixty-Eight
(Friday)

4.30 Child C asks me to sleep in his big bed. Do so. Spend the next hour saying "shhh" whenever he says anything, and when it does go quiet try to sneak out. Seems he's in a light sleep as notices when I move and instructs me to sleep.

5.30 Finally get out. Excellent manoeuvre. Extract one limb at a time. Then wiggle out and creep out of the door. Hard to get back to sleep at this kind of time. Child B coughing. Manage to drift off.

6.13 Wake up. Tired, but feel like I've cheated the system by getting some unexpected sleep.

6.18 Lie there for a bit. Then feel bad that Husband, who was away last night, might not wake up if I don't ring him as promised. He's up. Say morning. Head for shower.

Breakfast. All eat up. Child B has wobbly tooth so only soft cereals selected for him. Child A and B keen to play on the computer.

8.00 Child A ready super duper fast. Give him a tick on his chart. Child B narked that he hasn't got one. Child C still in his pyjamas.

Make lunch for Child C (staying for lunch at preschool). Leave for school at 8.15. Child C has been fairly docile until now, and becomes total nightmare. Screams over all of us in the car. Tell him he's annoying. Tells me I'm "annoynoy". Pull over and threaten to leave him there. At school takes on every child who comes anywhere near him on the wooden train. But does leave scooter on gate, where he is meant to.

9.00 Drop off Child C. Drive to Park And Ride. Catch bus, pop to supermarket, then to waxing. Hurts but a chance to put my feet up for a bit. Dash to buy 1980s accessories. Get loads. Find awesome fake pony tail, which makes me feel like I'm eight years old with swingy hair all over again. Pop to get new sports bra too. Reward for exercise.

11.00 Appointment at bank. Long long long meeting, as system keeps crashing. Make small talk with the nice bank chap about Match Attax and Fantasy Football.

12.05 Had planned on popping to M&S to get posh food for tea and treat myself to something different for lunch. Two more mins and won't get the chance.

12.20 Nice chap still not done. Download bus timetable on my phone while waiting (what did we do before mobiles with internet access?!). At this rate will miss Park And Ride bus and not get Child C from preschool. Leave office, go and find man who is with cashier. Tell him I've gotta go, sign two things, ask him to post me the rest and run like my life depends on it.

Just as well I've been doing workout DVDs. Running with rucksack (full of shopping and travel potty, even though Child C not with me) and two shopping bags, wearing clumpy knee length boots is no mean feat. Bus at bus stop. Run as much as possibly can. Make it just in time. Can't find ticket. Out of breath. Take seat. Find ticket. Show man. Collapse in a heap.

Get to preschool just in time.

13.15 Home, clear up from breakfast.

Quick trip to the supermarket required for couple of bits. Child C drank a lot of water on the way back from preschool so need him to do a wee before we hit the supermarket. Dialogue as follows:

Me: Please can you do a wee before we go to the supermarket?
Child C: Ok.
Me: There you go, please could you sit down?
Child C: Me no need a wee.
Me: You had a big drink, please try and do a wee.
Child C: No. Me told you. Me no need a wee.
Me: That's a shame. I was going to buy you a treat if you tried to do a wee.
Child C: Me want treat. Me no want wee wee.
[Last two lines and variation thereof repeated.]
Me: Fine, get in the car. You're a naughty little boy.
Child C: No. You're a naughty little boy.
Me: I'm not a boy.
Child C: Yes you are.
[Strap in Child C. Put keys in ignition.]
Child C: Me need a wee wee.

Child C will only leave house wearing Husband's size nine brown smart shoes. Try to make him see reason. Doesn't work. Five mins up the road he sees reason. Stop car. Change shoes.

Listen to *Never Smile At A Crocodile* on repeat, as requested for the entire fifteen minute journey to the supermarket. Strongly rejects any suggestion for another tune. He questions the lyrics en route: "his skin?", "his smile?". Do my best to explain the meaning / subtext. Don't think he gets it. Shopping trip goes relatively smoothly. Apart from Child C refusing to sit in the trolley. And throwing a tantrum that I won't buy a beach set, or a paddling pool, or a watering can. And needing a wee by the

DVD section, and causing suspicion with the security guard. Do get him a magnifying glass for quiet life / educational purposes, so goes around magnifying everything we buy. Falls asleep on the way home.

14.40 Leave (late) to collect Child A and B. Child C wakes in huge grump. Super clingy. Wants me and doesn't want me at the same time. Doesn't even know why he is grumpy from what I can tell.

Early tea. Beavers. Child B asks when I am "ever" going to sew on the Beavers badges he earnt ages ago. Promise I'll try and do them as soon as possible.

16.40 Have master stroke of genius that I'll give Child C a bath now, so that when we get back from cricket, I can almost just pop him into bed.

17.30 Cricket. Chat to other mums. Make interesting discovery, in the course of conversation, that we all eat Nutella from the jar. Don't feel so bad about it now.

Child C plays ball, throws sticks and follows the boundary rope. And no wet trousers. Hurrah!

18.45 Head home. Child C not convinced. Point out that the moon is out, so it really is nearly bedtime, and he is more interested in the idea of coming home. Friend bringing home Child A and B.

Convince Child C into PJs with incentive of beating Child A and B (who won't be home for at least an hour, but he doesn't know that).

19.30 Pilates DVD. I'm on a roll.

Tidy up. Boys still not home. Tidy up some more. 20.30 Boys arrive home. High on Pringles and cricket. Insist they are still hungry, which isn't surprising since they had tea more than four hours ago. Cereal, then bed.

21.15 Husband home. Dinner. Chill.

Show Husband clip on pony tail that I bought today. Says I look like a try-hard glamour model. Don't think it's meant to be a compliment.

Diet Cokes: 4.

Chocolate: 1 bar of Dairy Milk, 2 tsp of Nutella.

Glasses of wine: 3.

Day Sixty-Nine
(Saturday)

Wake up and look at clock. 6.20. House quiet. All asleep. Miracle. Need a wee but don't want to wake anyone up. Or jinx it all. Doze but can't get back to sleep.

7.20 Child A comes in saying he's just woken up and that it is Morning Time. Climbs in and starts talking football to Husband. Leave them to it and go to Child A's bed. Two mins in there before calls of "up time" from Child C. Not bad though. At least we got more sleep than normal.

Child B says he needs more sleep. Child C in a grump. Get brekkie.

8.25 Husband leaves for dentist appointment.

Washing all over the floor by the washing machine, so make a start on sorting it. Manage to get it into baskets and upstairs, but don't get to put it away. So soul destroying. A never ending job.

9.20 Husband home. Pop to supermarket. Alone. Only did teeny shop yesterday, with Child C in tow, so lovely to be able to nip around and get bits without worrying about child having a meltdown / screaming / eating half the contents of the trolley / sitting on half the contents of the trolley / running off / lying down. Get loads of food. £143 later (didn't mean to spend that much) we're all set for the week ahead. Apart from I'm not sure what I've got in the way of meat. And the fruit will probably run out within a couple of days.

10.30 Walk through the door with two of the shopping bags. No offers to help. Requests begin for drink / food / the second Wii remote ("we did call your mobile but there was no reply"). Wish I'd taken longer with the shop. Find the remote. Tell them refreshments will have to wait until shopping unloaded. Oh, and breakfast washed up.

Children and Husband play on computer. Clear up. Husband does workout DVD. Looks like he needs to lie down.

Pizza and chicken for lunch. Had urge to buy cooked chicken in supermarket (which, ironically, is same price as raw chicken), so huge spread for us all. Out tonight so want to eat properly now. Child C rejects most of his lunch, but don't care. Goal today is get kids fed, tired and in bed in time for the babysitter coming at 19.15ish. Child B's tooth falls out. Blood everywhere but he's delighted.

13.30 Clear up while others go back to TV. Play maths games with Child A and B. Major tantrum from Child B about not winning. Point out that it's about improving his maths, not about winning. Not worth the argument. Match abandoned half way through.

Attempt to cheer mood by practising roller booting down the street. Husband and children mildly amused. Much harder work on the legs than I remember, but haven't lost the old tricks. Well, I can start and stop (sort of). That's something.

15.00 Do Pilates DVD in attempt to ensure flat stomach at party tonight. Need everything in my favour so as not to adopt my nine months preggers look. So relaxing. Always start off feeling wound up, and quite chilled by the end. Despite Child A and B whooping at

Xbox, and Husband chasing Child C around the house pretending to be chasing a gingerbread man. That's enough to put off even the most well trained Pilates master.

Early tea and start getting ready. Miss the days when an evening out started in the middle of the afternoon, with a bath, face pack and all that. Nowadays, it's a waft of mascara and lip gloss (if I can find it) and out the door.

Get blue eye liner on, stick hair up with tonnes of mousse, hairspray, and clips, add large clip on pony tail. Green fishnets, Pineapple crop top, braces, puffball skirt, fingerless gloves, gummy bracelets. All the stuff I would have loved to have worn but would never have been allowed to. Would have loved all that. And to have been called Lisa. My '80s dream.

19.15 Babysitter due. Child C still not asleep. Stressing because he wants a neon necklace that have wrapped round my wrist to make bracelets. After three visits to his room let him have it with plan that I'll sneak it back. Then decide that's a bad plan, since he might:

- Choke on it.

- Break it.

- Not fall asleep then I won't get it back without a fight, and then that will wake him up even more.

Offer him a gummy bracelet swap which he goes for. He negotiates for four gummy bracelets. Calls me up two mins later, as now only two gummy bracelets. Questions why I'm dressed up. Don't want him to know we're going out as not sure how he'll react, so tell him Mummy and Daddy having special meal and Mummy dressing up for it. Sounds like a really lame reason. He seems to buy it. Wants to wear his cow costume. Eventually goes to sleep wearing full cow costume and gummy bracelets.

19.20 Babysitter arrives. God knows what he thinks when he sees Husband and me. Probably that we should know better.

Child A and B up and down every two seconds. Paranoid that they will wake Child C and then I'll have to go to party later. Taxi arrives. Kiss them goodbye. Lace up rollerboots. We're off.

Have such fab night. Despite some youth (who I couldn't see) shouting "ladyboy" at me when get out of taxi, brill night, spend it all on skates, and most fun I've had in ages and ages.

Dancing, laughing. Lovely.

12.18 Home. Husband falls asleep on sofa mid-game on iPad. Get ready for bed. Remember that the tooth fairy needs to visit. Following in his brother's footsteps, Child B has written to tooth fairy requesting a euro rather than sterling. Ransack Husband's funds and find last euro. Thank goodness for that.

Diet Cokes: 5 (rehydration for all that rollerbooting).

Chocolate: 3 handfuls of Minstrels, 1 bag of buttons.

Glasses of wine: Lots … probably too much.

Day Seventy (Sunday)

6.10 Hangover or tired. Reminded of why we don't go out much. Just over twelve hours to go until kids go to bed. Urrrrrghgggggggg.

Husband still out cold. Child C yelling. Bring him into our bed and stick the iPad in front of him so that he can do a painting thing on it. Feel like a bad mummy. Manage to claw an extra fifteen mins in a horizontal position before Child A comes in too. Husband sleeps on.

6.30 Take Child A and C downstairs. Hope they'll just watch TV and I can doze. Not so. Want feeding. Sort breakfast. Child B appears so feed him too. Move to lounge and do best to sleep on the floor. Child B chuffed with his euro. Slightly less chuffed when asks what its value is in relation to a pound, and realises he's got less. Manage to style out the "why didn't she leave me more?" with "well, you asked for a euro". Think he goes with it.

Veg in front of TV / computers until 8.50. Not actually sure where that time goes. All a huge blur.

Boys meant to have cricket training this morning. Not sure how that's going to happen. Suggest that they might like to miss it. Not a popular suggestion. Child A wails. Suggest he might like to wake Husband then. Gives it a try.

8.58 Husband "not up to it". That'll be me taking them to cricket practice then. Check with Husband that he is fit state to supervise a three year old child. And put spuds and chicken in oven. Says he is.

Rush to get ready. Shower, dress kids, peel spuds, fill water bottles. Text from friend asking if we can take her son too. Leave house at 9.55 for 10.00 practice. Written instructions re food. Dash out of the door.

Good to get some fresh air. Glad that we are there as there are only six children present and my car load is three of them. Watch from a distance that means I can see what's going on, but that I won't get hit by a cricket ball.

11.00 Didn't realise how cold it was. One hour in and I can't feel the end of my fingers. Seemed quite warm when at home. Tempted to go home and get another coat, but the coach says playing for just half an hour more so doesn't seem worth it. Call Husband to let him know about timings etc. Check he put the chicken in the oven ok. "What chicken?" he replies. Seems he thought it was just potatoes he had to put in the oven. Question what kind of a lunch he thought we were having. Asks if he has to touch the chicken. Er. Yes.

11.30 Race home. So so so cold. Just want to warm up. Husband mentions that Child C has been feeling ill. Take his temperature and he has a fever. Administer medicine. Get him comfy on sofa under blanket.

Finish off lunch bits. Child C falls asleep. Take Child A to party. Dash back and serve up roast.

12.45 Roast yummy. Makes me feel better while I'm eating it. Then instantly feel hungover and like I need to sleep again. Child C still asleep, so Husband and I doze while Child B plays on iPad. Only rest for twelve mins, then feel bad for ignoring Child B and not washing up. And worried I might sleep through picking up Child A. Husband sleeps on.

2.30 Collect Child A. Happy and brings home big bag of sweets.

Husband, Child A and B all watch last footie matches of the season on tele. Popcorn, chocolate, and Jelly Babies served. Kids high on sugar within ten mins. Child C perks up and happy watching kids' TV or playing in the kitchen. Good to see he's on the mend.

None of them want much tea. Not surprising. All in bed by 19.00. Child C goes to bed with cardboard box and laundry basket in his cot, insisting that he is addressed only as "baby cow".

Husband books flights for a few nights away next month, for the two of us, on his Airmiles. Staying at my parents' flat in France which they are selling, so now's a good time. Will be so lovely to spend time together and wake up to silence. Can't wait. Feel bad leaving the children, but it will do us both good. Plan on doing nothing but sleeping for three days.

Husband off for early flight and away for the week, so shirts folded, bags packed and to bed early. 22.30 by time lights go out. Beginning to think an early night just isn't possible these days.

Diet Cokes: 3.

Chocolate: Half my body weight. Only way to get through the day.

Glasses of wine: 0 – the benefit of having too much the day before. Actually, last night's intake probably still in my system, so perhaps zero isn't a fair assessment.

Day Seventy-One
(Monday)

My alarm goes off for Husband at 5.00. His alarm follows one minute later. Vaguely hear him have shower and get ready for the day. Wakes Child C.

Half tempted to get Child C used to sleeping in a bed this week, since Husband will be away for the rest of the week. However, can't quite decide if I'm ready for that. He doesn't show any desire to escape out of the cot, but he's getting rather heavy to lift in and out, and doesn't need cot sides any more. Also, thinking about holidays etc., he won't fit in a travel cot for much longer. Maybe I'll leave it just a little longer …

5.36 Child C's mutterings louder now. Don't want him to wake Child A and B. Wants his dressing gown on, in bed. Still only answering to "baby cow".

5.45 Husband leaves. 5.50 Child C calls for a wee. Then wants to go in my bed. He might as well as there is no way he'll go back to sleep. Plays with teddies.

6.15 Get up for shower. Child A and B off to Legoland on school trip today and need to be in a bit early. Child C decides he'd like a shower with me. Shower colder than normal, not as refreshing as normal and being in an enclosed space with a young child is never that much fun. However, on the plus side, both clean, and perhaps

I can avoid having to give him a bath tonight. See how much snot and food he manages to accumulate over his face by then.

Child A and B come in with lists they have made from the Argos catalogue of things they would need for a camping trip. At 6.30. Page numbers, item numbers, description and price all written down in a table they have each made. To include sleeping bags, tents, camping chair, camping stoves and bags. Praise their enthusiasm, and chart making skills. And remind them that we are not planning on going camping.

Child A and B still in Beat A Brother Til Death Us Do Part Mode. They encourage Child C to race them to eat breakfast, in part trying to get Child C to eat rather than shout at everyone. Child C starts shovelling food in, and then wretching. Competition terminated with immediate effect.

7.45 Child A and B decide to play on their electronic secret diaries. A girl's toy really but both wanted them for Christmas a few years back, and they enjoy playing the games from time to time. Child B gutted at Child A's discovery that he can open his brother's diary by imitating his voice. Child A gloats, until Child B manages to pull off the same spectacle. Child C frustrated that his voice won't open either of them. Child A and B call a truce and play the games instead.

8.00 Batteries running out on one of the secret diaries. Child B wants to know where his voice changer is. Meant to be leaving the house in ten mins. Bottles to fill, lunches to pack, stuff to gather. And now mini screwdrivers and batteries to find.

8.10 Leave for school. Can't find Child A's coat, so he wears one from when he was in Year R. Can just squeeze into it. Swears blind he had the other one over the weekend. Find it at school.

Drop off Child A and B. Bit of time to spare before preschool for Child C, so chat to other mums. Lots of "I don't want to go to school" from Child C but think he's saying it for effect. Seems totally fine when we get there.

9.20 Home. Where to start? Pressure off a bit as Husband away so have got a few evenings to sort stuff too. But can't see the wood for the trees. So many papers. So many toys. So many abandoned pieces of clothing. So many bits that don't really have a home. Make an executive decision to temporarily ignore the ironing board, the breakfast dishes and everything and get a few bits online that need for the children, before a number of promotional codes expire.

Almost an hour later, and lots of lovely clothes will be winging their way to us soonish. And none of the other jobs have been done at all. Denial is a wonderful thing.

10.20 Feel bad that I have avoided doing anything useful.

10.30 Hungry. Must have stretched my stomach over the weekend. But figure that if I feel this hungry then I can eat legitimately as my metabolism must be working super fast, that this is why I am starving, and therefore anything I eat won't count and will be instantly burnt off. Cook two pieces of toast, and two poached eggs. Yum.

11.00 Feel like something to finish off with. Ben and Jerry's Chocolate Fudge Brownie Ice Cream. Always think that it's got to be better to have a little of what you fancy than denying yourself what you really want and then gorging on everything else.

11.05 Ice cream been in the freezer an age, and is still frozen. Consider putting it in the microwave to defrost it a bit, but figure that the constant defrosting and refreezing can't do it or me much good.

11.12 Ice cream ready to eat.

11.22 Finish off ice cream. Seemed a shame to leave a tiny bit in the freezer, and I have all day to work it off.

11.23 Feel a bit sick.

Collect Child C, having not achieved half the things I wanted to this morning. Have made list, however, of all the things I need to try and do over the next few days while Husband away. Must keep remembering that "Rome wasn't built in a day", and that I can only achieve so much.

12.30 Make lunch for Child C. Not interested in any of it, apart from the yoghurt. Wants more yoghurt. A fine line between giving him what he wants because he's under the weather, and making a rod for my own back. Deny him the yoghurt.

13.15 Call from teaching assistant on school trip. Heart stops for a moment. Only asking when Child A should take his travel sickness pill. Phew.

Suggest to Child C that we do puzzles together. Then attempt some jobs upstairs. Child C finds Child B's gingerbread man cutter and wants to make biscuits. Attempts to fob him off fail, so google "easy biscuit recipe". Child C happy that he's baking and I feel like I'm doing wholesome constructive activity with a child who generally watches too much TV.

14.30 Suggest to Child C that he might like to go in the garden, while I tidy up. Move the slide to where he wants it (with gargantuan effort) and he plays on that for a while. Then draws on the patio, with outdoor chalks. Then draws on the brickwork and windowsills. Then gets told off.

Comes inside to watch TV. Put bins out. Find dead mouse. Decide that karma is having to clear up the dead rodent you have evidently poisoned. I blame having watched too many thrillers for making me think that dead things are never quite dead yet. Always one more limb likely to reach out and try and get you before the final moment of doom. Luckily this one is dead and doesn't reach for a large knife.

15.00 There are disadvantages to having lunch at 10.30. Even when followed by a quarter of a tub of ice cream. Hungry again. Eat avocado. Receive text saying that the coach will be back late from school trip.

15.15 Leave to get Child A and B. Was going to scoot, but large black cloud on one side of the sky so decide to drive. Bad move. Can't find space anywhere near school, have to loop round all over again, and end up late, and parked almost back home. Serves me right for being lazy.

Must must must must, above all other things, get some early nights this week. Another mum comments how tired I look today. Hadn't realised I look that bad, but think too many late and interrupted nights catching up with me.

15.35 Child A and B full of excitement from their day at Legoland. Head back to the car full of chat. Child C scoots across a main road by himself. Luckily not hurt or killed. Give him a talking to, but he remains totally disinterested.

Child A and B starving. Give them snack. Child A shattered and just wants to collapse in a heap. Child B uses the computer to plan his Fantasy Football for next season. Point out that the current season only ended yesterday.

16.30 Serve up tea. Child A and B eat a tiny bit. Makes me mad bearing in mind they were SO starving they *needed* a snack. Child C has two spoonfuls of spaghetti then declares he is full.

Children potter for a bit in garden and watch TV. Child C in bath by 17.00. Happy to have a bath tonight, which makes a nice change.

Come downstairs to find that Child B has "found us a campsite". He declares that his search was quite tricky as he really wants a campsite with a TV set available to watch. Suggest he might like to start by camping in the garden in case he doesn't like it. Never mind the fact we don't have a tent, and the ones they are looking at cost over £300. Plus, if he wants to watch TV, he might as well stay at home.

Up to bed at 18.20.

18.30 Add four foot stick to the list of items that I shouldn't let a child take to bed. That and a harmonica, which was already on my list. Child C whacking the hell out of the cot with aforementioned huge stick. Must remember to check on him later to ensure he's not impaled on it. Quietens down when threaten to take it away. Twice.

Read bedtime story to Child A and B, at their request. Child A spends time packing case, presumably for fictitious camping hols. Child B tests felt pens to put in his case.

Both sleeping in Child A's room. Warn them not to stay up chatting.

19.20 Husband calls to say that his bank card has been refused. Has called bank and they say it is because a new one has been issued. Oops. That will be the one I put in his cupboard and didn't tell him about.

19.40 Child A and B still chatting. Tell them off. Child A complains that Child B is being mean and wants him out of his room. Declares that "his behaviour towards me hasn't been very nice, and this way he'll learn to improve, so we'll see how he gets on tomorrow". Can't think where he's learnt to talk like that.

20.00 Child B calls down. Still can't get to sleep despite "trying really hard". Tell him to imagine he's lying in his tent and send him on his way.

Do various life maintenance tasks. Still 22.34 by the time I get to bed. How can that be, when I had such good intentions?

Diet Cokes: 4.

Chocolate: Quite a lot of Fruit and Nut. Ben and Jerry's Chocolate Fudge Brownie Ice Cream. Must try harder tomorrow. And one biscuit as made by Child C.

Glasses of wine: 1.

Day Seventy-Two (Tuesday)

4.52 Woken up by Child C. Thankfully he goes back to sleep. Or maybe he doesn't and it's just me who does. Wake again at 5.50.

Lay there for a bit. Ignore the fact that Child C is getting louder and probably waking Child A and B. Go for shower at 6.00 in attempt to have shower in peace, on my own.

By time out of shower, Child C calling loudly. Get him up. Say hello to Child A and B who are now awake and making lists of toys that they want from the Argos catalogue. Metal detector, fossil set and lots of Lego models seem to feature quite heavily on both lists. Remind them for the millionth time that it isn't their birthday any time soon. They go back to talking about camping.

Breakfast for all. Child C takes toy worm from Child A and won't give it back. Child A cross. Child B tries to tell me something. Child C screams over him. Child B cries. All before they have even started their cereal. Remove worm and put it well out of reach. Console Child B. Peace restored. Where would I be without high surfaces on which to perch confiscated objects? Maybe that's why the house is a tip. All out of reach surfaces are full of things I don't want small people to have.

Ready for school by 8.00, so time to spare. Both Child A and Child B tired from school trip yesterday. School run uneventful. Makes nice change. Child A forgets about going in early so goes in with everyone else.

On mission to get to Costco for long-awaited stock up. Drop Child C at preschool and on the road by 9.20. Pop home to grab a drink and totally forget to empty boot. Will have to sort that out when get there, to make space for my money-saving bulk purchases.

10.00 Arrive. Journey not too bad. Rearrange boot and head inside. Eat loads of samples and buy much more than I planned to, including new paddling pool and large holdall on wheels. Feel can justify the first, as we get through one every few summers and need new wheely bag as current one may not make it through another summer after the amount of stitching I had to apply this year. I'm very conscious of the fact that if there is one delay I may not make it back in time to get Child C. Keep looking at watch. Must be out by 11.00. Look forward to a day when my every movement isn't governed by the clock.

11.10 Leave car park. Should be fine. So nice to listen to the radio and not have to listen to kids' music. Flit between radio phone ins, pop music, and cheesy classics. Refreshing change.

11.45 Arrive home. Just in time to unload car into hall, find space in freezer and fridge for any cold stuff, make snack for Child C and head off to collect him. Good job done, but three hours gone, and thus a day's free time, just like that.

Apparently Child C did better listening today (apparently yesterday not so good). Seems to have had a good time, and trousers and pants totally dry for second day in a row. Not sure if he's chronically dehydrated or if we're cracking it. Just need to work on him coming to the potty rather than potty coming to him at home. A problem of my own making.

Lunch and TV. Suggest to Child C him that he might (gulp) like me to take the sides off his cot. He agrees. May well regret it, but got to make the move at some point. Helps me hold the nuts and screws etc. and we make the change. He seems thrilled. But then again, he was last time, and that was a disaster. Kept getting up at 4.00, and screaming, and none of us got any sleep. There is a stairgate on his room, but no point closing it, as he'll just stand there and scream, as he shakes the stairgate. Think I'd rather he wandered into our room than that. Keeping fingers crossed that he stays put. Think I'm in the right mindset this time.

14.00 Remember I promised to post Child A's drawing competition entry for kids' TV competition, which closes tomorrow. Write name, address etc. on the back, and also a note of what it is – someone from *Bubble Guppies* (do they have names?) standing by a big wheel. Not sure they'll know otherwise. Suggest to Child C that he scoots down the road with me to the postbox. Insists that a plastic storage box is his scooter, so he leaves the house with that in hand. Take his with us just in case. Ten metres down the road, and he opts for the real scooter, while I carry letter and plastic storage box.

Child C watches a bit of TV while I clear up, peel and cook potatoes, make a curry with chicken left over from the weekend and get ready to collect Child A and B.

15.10 Rainy but looks like it should pass, so head out on scooters. Child C insists on taking turns on all three scooters. Also throws a strop in for good measure at me not having brought the strap with which to pull him. Get to school just in time. Collect Child A and B. All three play in playground. No rush back so leave them to burn off some energy.

Friend of Child B's asks if he'd like to come and play at his house soon. Discuss with friend's mum and agree we'll sort out a date. Child B super excited but a bit quiet in front of Child A. Child A a bit glum, so reassure him that we'll find something fun to do when the time comes. Remind them both that it's a win-win situation, and that they will both have fun. Too convincing, obviously, as Child B then worried that he's going to miss out on something fun at home and makes me promise that Child A and I won't go for a hot chocolate without him.

16.20 Arrive home. Child A and B go out to practice cricket in garden, as they are selected for match on Friday and need to practice their bowling. Child C gets as much as possible out of the shed, wants the slide moved, and keeps stealing Child A and B's stumps. Fight breaks out between Child A and B. Shoes thrown, bruises inflicted. Match abandoned less than ten minutes after it started.

Child B comes in and decides to start a sewing project. Point out that this may not be the perfect time. Carries on regardless and, in quick succession throws the following at me, while I'm trying to clear the table for tea.

1. Can I have the scissors?

2. Can you thread my needle?

3. I need something shaped like a circle to draw round.

4. Can you rethread my needle?

5. Please can I have a drink?

6. This is rubbish it's all knotted.

7. Oh I think I made a mistake.

8. Can you unpick this for me?

9.   Can you tie a knot please?

I'm all for modern man, and learning to sew will be a very helpful skill, but it's just the timing that isn't so helpful right now.

17.10 Put tea on. Child C presents himself in kitchen with nothing on his lower half. Wants sandpit base filled with water. Refuse. Rants. Figure that the worst that can happen is that he realises that the water is freezing and goes off the idea. Put some water in. Doesn't care that it is freezing. Strips off and plays in it. It can only be about fifteen degrees outside. And this is the child with a cold.

17.30 Serve up mince, mash and broccoli amongst a sea of abandoned needlework. Child C eats half of his portion, naked, after much encouragement (and minus the broccoli). Child A and B eat most of it up. Surprised as Child A supposedly hates cottage pie. Makes no sense if he likes all the bits that go into it.

Baths for all three children, on a rotation basis. Reading for Child A and B. Both make lots of silly slip ups. Must be shattered.

19.00 All in bed. Didn't rush it, as want Child C to be as tired as poss for his new bed set-up. Child C and B drop off almost straight away. Child A complains of sore throat. "Rest it" advice given and reassure him that he will feel better soon.

20.15 Make dinner. Way too much food. Set up parental control on home network, now Child A and B using the computer a bit more. Half tempted to block all football sites, just for a laugh. Since I'm the only one who knows how to undo it. Ha ha ha.

21.30 Must clear kitchen. Meant to be in bed as early as poss. Husband calls. Good to catch up.

22.45 Not in bed by 22.30 again.

Diet Cokes: 3.

Chocolate: Tonnes. Lost track. Restart healthy eating regime tomorrow.

Glasses of wine: 1.5.

Day Seventy-Three (Wednesday)

Woken in night by calls from Child C. No idea what the time is. Stumble into his room. Dump down in bed. Fall asleep. Wake up. Go back to my bed. Clock says 1.46. At least plenty of the night left.

Wake at 5.54. Not a sound in the house. Only the birds outside making a noise. Doze.

6.10 Can hear Child A and B, but still no Child C. Hope he's still alive.

6.20 Get up for shower. Have shower, clean teeth, get dressed, dry hair. Child C trots through at 6.30. A total miracle. Kept him up a little late and he's got a bit of a snotty nose and cough, but even so. Big congratulations all round, and he's super happy to have got out of his own bed at this time of day. Tells me he's been reading books, but can't have been doing it for long as it was so very quiet. Hope this is the start of things to come rather than beginner's luck.

Finish getting dressed, Check on Child A and B, and go downstairs. Child C only eats a little, Child A and B eat but full of chat, so takes a while. Discussion gets onto starting new school in September. Child A and B practice their bubble writing, and we chat about schools, gum shields, girls only being allowed to wear scrunchies in a certain colour, and what a blazer is.

8.15 Leave for school. Children argue about who sits in which seat in the car. Got in a muddle with swapping them into Husband's car and now Child A, B and C are territorial, confused and angry. So bored with the politics and bickering. Can't they see that if they all just got along, our mornings would be so much happier?

All children happy to be dropped off. Meet another mum in our road, and catch up about schools, kids and work.

9.20 On a mission to blitz house. Well, part of it. Working through my twenty point To Do List, and determined to make progress this week. Workouts and work going to have to wait until everything else is a bit more sorted. Lounge is main focus this morning. Tidy toys, put some in loft, chuck a load, and move a sideboard. Looks great. Rest of house looks like a total bombsite. Takes ages. Get nothing else done.

Call school office re dinner money I owe. Letters have been sent through twice, but not sure where they are and worried the bailiffs might be next.

12.00 Time runs away with me, as always. Three hours just isn't enough. Pick up Child C with lots of paintings he has created. Read book he has borrowed and make lunch. Tidying lounge has left huge wall exposed with nothing on it at all. Looks far too blank and is bugging me. Have a brain wave that could get kids' hand prints, and foot prints in different colours, in set of six on box canvases on wall. Could look fab. Could look awful. Research canvases and order, while Child C yells at me to read another book.

13.20 Place order. 13.21 Confirmation email through. 13.23 Realise that 20cm x 20cm is not going to be big enough for a seven year old's feet to look unsquished. Ring to cancel. Ordered express delivery, so need to sort ASAP. Reassure me that they will sort it and email me to confirm.

Hang out washing with Child C's help. Load car to take a load of old boxes and wrapping to the tip. Child C plays with fishing net in front garden catching pea shingle. Wrecks driveway. Total mess. Won't listen when I tell him off.

14.20 Head off to the tip. Child C brings bucket full of stones and fishing net, which stretches the width of the entire car. Tell him not to put it over my head as I'll crash. Doesn't stop him trying.

Get rid of everything. Child C throws tantrum at not being able to get out and help. Explain that children aren't allowed. Screams more. Only stops when I labour the point about how terribly smelly it is.

15.15 Not heard from shop re canvas delivery. Ring them to chase. Apparently takes longer than that to go through.

15.55 Leave to collect Child A and B. Child C insists on bringing piece of ribbon he has found, approx. eight feet in length. Tries to hang it out of car window as drive. Insists ribbon is tied to scooter on arrival. Footie practice ends. Child A chirpy. Child B in a grump but unsure whether it is because I brought a raspberry yoghurt as a snack (he wanted a cake), because I didn't bring his scooter (never seems like a good idea in footie studs) or something else. Have lost Child C.

Find Child C. He scoots off in the wrong direction with another child. Child A follows my request and gets in car. Child B lies down on the grass, two road crossings away from where we are heading.

Retrieve Child C. Two down. One to go. Out of corner of my eye, see Child B running across the two roads. Albeit he checks for traffic (Child A tells me that he looked left, right and left again), but still shouldn't do it. Can't be doing with tantrums at pick up. Or anytime, but at pick up just so annoying. It's like all their frustrations of the day, and hunger taken out on the person who is (or was) most pleased to see them.

16.30 Arrive home. Neighbours walk past on their way home. Five boys all play in front garden. Get out as many toys as they can, and prove that it is still possible to have energy after a day at school. Remind me of a bunch of savages. Happy though. Friends depart and Child B returns to grump. Transpires it was something to do with Child A scoring a goal which should have been for Child B to take.

17.00 Email arrives saying first order of canvases has been sent. Nooooooo. Ring to sort. After three failed attempts to get through turns out that they will try and stop it with the courier.

17.10 Serve up chicken nuggets and pasta for tea. Not going to win *Masterchef* with that one. Barely talking to Child A and B after all the arguing and cheek. Child C (who has been very dry for the last three days) has wet trousers but won't hear that he needs to be changed. Also a large quantity of snot and mud smeared across his face, which he won't let me wipe off. It's a wonder he doesn't contract cholera or consumption, or some other disease from olden times. Genuinely surprised that he doesn't, at least, have scurvy.

Eat tea. Child A and B go outside to play as lovely sunny evening. Child B moans that the basketball hoop is too low, and that's why he can't get the ball in it. Point out that his accuracy should allow him to get it in from anywhere. Bath for Child C, who doesn't want a bath. Again. Insist on washing face and bottom. New PJs. Hardly ever gets anything new so sometimes lovely to see him in something which is really his.

Child B decides he wants a bath too. Then Child A complains of being hot, and that his boys' bits feel uncomfortable. Where's a husband when we need to ask about male personal hygiene? Suggest he has a bath and wafts his bits around a bit. Give him wet cotton wool in case he needs it. Make mental note to look up proper details of how he should clean. Am guessing will need to switch off parental controls for that one.

18.35 Husband calls as Child A getting changed into PJs. Enquire as to whether I've given the right advice. Seems I have, more or less.

18.45 Child C on iPad. Child B on computer. Looking on Amazon for "fantsy dress coschoms". Ahhh phonics ... you bring a smile to every day! Don't know where he thinks he's going in fancy dress. Camping, perhaps.

18.50 Child B calls out "What is a giant inflatable cock?" Rush to computer and put a stop to Amazon search.

19.00 Child C to bed. Read to Child A and B. Can't find book we were reading, so read the start of *The Enchanted Wood* to them. Don't remember Enid Blyton sounding so old fashioned when I was young. They half listen, but not sure Moonface and Silky the Fairy have the same appeal that they did to me when I was their age.

19.35 Make determined effort to clear up before I have dinner so not left doing it all last minute. Get washing in, put curry on, clear up from kids' tea.

19.45 Wonder whether Husband will mind if I have cheeky mini bottle of champagne. Figure it is managing what I drink, as it is only one glass, so that's got to be good, right? Tastes superb. Reminds me why I'd like to have champagne as my only choice of alcoholic drink.

Tomorrow will start doing workouts again. Want to tackle kitchen tonight. Settle down with dinner, wine and *Masterchef*. So far behind it could take me six weeks to catch up. Child A comes down to say his bits are still hurting. Tell him to "rest them". He wants to watch *Masterchef*. Tell him I'll save it.

20.05 Grandma and Grandpa call from Scotland. Catch up on what they've been up to.

Pay for school dinners, pay gardener. Hurtling towards 22.00. Haven't done kitchen. Haven't done laundry.

22.23 Find children's school uniform from football bags. Do damage assessment. Figure they can wear most of it tomorrow.

22.24 Damn. Remember I'd promised Child A that I'd leave some hard maths questions for him. Did it as ploy to get him to bed, as he wanted questions there and then. Figured I'd have time later. Didn't. Write out sums for Child A and B. They include:

$592 + 87$

$327 - 152$

$408 - 421$

$482 + 92$

$311 - 207$

Will have to work out answers in the morning. Brain too addled now.

Diet Cokes: 3.

Chocolate: Tooooo much. 3 bags of chocolate buttons, and lots of Fruit and Nut.

Glasses of wine: 1 mini champagne bottle.

Day Seventy-Four
(Thursday)

Wake naturally at 5ish. Does that mean I've had enough sleep by then? Find that hard to believe, but nothing else woke me up, as far as I know. Child A comes in at 5.15. Tell him to get into Husband's side of bed if he wants to but that he has be quiet as need more sleep. Both drift off to sleep until 6ish.

6.04 Child C comes in needing a wee. Vaguely aware of him reading books in bed before that, but thrilled that Operation No More Cot has gone better than expected.

Child B follows shortly afterwards. Take a shower. Dressed. General unrest about me not having bought the "right kind of brioches".

8.20 Leave house, after pinning down Child C to clean his teeth. Forget Child A's coat. And his hearing aid. Give them a talk about the fact that I have to get everything ready. My frustration rather than their fault, but I'm still cross.

Leave car with feeling of having forgotten something. Get to playground. Realise have left school bags in the car. How on earth did I manage to forget them? Child C unwilling to come back to car with me. Child B can't be left in charge. Child A playing football. Another mum kindly offers to watch Child C. Dash to playground gate. Hop on scooter. Head back to car at top speed like protagonist in comedy movie chase scene.

Children all dropped off fine. Home and blitz laundry pile, sort hospital appointments that need changing for Child A's ears and Child B's feet. Hang out washing and fold dry laundry that was all over the floor. Yet to put it all away. Then exercise DVD.

10.30 I thought that there would be some muscle memory. Seemingly not. Almost die. Have to add in lots of extra breaks. Thirty-six long minutes later have to cool off in the garden and then take a shower. Better be doing me some good and getting me into those lovely black trousers.

12.15 Pop to garden centre on way home from preschool. Grab two grobags and some different lawn food. Child C steals four large stones from the car park.

Child C seems pretty tired. Sits on sofa while I make lunch. Have lunch, more TV, read a book. Four wees in the potty. Start cooking spuds to roast at teatime.

14.30 Leave for second hand uniform sale at Child A and B's new school. Feels very weird. Not as ready as I thought I was for the transition. Get two jumpers. Too bamboozled to get much else. At least have made a start. Child C rants on the way home about wanting to listen to *Twinkle Twinkle Little Star*. Then promptly falls asleep.

15.45 Leave home to get Child A and B. Child C still asleep. Put him in buggy, wheel up to school, collect others, wheel back, waft biscuit in front on him. Still asleep. Was hoping that biscuit might wake him in style of the Bisto Kid. Doesn't. Only wakes up at 16.30 when taken out of the buggy. I accidentally bang his head on buggy frame. Might have something to do with it.

Child A and B play cricket in front garden. Child A's favourite ball gets lost in hedge. Huge mood and tears and stamping ensue. Try to look for it but tea is cooking and can't find it. Try to placate him by saying we'll wait for leaves to drop in winter. Doesn't help.

16.50 Child A finds ball. Mood improves.

17.00 Child A has stuffed his face (three biscuits, one mini cake, one banana) and can't see him wanting tea. But proves me wrong. Eats good helping of beans on toast. Others wolf down bangers, mini roasties and beans.

Baths for all.

17.25 Child A and B look for jokes for school joke competition. Fight over who has which one. Eventually settle on the following:

Child A: There are two goldfish in a tank. One says to the other "how do you drive this thing?"

Child B: What's the difference between a fish and a guitar? Can't tuna fish.

18.30 Child A and B decide they forgot that they wanted more food. Point out silly to have to eat and then brush teeth. And ask them to kindly remember that I'm not an all day café. They don't care.

19.00 Night night to all. Wee wee call from Child C. Child A and B decide that now is the time they need to share news from the day.

19.03 Child C not even mildly interested in going to bed. Says its "bore bore" and tells me he wants to "go to the moon". Fan. Bloody. Tastic. The one night I have a mum's night out. 19.04 Husband calls to say his flight home tomorrow evening has been cancelled. So he'll miss Child A and B's cricket match.

Child C proceeds to run around a bit, disturbing Child A and B. Child A and B let me know, which means they are then out of bed. Give them a lecture on modelling behaviour and that they need to stay in bed to show him what we do. But thank them for letting me know anyway.

19.45 Child C claims to "need wee wee and poo poo". I have my doubts. Babysitter arriving in five mins. Tell him I have a friend coming round. Exchange as follows:

Child C: Who friend coming round?
Me: His name is Alasdair.
Child C: Which friend?
Me: Alasdair.

Doesn't seem happy with this response. Frankly it does sound a bit odd. Throw in another name to see if that appeases him.

Me: … and maybe Luke's mum.
Child C: Nooooooo. Not Luke's mum.

Obviously not very convincing then.

Child C: What you talk about?
Me: Boring jobs.
Child C: I knoooooow. Not your friend come come round. Jake and the Neverland Pirates come come round.

Agree with him. Resistance is futile. Goes to sleep fairly swiftly after that.

19.50 Babysitter arrives. Go upstairs to change. Child B and C asleep. Child A playing cricket air shots on landing with homemade bow and arrow. Send him back to bed.

20.20 Drinks, crisps, chocolate out. Leave my number. Finally leave the house.

23.16 Back home. Bid farewell to the babysitter and start getting ready for bed. Realise I need to finish Tesco shop or will end up with a few high value items I shoved in the basket to get the price up as holding items for the delivery slot, and nothing else. Briefly speak to Husband to say "night night." Then remove from my online basket five bottles of washing detergent, three bottles of fabric softener, six family packs of toilet roll, and six bottles of wine, and replace with things that we actually need.

Diet Cokes: 4.

Chocolate: 1 heaped tsp Nutella, 2 bags of buttons.

Glasses of wine: 1 small one.

Day Seventy-Five (Friday)

4.00 Child C awake. Ready to party. Wants a wee. And to read a book to me. And to come into our bed. And to read the Argos catalogue. And to go camping. And to play with his Little People on the landing. And a poo. And to come back into my bed. And go downstairs.

6.00 Child B comes in looking for Argos catalogue. God help me.

Drop children at school and don't even take my coat off before I lay down on the sofa and doze. Wake up every ten mins or so but lovely to get a tiny bit more sleep.

10.20 Woken by Tesco man ringing on the doorbell. Conscious that I probably have creases and dribble down my face.

Unpack shopping, and make early lunch of tomato soup. Too lazy to put tray on table when reaching for remote. Balance it on sofa instead. Spill entire contents of bowl of tomato soup all over the carpet. Carpet turns orange before my very eyes. Use all of the carpet shampoo which remains in the bottle. Move onto washing whitener. Says don't use on wool. Anything is worth a shot. Heat up steamer. Carpet so wet can't tell what colour it is anymore.

Post my distress on Facebook, in case anyone has any tips for removing horrific tomato based stains. Friend offers to bring round a different brand of carpet cleaner. Use up what's left of that. Looks a bit better. Arms exhausted. Just an orange tinge remains. Hope that muddy feet will get rid of the worst of that in time. The whole carpet will probably need a clean at some point. With the amount of wee and mud and food it has had on it, it would probably be best for health reasons, if nothing else.

Screw the healthy eating soup option. Have two sausage rolls and a huge triple chocolate cookie.

13.00 Collect Child C. Clean some more. Child C tries to help.

13.20 Set about getting all the stuff ready for later. Beavers kit. Check. Cricket trousers. Check. Cricket tops. Can only find one. Search for the other. Find it in the bottom of the linen bin, bit damp and smelly. Think it was next to some of Child C's wet pants for a day or two. Quick wash and tumble dry.

15.00 Collect Child A and B, head home, quick tea, change and out to Beavers again. Musical Instrument Night tonight.

17.30 Pick up Child A and B from Beavers, complete with Pringles tube guitars. Drive to cricket club and Child A and B jump out.

Have come prepared this week with large bag full of toys for Child C to share, and a small range of snacks. Child C demands Cheerios. Have forgotten Cheerios. But do have packet of mini smarties in my bag. Child C opens them, then pours them all in a patch of mud. Adds water and stamps. Question what he's doing it for. Answers "for the ducks". Of course. Confrontation ensues between Child C and another child of similar age. Other child wants to stand on the same mud patch as Child C. Child C chest barges him. Exchange calls of "you're nor nor" (Child C), "no you're naughty" (other child). So it continues for approx. fifteen repetitions. Until the mothers intervene.

19.00 Husband arrives at cricket. Am relieved to see him. Head home with Child C with aim of getting him to bed ASAP.

Child C thinks we're racing Husband. In, changed, in bed quickly with cries of "me win, me win". Don't bother to correct him. Realise have Husband's phone. Leave message with friend to let him know.

20.10 Husband, Child A and B all return home, full of chat about the shots they made and the catches they took. Quick snack and bed.

22.00 Fall asleep watching TV. Must be tired. Wake up fleetingly, then not properly until almost midnight. Too tired to wash up. Put blanket over Husband and go to bed.

Diet Cokes: 3.

Chocolate: Lots. Purely to compensate for the stress of the whole soup incident.

Glasses of wine: 2.

Day Seventy-Six (Saturday)

5.12 Wake up.

6.34 Child C trots in. Comes into bed, and plays with iPad. Child B follows shortly afterwards. Followed by Husband. Then Child A.

8.20 Take Child A and B to their swimming lesson. All fine. Tick that off for another week. Wear shorts as meant to be warm day. Get cold. Husband says that my pale legs and creamish shorts are such a similar colour that I look like I'm naked. Not the look I was going for.

9.40 Back. Rush around to get Child C ready for a cowboy themed party. Change into jeans to warm up. Takes a while to get from car to house as Child C insists on riding his hobby horse and carrying a hair brush. One of Child C's preschool friends there, so they spend time chasing each other round the garden. Cake, crisps and pass the parcel. Happy children. Doesn't stop Child C trying to barge big kids, and push the birthday girl off her scooter. Boiling hot now. Should have worn shorts.

12.15 Get home. Plan to put the lunch on. Child C wants the paddling pool out. Lovely and warm. Try and fob him off with small sandpit, full of water. Not having any of it. Wants the large blue paddling pool. Turn house upside down looking for electric pump. Lunch on hold. Find it and pump it up. Leave Child C in charge of adding water. Get lunch. Eat too much.

Child A, B and C go out to play with water. Lovely that Child C is now an age when he can enjoy running around and spraying the hose. All have lots of fun. Husband and children play with water pistols. Lots of laughing. Happy times. Wash up and clear up. Takes ages and ages.

14.00 Happy quotient used up. Child A and B turn totally vile. Husband brands their behaviour as "atrocious". Am sure neighbours wish they had already moved out. Argue about everything. Child C not argumentative but being a pain in his own way. Puts Husband's shoes on to pretend to be a troll. Fills them with wee. Thirty mins later wees all over brand new bean bag. Can't decide if he is really tired or it's a cry for attention.

15.40 Go into village to get some bananas and strawberries. Tell Child C he's not coming because he keeps weeing over everything. Tell the others I'm going. Ask if they need anything. Husband suggests "a non-grumpy wife". Child C wails. Decide he can come as long as he doesn't wee all over everything. Climbs on every rock outside every house. Keeps scooting out of sight and have to run to catch up.

Get new toothbrush for Child C since he has chewed the other one too much and buy some fruit. Insists on scooting inside the chemist and greengrocer. Tell him not to but he doesn't give a stuff. And it's either that or he'll trash the place in a rage.

16.40 Home and sort out tea. Call the children in. No one comes. Fed up of them not listening. And not respecting the requests of parents. They don't get that it's just plain mean to have to be reminded three or four times to come to the table, when the person calling has just spent time preparing the food. Fed up with their fighting with each other. And with Child C peeing all over the place for no reason when he is perfectly capable of not doing so.

Bedtime a fiasco. Keep asking Child A and B to do various things, such as "come in", "get changed", "clean teeth" – though obviously with all the pleases and thank yous in the right places. All requests ignored or met with "in a minute".

19.00 Put Child C to bed, who is the only one behaving himself, and tell the others to sort themselves out. I give up.

Child A and B eventually go up about 19.30. Both up and down for the next hour, complaining of feeling sick, hurting eye, hurting leg, too hot and range of other ailments. Tell them that if they still feel ill in the morning, they will not play on computer and will miss party, so that they can rest. Seems to do the trick.

20.15 Husband does workout. Too tired to join in. Have dinner. Nothing good on TV, so watch recorded stuff.

21.30 Both totally shattered. Clear up and in bed by 21.44. Saturday night rock and roll.

Diet Cokes: 3.

Chocolate: 2 fun size bags of buttons, the rest of Child C's Easter egg (just to help him, obviously), mouthful of chocolate cake at the party.

Glasses of wine: ⅓rd of a glass, left over from yesterday.

Day Seventy-Seven (Sunday)

Eight hours sleep. Woo hoo!

6.14 Child C climbs into bed with some books.

6.16 Child B comes through. Wants to play on iPad. Seems a bit early for that, but no worse than watching TV I guess.

6.20 Child A comes in. Round them up and head downstairs. Husband mentioned something yesterday about him having a lie in, and then me going back to bed. Feel like I've been drugged, so am up for that.

6.34 TV on, Child C watching. Child A and B playing on iPad. Sneak some cereal in peace.

6.36 Hear argument from the kitchen. Screams from Child C about the sofa, covered in cushions, being "MY bed". Child A and B having a lively discussion about who has had more time on the iPad. Not even 7.00.

Do a few jobs around the house. Conscious that cleaners coming tomorrow. Haven't been in a month, and I have some serious ground to make up before they can start cleaning.

8.45 Husband appears. Takes over childcare duty while I sneak back to bed.

9.50 Re-emerge. Feel much better for the extra sleep.

Husband, Child A and Child B keen to go on a bike ride. Tyres flat on Child B's bike. Ten minute search for bike pump. Fifteen minutes spent accidentally letting air out, and pumping air back into tyres. Balance Child C in seat on back of my bike, and head off. Hadn't realised how tricky it was to balance on a bike with a three year old on it. Other mums make it look quite easy. Wonder whether it's because I haven't ridden a bike in ages, or whether my tyres are early '90s style, and too thin to be child weight bearing. Wobble a bit and worry about Child C's head also wobbling too much, but he seems ok. Do a circuit of local common, and back home. Feels like we've cycled miles.

12.45 BBQ on for lunch (excl. Child C) while Child A and B build a bike stunt course in the garden.

14.00 Boiling hot day, so set up paddling pool. Child A and B make perfume from petals in the garden, bug houses from margarine tubs, for whatever creatures they can find, and Child C makes mud pies.

Lovely afternoon in the garden. Parental intervention required from time to time, but a state of relative calm achieved.

15.15 Make the most of relative peace and quiet to sort through some family photos. Want to get some printed at some point soon rather than always leaving them on the computer. Child C enjoys looking at photos of himself, and surprises me with how much he remembers of where and when they were taken. His words might sometimes be hard to understand but his face lights up with memories of things we have done and places we have been. Guess it's largely the frustration of not being able to get the words out to explain all that that makes him so cross.

Child A and B take a break from the paddling pool and stumble upon some of their baby and toddler photos. Spend the next forty-five minutes going through photo back catalogue with them trying to work out which one they are in the pics. They both get it wrong nine out of ten times, and are shocked, disbelieving and amused to be told that they are wrong each of those times. Since I dressed them, where there is any doubt, I can remember what each one wore, but I guess that's what happens when you're used to looking at a mirror image of yourself on a daily basis … you end up knowing your identical twin's face better than your own. Child A and B start to lose interest once they realise that they don't know their own younger self's appearance very well at all, and comments like "that's not me, look at that silly face" (er, yes it is you), and "that's definitely him, look at his fat tummy" (er, no, that's you) leave them a bit disgruntled and confused.

16.45 Make quick tea, since no one seems very hungry in the heat, and kids excused bath on account of them having got clean in the paddling pool.

18.45 Duvets replaced with a sheet as all complaining that "it's too hot to sleep". Explain that I can't control the weather, the sunlight, the breeze nor the sound of passing cars and reassurance given that it will cool down soon.

19.15 Downstairs and start bag packing process for week ahead.

Diet Cokes: 3.

Chocolate: 2 bags of buttons, 1 large chocolate cookie – but am sure I burnt them all off cycling.

Glasses of wine: 0.

Day Seventy-Eight
(Monday)

Husband needs to be in work early. Get in shower at 6.08. Child C trots into our room and looks through books with Husband. Grateful to have Child C occupied while I get ready to face the day.

Hot weather forecast so brave shorts again. No time to fake tan. Vague waft of razor over legs.

6.40 Breakfast for children. Take up banana and crumpet for Husband. Seem to have loads more time than normal. Manage to do some last minute putting stuff away before the cleaners get here.

7.45 Put sun cream on Child A, B and C. First application of the season. Child A and B meant to take their own bottles of sun cream to school. Can only find one bottle of SPF 50 and one of SPF 15. Wonder whether it is favouritism to give one child the bottle with the higher SPF. Decide it probably is, and ask them to swap at break time.

8.15 Time to go. Child C refuses to move. Puts TV back on. Smears snot, tears and sun cream all over his face. Not sure if the sun cream is causing additional tears and snot, or not. Grab tissues for the school run in case he is suffering some horrible allergic reaction.

8.20 Eventually coax Child C into the car with food. Strikes me that it's a bit like having a baby tiger. Grumpy and likely to lash out, but waft the equivalent of a juicy steak in front of him and he's more open to discussion.

Child C insists on playing where he's not meant to in the playground, meaning that Child A and B get largely ignored, while I try and retrieve him. Try my "Come back quickly, the man's coming" threat which used to work beautifully with Child A and B. Not Child C. His attitude smacks of "bring on the man … and his mates".

Have forgotten sun hat for Child C. Must remember tomorrow. Happy playing with water and cars with his friend when I leave him at preschool.

9.15 Home. Answer machine message. Cleaners can't make it today and would like to reschedule for tomorrow. Don't know whether to be happy or sad, after the time spent tidying up in anticipation of their arrival. Boxes on beds, so that they can vacuum the floor, and for nothing. But does mean I've gained a morning which can't be a bad thing. Call them back. Give them the ok for tomorrow. Will be around lunch, but that's ok. Child C and I can go out for a walk. Will make me do something outdoors and non-houseworky with him.

10.00 Respond to some work emails. Nothing really mega urgent but have remembered some bits which need doing, so time to crack on.

11.20 Takes forever to put up canvas pics that we made the other day. Never has hanging pictures taken so much time, patience, paper, measuring devices, string, pencils, pliers, spirit level and chocolate. However, pleased with the end result. Think I like it. Though does look a little like we are running a Montessori nursery or possibly a hospital children's ward.

Have an early lunch. Two seeded rolls, two boiled eggs. Feel a bit that I have gone wrong with portion size. Perhaps I should have just halved that lot to get in those trousers I want to wear.

12.00 Collect Child C. Insistent that he wants to bring home hat which belongs to school. Despite "it's not yours" / "you're not allowed to" / "it's a sharing hat" / "we have lots of hats at home" / "other children might need it" / "you can choose any hat you like from the shops" (realistically, not going to happen, but getting desperate), he still wants to wear it and is finally allowed to borrow it until tomorrow.

Out of fruit, so pop to the local shop. Get bananas, grapes and chicken (since forgot to get it out of the freezer last night). Give Child C four different reasons why he can't have an ice cream. Receive congratulations from passing elderly lady, despite Child C stamping his feet and saying "want one NOOOOOWWWWW".

Pass library on way back. Selling books and CDs outside. Child C wants a DVD. Refuse. Then see that they have one about farms. Child C loves farms at the moment, so spend £2 on DVD. Head home for lunch.

13.20 DVD a wise investment. Child C super happy eating his lunch (very slowly) in front of DVD. Sit with him and do Tesco shop to come tomorrow. DVD ends. Child C wants to watch it again.

13.45 Here we go again. Child C asks if milk comes out of the "cow's bot bot". Hard one to explain. Then tells me that "poo makes milk and tea". Not sure this DVD's going to help him much. Try to point to his chest and say it comes out of there, but he's not having any of it.

So lovely and sunny outside. Come on summer … hurry up. Should be out there really but lots of bits to do inside too. Tempted to set up the ironing board in the garden somehow, but can't be bothered with all the faff. Opt to leave ironing until later.

14.00 Child C finishes lunch. Rally him to come outside and water the pumpkins. That takes a while, then leave him playing with a very slow running hose to "put out fires". Evidently the fence, the climbing frame, the flower beds and the walls are all on fire. He's happy so that's just fine with me.

14.30 Decide to try and be nice and fun and kind mum. Pack three ice creams and two freezer blocks (which take ages to find) into mini cool bag and set off on scooters with Child C. Five metres up the road Child C says he is tired. Repeat "once you get there you can have an ice cream" approx. fifty times. In foul mood. Says I'm not allowed to scoot. Then decides I can scoot. Whatever.

Arrive at school. Give him his ice cream.

One down, two to be delivered.

Total anti-climax. Child B has it but "doesn't like the flavour". Child A "doesn't like the flavour but wanted something to cool down". Child C drops his four times, covers it in small stones, and demands a bowl in the playground. Luckily I have one, in my bag, left over from his strawberries which he ate on the way home from preschool. It truly is a real Mary Poppins bag.

Home. Carry bags, jumpers, water bottles, ice cream sticks, sticky bowl and ukuleles. And my rucksack.

15.40 Child A and B want to play on computer. Child C wants to watch DVD again. Let them all get on with it while serving things to eat, and putting on tea.

16.30 Serve tea. Child A and B starving and eat it all. Child C eats three pieces of pasta and demands chocolate buttons. Drags chair over to where they are kept on top of cupboard to try and get to them. Fails.

Have decided that there is too much bickering over computers, so encourage Child A and B to play with something else. They suggest *Monopoly*. I suggest *Cluedo*, as less likely to cause inter-sibling friction.

Bath for Child C. Reading with Child B. After two paragraphs wants to stop. Won't let him so reads on in monotone voice. Complains that Child A is making too much noise with boxes. Complains that he wanted one of those boxes. The ones that have been sat there for over a month and no one has touched them.

18.30 Bed. No story. No one asks for one. Have to put all children back in bed at least three times. Child C only gives in when threaten to shut gate on his room.

Dinner and chill. Should be ironing.

Husband stressed that he can't find any of the things I have hidden for the cleaners. Rush around trying to find all his things and take boxes off bed.

22.30 And sleep.

Diet Cokes: 3.

Chocolate: 2 bags of buttons.

Glasses of wine: 1. Had forgotten how good it tastes.

Day Seventy-Nine (Tuesday)

5.19 Enter Child C. Spends the next hour doing anything but sleeping. However, count my blessings as does look through books, carry through his Little People house and boat, plays with them and carries through a toy train puzzle, so whiles away an hour fairly quietly. Husband, Child A and Child B sleep on.

6.20 Alarm goes off. 6.21 Child A comes in. Get in shower and leave Husband and Child A and C to chat.

Debate about wearing my nice new summery top and wonder whether Husband will get cross at a new item of clothing. Conclude that he'll see it sooner or later. Put it on. Feels lush.

Downstairs for breakfast. Put on apron to protect top. Child A inspects his bug house and cradles dead / sleeping centipede, wondering what might have caused it to stop moving.

7.15 Child B appears. Woken by Child C and A. Still sleepy. Suggest he lies down in the lounge for a bit.

Pop upstairs. Husband notices new top with "That another new top?". Give him full list of everything purchased:

- Two bikinis

- Two tops

- One dress

- Two pairs of shorts

- One pair of trousers (though at this rate will be sending back as can't breathe in them. Chocolate not helping).

There. It's all out there. I have nothing to hide. He's not ecstatic but he's not gone mad.

Child B suffering from computer withdrawal further to thirty-six hour amnesty. Makes me realise what a good idea it was. If he's that reliant on it for entertainment, then all the better to get rid for a day and a half.

7.35 Kiss Husband goodbye.

7.40 Child B asks to text Husband. Can't use the computer, so he's obviously realised that the phone is the next best option.

8.15 Leave for school. Child C proudly wears sun hat even though not that sunny. Child A goes into school in tears after another child accuses him of cheating at football. Tell him they're just jealous and to ignore them.

Get chatting to a mum at the gates and realise that it is 9.10. Arrgh. Hairdresser coming for fringe trim after drop off. Get a wriggle on and drop off Child C. Have forgotten wellies. Will cross fingers for no rain. He's still wearing the sun hat.

9.23 Arrive home. Hairdresser sat in driveway. Apologise. Quick trim and done.

Spend next two and a bit miserable hours tidying the house again. Seems like such as waste of time when I've done it all once already. Feel like I have achieved absolutely nothing other than lift stuff up onto higher surfaces and throw a few things in the bin. Husband will be stressed again that he can't find anything and it will be déjà vu.

Carrying on in the vein of computer avoidance, have bright idea, of building a den in the garden, or rather letting the children build a den, or a combination of both.

10.45 Pop to B&Q. Buy four long bits of wood and some rope. Den building kit started. Post request on local Facebook group to see whether anyone is throwing away any bits of wood.

Collect Child C. Head home. Cleaners still not here. Read books. Feel like sleeping. Make lunch. Shop online for den making stuff while Child C eats. Perfect garden for making a den, just not enough trees. One camo net, and two responses to my free wood request later, we'll be sorted.

13.30 Call cleaning company and leave message checking that they are going to come. They said lunchtime but that's a bit vague.

Read, on Facebook group for slow cooker enthusiasts, about cooking a whole chicken. Inspired, get to work. Intrigued to know how it will turn out.

13.40 Cleaners arrive. Yay. Make tea for them. Go with Child C to take replacement carpet shampoo to neighbour. Go to shops to get shoelaces. Not sure we have time for the whole scooting fiasco, and think Child C probably too tired anyway, so get the buggy out. Child C wants to "Play Peppa on phone". Over next thirty mins I become the mother I said I'd never be, as he plays kids' games on the phone. That said, I have the easiest trip to the shops ever with a child in the last three years. Sometimes needs must. This was one of those times.

15.00 Arrive home.

15.10 Shoes back on to collect Child A and B from choir. Child C gets in car. Then wails "poo poo". Stands in driveway shouting "Bring potty HEREEEEE". Refuses to come inside like a normal person. Does his business. In the driveway.

Collect Child A and B. Straight into town to get passport pics done for football club. Get pics done with just a four out of ten on the fuss and chaos scale. Always wonder whether we could just use the same passport photos for Child A and Child B and whether anyone would notice the difference.

16.40 Arrive home. Cleaners only just packing up.

Child A and B decide out of nowhere that they want soup with their tea. Didn't even know they liked soup. Child B writes down his order and leaves it for me in the kitchen.

Slow cooker chicken looks ready. Try it with Child A and B. Tastes yummy. Success.

Sort dinner – and soup. Fight over who has let whom have a try of their soup, and how much. Child A decides he doesn't like his flavour soup and wants what Child B is having. Child A's goes in the bin.

Dippers and chips largely uneaten. Totally uneaten by Child C.

Send Child A and B into garden to plan den. Can't be bothered to bathe Child C and wearing a hat nearly all day seems to have kept the grime off. 17.40 Put PJs on him.

Clear up. Lovely to see Child A and B outside playing in the trees, rather than inside looking at a screen. Long may it continue. Hope that they will show the same (or more) enthusiasm when the den supplies arrive.

All kids in PJs by 18.20. Read a chapter of *Matilda* while Child A and B text Husband, and Child C makes as much noise as possible. Not sure anyone was listening.

Put Child C to bed, then Child B, put Child C back to bed, then say goodnight to Child A. Focusing on the race element of my Beat Your Brothers To Sleep Technique seems to work.

19.00 Kids in bed.

19.19 Child A calls down to tell me that he has been drawing pictures and writing. Ask to see. He's started a little book with a page for each child in his class, and the teachers, thanking them for being so nice. Front cover reads "Kinds (sic) wishes to green class". Gulp. Poor thing. Moving schools is intimidating at any age, but hard when your child is going through it and you can't really do much to make it better. Despite the fact that they have been in different classes since Year R, feel bad for splitting them up in separate classes, at a time when they could probably do with each other. They can be such a strong whirlwind force when together (hence one of the reasons to split them up), but really notice their vulnerability when faced with being apart at times like this. Give him hugs and a kiss. Wish him goodnight. Gather up another load of washing.

Sort dinner. Husband comes home. Has phone calls to make. Serve curry. Eat and watch TV. Contemplate doing the ironing.

Just as going to bed, Child C stirs and calls out a few times. Lie in Child C's room in case he keeps waking. He doesn't and I start dozing off, so go back to our room. 23.00ish Zzzzzzzzzz.

Diet Cokes: 3.

Chocolate: 2 bags of buttons, 1 Mint Magnum.

Glasses of wine: 1.5.

Day Eighty
(Wednesday)

5.10 Wake up. Child C coughing loads. So tricky with coughs. Can't give him anything other than Calpol and just have to hope that it's not a chest infection.

5.20 Pop in and give him more water. He'd dropped it under the bed, but hadn't called out. And he needs a wee.

He goes back to sleep I think. Or I do. Or we both do. Keep thinking that I can hear him coming into the room. Look up but he's not there. Just my imagination.

6.20 Alarm goes off. Hit snooze. 6.25 Goes off again. Get up. See Child C on landing. Ask if he's ok.

Me: Are you ok?
Child C: No. They wake me up.
Me: Oh dear. Do you want to come in Mummy and Daddy's room?
Child C: No. Me go tell them off.
[To Child A and B] You wake me up. You wake up the whole house. [Equivalent of "humf"].

The irony is not lost on me.

6.23 Take shower. Child C decides he wants a shower. Get him out of his PJs. Then he decides he doesn't want a shower anymore. Wants me to shower with the shower door open. Not keen on the idea. Floor gets soaked every time he opens the door, and I get cold. Meanwhile he's naked. And cold.

Get out. Get him dressed. Get me dressed. Child A busy showing Husband the full book he has made for his class. Take a read. So extremely sweet. Brings a tear to my eye. A few pages need reworking (particularly the one which asks a child to "work on your attichood"), but very well meant. Has spent time thinking about each child individually and has made a thoughtful and honest comment about each one.

Breakfast. Take up toast and banana for Husband. Put shorts in tumble dryer for Child B. Wondering how many pairs of shorts we own. Can only find two. Will have to check back online to see if ordered more, since can't find any. They could be tidied somewhere.

Staple book for Child A. Then realise there is a child missing from his book. And another. And another. Child A writes the extra pages. Unstaple and restaple. Twice.

Wish Husband a good day, good flight and a "see you on Friday".

Child B asks to use computer and starts a Powerpoint presentation on woodlice. No words. Just lots of pictures of woodlice.

8.00 Running late. Am guessing it is because of the shower and book incidents. Either way, tops not ironed for Child A and B, fruit not packed, contact lenses not in, teeth not cleaned, and lots of other things not yet done.

Sunny day. Child C refuses to wear sun cream. On his feet will only wear wellies. With no socks. With a view to picking my battles, I can't be bothered. Screams over all of us on way to school. Choose to fight that battle. He stops for a bit.

8.20 Car leaves the driveway. Child C ratty again. Child A and B behaving, but still had to ask them too many times to get ready. Stressed.

Explain to teacher that Child A's book for the class has been proof read for anything contentious. Child C picks fights and refuses to share. Child B just fine. Both Child A and B just a bit ignored due to me dragging Child C off everything and everyone.

Drop off Child C. Home for chocolate and ironing. Call Grandpa and wish him a happy birthday.

10.00 Pop round to collect den building wood, following on from Facebook appeal. Feels a bit weird taking someone else's rubbish, but if it has the desired result then it will be worth it.

10.25 Home. Take all the wood out of the car. Can't help but start building with it. Have the start of something fab. Hope the kids are as excited as me. Stop there. Building it is half the fun and don't suppose they'll want to spend any time in it if I do it all.

11.00 Workout DVD. Don't want to do it, but will feel even less like it tonight. So horribly hot, and shorts keep riding up, so resort to exercising in my undies (with socks and trainers). Keep glancing round to check that there isn't a delivery man or builder or anything at the door.

11.45 Feel better for the workout. Really hard work. Feel energised though, and pleased to do something non house-orientated, for me.

12.00 Pick up Child C, come home, read book, make lunch.

13.15 My uncle calls, returning call from yesterday. Child C so noisy that lock myself in the loo. He turns light off from the outside and cranks handle up and down, so attempt to conduct conversation in the dark over the noise of banging handle. Can't hear much at all, and have to end conversation over the screams of "Let me in, Mummyyyyyyyy". Such a "spirited" little chap. His way or no way.

13.45 Bit more den building with Child C. Quite proud of what we achieve. Only prob is that Child C says it is *his* house. Has no intention of sharing with Child A and B. Point out repeatedly that it isn't his. Threaten to make a bigger better one for Child A and B, and fill it with cakes. Goes with that idea. Damn, That wasn't my plan. Go back to "it's not yours, it's for sharing".

14.50 Settle Child C down to watch some TV while tidy up and get ready to collect Child A and B.

15.45 Time to set off. Child C tired, snotty, coughy and vile. Bad mood about everything: the CD in the car, the tunes on the CD, not walking to school, anyone talking to him … and so it goes on. Pick up Child A and B and two friends who are coming to play.

16.15 Home. Children put toppings on their own mini pizzas. Carefully put them in the oven, though toppings weigh more than the pizzas themselves on some of them. One friend asks if there is "just somewhere we can put" Child C (who decides not to eat), as he screams at the dinner table.

Older children embark on ambitious junk modelling project. Child C perks up and decides to start eating once everyone has finished. Don't care. At least he's eating. Child A and B fall out over who was using an empty tissue box first. Child B sent to his room. Child A in a grump. Friends (who evidently don't express their dissatisfaction through the medium of rams-locking-horns style verbal / physical interchanges) left a bit bewildered at the performance of Child A and B (who evidently do).

Once Child B released and Child A given stern talking to (" ... never have friends round again if you leave them just to play by themselves, very disappointed by behaviour ... blah blah blah") junk modelling reaches climax, and all four older children emerge wearing zombie outfits fashioned from a range of discarded household items.

18.15 Parents of friends collect their children, complete with costumes. Remind Child A and B that it would be nice if they waved and said goodbye to their friends at the door (" ... or will never have friends around again ... blah blah blah").

Child C keeps shouting and screaming over all of us. Try and be nice. Try and be rational. Takes no notice whatsoever. Tell him off. Gets the message. Then wets himself. Feel bad that maybe I was too harsh. He has to understand that it's not nice to be screamed at, and talked over the whole time. He's so tired by this time in the day, too, there is just no reasoning with him. Child A and B ask me not to cry. Can't help it. Pushes me to the limit.

Bath for Child C to rid him of the layer of grime, combined with smell of stale urine. Delightful. Bath water turns brown / grey colour. At least he's clean by the end of it. Indulge in fresh water for Child B. Lovely to catch up with Child B and hear his news. Child A and C play together in the garden. Child C mainly bossing Child A around, pretending he's a fireman.

Then bath time for Child A. All clean. Child A and B want to text Husband on my phone. Clear garden a bit.

Repeated requests to Child A to get ready for bed. Loses tick off reward chart. Child B resists tooth brushing. Lost tick for him too. And finally bed. Pour wine. It's never tasted so good.

Had enough today. Loads of things I could / should be cracking on with, but would really love to just finish my wine and crawl into bed. Pizza toppings everywhere in the kitchen, from where they fell off the pizzas, or the children were shovelling them in their mouths, school bags still in the car, clean washing all over the lounge floor.

Don't think it's helping that I've lost the book in which I write my To Do List. Think that's sent me off task. Try to book Tesco shop to replenish fruit / milk supplies after today. No slots for tomorrow. Damn. Will have to go to actual shop. Can't fit that in in the morning. Will have to be afternoon outing with Child C. Assures me that "me love shop shop", so at least he might start in a good mood.

22.07 Watching *Masterchef*. Remember school cake sale tomorrow. Better look at what's in cupboard.

22.10 Find left over bars of white and milk chocolate. Cornflake cakes it is. Problem solved.

22.17 Put frozen salmon on low in the slow cooker. Figure it might be a success. Then google it and figure it might not be. Too late though. Already warming up and defrosting, so add a load of stock and a damp tea towel. Might be scraping flakes of dry fish off the slow cooker for days to come.

23.00 Get ready for bed. Requires several trips upstairs, since need to bring up:

- Woodlice house for Child B.

- Book Child B is writing for his class (not to be outdone by his brother).

- Potty for Child A (empty wee first).

- Long bench cushion from landing which Child C used to ride down the stairs, earlier on.

- Water for me.

- Phone and charger (to speak to Husband in the morning).

- Laptop (to finish writing this).

Wash face and moisturise. Slap loads of coconut oil in my hair. Read somewhere that it's a great nourishing treatment. Will probably regret it when pillow smells like a macaroon. Since that needs washing anyway, and no one here to see me looking greasy, what the heck.

23.32 Shut bedroom curtains. Night night time.

Diet Cokes: 4.

Chocolate: 2 bags of buttons, 1 Mint Magnum (should never have bought them), a large quantity of Fruit and Nut. What's that they say about eating more than you have burnt off and that that's why you're not losing weight as you should?

Glasses of wine: 2.

Day Eighty-One
(Thursday)

1.19 Wake up. Can hear something. Not sure if it's the pipes or rain. Been so long since it has rained that I can't remember what it sounds like on the house. Turn over to go back to sleep.

1.21 Remember that the skylight is open upstairs. Go and close it. Towel required on the floor. Worried about my fish in the slow cooker. Decide might as well go downstairs and switch it off. It looks edible. Put it in the fridge. Back to bed.

3.20 Hear loud sobbing and calling out. Head to Child C's room. He's fine. It's Child B. Having a dream about being run over by something or other. Reassure him and lie down with him for a bit.

3.33 Go back to my bed. Need some sleep.

6.14 Wake up. Hear Child A and B. Child C asleep. Tell Child A and B to keep it down. Hear familiar sound of cricket ball hitting skirting board. Tell them to stop.

6.20 Child C calls "Morning Time Mummy" repeatedly. Have reset his clock to match my getting up time to make it more realistic. Gives him a better idea of what Morning Time really means. Wants a tissue. Leave him reading in bed.

Go to have shower. Weigh in. Have lost weight. How does that work? Hair feels refreshed, and am sure will be glossy. Lovely fabric headboard is, however, totally trashed. Hadn't thought about that.

Downstairs for breakfast. Child A and B are making a set of trading cards with their friends' names on them (and ranking their characteristics accordingly). Point out that they may not have many friends if they carry on. Just me and Child C for brekkie. Child B showing serious attitude. Moans that he wants to carry on playing upstairs. Moans that he wants to eat the other half of the cereal bar that I gave to Child C last night, when I thought it might as well be used up, and not go soft. Lots of shoulder shrugging, and general "I don't care"-ness. Shout at Child B that there are people dying, and that he is worried about a cereal bar. Child C joins in, and tells them off too.

7.30 Make attempt to clean headboard, which has a huge greasy circle on it. What was I thinking? Cleaning attempt unsuccessful.

Child C refuses to do wee before school, despite drinking huge amounts of liquid. Several trillion reminders to Child A and B to put their socks and shoes on and clean their teeth. Will be nice next week when they are on holiday and I don't have to moan about this every day. Pack car with book bags, shoes for Child C, change of clothes bag and fruit for Child C too. And cakes.

Get to school. Drop off Child A and B and cakes. Giving the cakes in was a huge deal in Year R. Now they're more like "Mum, you can do it". Round up Child C who has soaked trousers from sliding down wet slide, which he's not meant to slide down anyway. Taking his friend to preschool while his mum helps gather cakes.

Seem to get back to the car quicker with two of them. Think the competition element speeds them along. Drop them off at preschool and both happy.

9.20 Back home and do some paperwork. Forms for school football, for out of school football, for school BBQ, finance stuff … just all takes ages. Check on headboard. Now oil mark, and massive water mark. Try again.

9.45 Window cleaners arrive. Hoping that it won't take too long, then I've still got time to do workout DVD. Close a few curtains to hide mess inside.

11.45 Window cleaners still here and still quite a lot of windows left to clean. Very thorough. Or they have nowhere else to go. No workout DVD done. Will try and do it tonight, though resolve tends to weaken by then, so not counting on it. Use my slow cooked salmon in a sandwich, and pray I don't get food poisoning. Eat Magnum. Packet finished now. Probably just as well.

Even bigger water mark on what was lovely headboard. New strategy required. Google "getting grease marks out of upholstery". Formulate plan. Seems I need to try washing liquid that I'd use in the machine, and if that doesn't work then washing up liquid.

Child C full of chat on collection. Home, carry logs down garden for den while Child C sings "What's going to work? Teeeeeeeamwork". Make lunch and prepare for Tesco shop. Window cleaners leave.

14.10 Set off for Tesco. Child C insists that we role play *Jack and the Beanstalk* the entire way there, shouting at me to turn my head as much as possible. Due to that. I reverse down the drive with the handbreak on (didn't actually know that was possible). Point out repeatedly that I will crash if I turn round. Doesn't care. "Turn round NOOOOOWWWW" just keeps getting louder.

Parent and child space free, and trolley with car underneath right by it. Hurrah. Always wished that they did a twin version as other people's children always looked so happy in them. Child C is happy some of the time, wants to get out some of the time, and *is* out the rest of the time. At least he can't see so much of the food on the shelves down there. Get away with only adding Babybels (I explain he doesn't like them) and marshmallow tea cakes (explain he doesn't like them either) to the list. Not bad going. And find mini mint ice creams. Figure that's a calorie saving idea. I'll wean myself off the big ones gradually.

Pack up shopping. Child C throws strop about wanting to hold his stuff. Give him a bag with his bits in. Unwrap a Babybel as requested. Doesn't want it to be unwrapped for him. Wants another. Try to pack. Give him another. Sits to unwrap it. Last few bits in bags. Pay.

Huge storm while we're in the shop, so get drenched on way back to car. Child C rejects Babybel which he hasn't even tried, and says he doesn't like it. I eat it.

15.00 Home. Need to unpack. Child C tells me it's boring and wants me to read a book. Read a book, then back to unpacking. Stick leg of lamb in slow cooker. Am getting hooked. Will slow cook anything that stands still long enough. How did it take me so long to catch up with this invention? Wish I'd had one when Child A and B were first born. Or when cooking stewed apples and all that for weaning. Might have saved some burnt pans.

15.45 Leave to pick up Child A and B. Park near school and scoot the rest of the way. In the course of twenty mins the following takes place:

1. Child C jumps in puddles to the extent that his trousers are wet up to the upper thigh, front and back.

2. Child C finds two large bricks from somewhere and puts them in the middle of the road. Negotiation follows as to why that's a bad idea. Doesn't agree, so move them anyway.

3. Child C nurses a teacake all the way to school. Drops it more times than he takes bites.

4. Child B falls headfirst over scooter handlebars and cuts his knee and arm.

How can one short walk cause so much trouble?

16.20 Lamb looking and smelling good. Think it'll be ready for children's tea. Put some spuds on and start putting sheets back on beds. Always hate realising I've still got that to do at end of long day. Headboard still looking bad. Will have to wash the whole thing, to get rid of water marks.

Lamb turns out really well. Child A and B wolf it down and have seconds. Child C isn't fussed, but with threats of no pudding he eats a few green beans, three potatoes and a teeny weeny piece of lamb. He can do it. Which is what makes it so annoying when he won't.

Clear up after tea while Child A and B play outside. Child B comes in and asks "Have you got any Vanish?". Reveals that he has put his hand in bird poo and wiped it on his T-shirt. Stain removal assignment three. They should have taught it at school instead of chemistry.

Bath for Child C – though refuses at first, insists I run the shower, and the opts for bath after all. Child A and B still outside at 18.50. Enjoying being in the den. Should be careful what I wish for.

Make up rest of beds. Child C jumps on them while giving his rendition of *Gangnam Style*. Can best decipher lyrics as "Woop woop. Drive in Grandpa's car" or similar.

19.05 Child C goes to bed fairly well. Apart from insisting on wearing dressing gown. Must remember to take it off later so he doesn't boil.

Child A and B keen for story, so settle down to read to them. 19.31 Give up. Feel a bit bad for being mean but when someone's reading to them, they should listen, and their headstands and ball kicking suggest that they weren't.

Various call downs from Child A (headache, sore knee) then Child B (wants his Big Dog teddy to cuddle), but all asleep by 19.45.

Had so many plans for this evening. Not least of all exercise. None of them achieved. Not enough hours in the day. Ever. Finish off finance stuff so Husband will, at least, be pleased. Eat too much dinner and want to go to sleep.

23.14 Go up to bed. Headboard looking bit better. Probably needed a clean anyway. Forgotten to put pillow cases back on our bed. Want to crash.

Diet Cokes: 4.

Chocolate: 2 bags of buttons, Mint Magnum, loooonnnng line of Fruit and Nut, lick Nutella knife.

Glasses of wine: 1.5 … or maybe 1.75.

Day Eighty-Two
(Friday)

Child B up in the night, complaining that he's too hot.

5.50 Child C all chat chat chat. found his voice and now won't be quiet. Think I'm getting Child C's cold.

Sort out cereal. Pop to toilet. In meantime, Child A drops his cereal all over the floor. Something to do with pretending to shoot people with an empty chocolate raisins jar. Either way, and in the interests of teaching responsibility ask him to clear it up. Wants me to help. Child C helpfully tells us that "the cleaners need to clean the floor". Point out that I clean too. He laughs.

7.32 Child B and C all finished. Child A still going on cereal, take two. Wants to ask me something. Just explain to him that I'm sending text to Husband and that will be with him in a minute. Starts asking me "How many bite marks does it have?". Haven't the foggiest what he means. Eventually ask "What are you talking about?". "You know, your phone. How many bite marks has it got?". Ahhhhhhh. Got it. "Do you mean mega bytes?". Sweet.

Ten minute before-school-limit on iPad each. Feel a bit mean, but actually much nicer without it. Once past the initial "whadyamean only ten minutes? Sooooo unfair" stroppy attitude.

9.20 Return home. Time to attack some long overdue work emails and some other computer bits.

11.30 Postman brings camo netting delivery. Spend time on the den which I should be spending on ironing. Too irresistible. Roof all in the right places and secure, netting draped over. Will get boys to paint the bare bits of wood over the hols. Awesome.

13.00 Collect Child C. Feet barely through the door, when he announces "Let's make cakes. I want to make cakes". Try to find a reason that he might understand to not make cakes today. My silly fault for having left out the cake tin from the cake sale cakes I made. He spots it and has been suitably inspired. Check the clock. We probably do have time to make something quick. I opt for Duck Death (broken biscuit cake, so called as Grandma and her siblings fed it to the ducks when they were little, and when they went back the ducks had all gone. The cheery bunch presumed that they had all died from eating the cakes). Send Child C off looking for a toy hammer or rolling pin to break biscuits while I gather the ingredients.

15.20 Pick up Child A and B. They love the camo netting on the den. Great to see them so excited.

17.45 Arrive home from Beavers. Just taking off shoes and Husband arrives home. Children all delighted to see him. They can't wait to show him the den. He suggests improvements in male "you've missed a bit" style. And asks me how much the camo net cost.

18.10 Husband asks Child C if he wants to go to cricket. A child who is covered in tea and snot. Who has been carted in and out of the car fetching and carrying Child A and B countless times today. Who we are taking to the cinema for the first tomorrow, and so who has to sit still and nicely for one hour and forty mins (have checked the running time). Who is tired. Who will drain all his caregiver's attention so that they can't watch the cricket. Husband suggests that I could go with them. Point out that's exactly what I was trying to avoid. Now I feel selfish.

18.15 Child C climbs in the car. Point out all the reasons he shouldn't go. Big watery eyes stare back and he utters "Me want to go with Daddy". Normally would take him out of the car with a "too bad" but can't deny those big blue eyes from a child who hasn't seen Husband all week – and who normally won't give him the time of day.

Child A bursts into tears with "But Daddy will have to look after him and won't see us play". Child B bursts into tears because Child A is crying, supposedly, but think it has more to do with the reasons given by Child A.

Give Husband travel potty, change of clothes, botty wipes and all the other paraphernalia. They set off. Wash up from tea. Sort some laundry.

18.33 Call Husband. Reiterate that he is to call me as soon as Child C becomes too much. Husband informs me that Child C has wet himself and won't be changed. And that it is Parents Join In Night. Suggests that I might like to come down. Politely decline.

18.35 Feel bad. Husband been away all week and doesn't need an evening with a tired three year old. Call Husband and let him know that I'm coming to get Child C. He replies: "I have asked him and he doesn't want to go home". Rule One Of Parenting: Never ask in these situations unless you know you are going to get the answer you are looking for.

Drive to get Child C. Couple of mums ask how I am. I rant about Child C. Meanwhile Child C has led Husband off to the other side of the pitch. Gesture wildly to Husband to pick him up and march back. Rule Two: Don't negotiate with tired toddlers. They come back over and I start on trickery and deception. "Let's race" I say. "We've got to get back and to bed before the others". Takes the bait. Wants to sit in space in the car which doesn't have a car seat.

Try being nice. Then just plonk him in a car seat, remembering the Tired Toddlers Rule.

19.15 Child C in bed and sleepy. One call for more water, but other than out for the count. Job done.

More ironing to be done. Feel like I'm on a washing / ironing / washing hamster wheel. Not sure it will end until kids move out and Husband retires, so no shirts to iron.

Definitely getting a cold. Seem to recall that, last time, drinking didn't really help. Worth a second try.

19.59 Had better get PJs ready for Child A and B coming home.

20.15 Arrive home. Eat half the fridge. High as kites. Bed just before 21.00.

Watch bit of a film. Husband has some work to do.

Super coldy. 21.50 Go upstairs to put some pillow cases on Husband's pillows. Put head down. Wake up forty mins later.

Diet Cokes: 3.

Chocolate: 2 bags of buttons, 1 mini ice cream, bit of Duck Death.

Glasses of wine: 1.

Day Eighty-Three (Saturday)

5.45 Child C comes in wanting to play. Ask him to go and get some books.

5.47 Child A comes in. Then Child B.

Announce to the children that we will be taking them to the cinema for the first time, today. All excited, as am I. Love The Firsts. So many things you can't do when they are little, that it is always exciting when you can finally do something for the first time. Plus it's lovely to be doing something that grown-ups can enjoy as much as the children. So it's *The Lego Movie*, but I'll take that over two hours in a soft play centre.

8.15 Take Child A and B to swimming. Both want to stay home and watch TV. Remind Husband we need to be ready to leave at 10.00.

9.30 Receive text from Husband. He has loads of work to do and might not be able to make cinema. Hasn't had a chance to get ready yet. Asks what time we need to leave. Explain to kids it might just be us. And hope it isn't. Was really hoping for a family trip.

9.40 Arrive home. Husband needs shower, but ok to come to the cinema. Children (and me) super happy.

Forget every time, that with The Firsts, comes the expectation of a fantastic photo moment in my mind, of a happy, smiling, laughing family, with children who are brimming with joy and gratitude, and parents who are proud to have such warm, caring children. Never quite happens. Cinema trip good, overall, but photo moment blurred a little by:

- Child A and B using the trip as an opportunity to spend as much of Husband's money as possible on food and drink.

- Ask Child C to wait just outside cubicle in toilet, while I just go for a wee. Exit cubicle and, after search of every other cubicle, find him going into Screen Two.

- Child C complains that it is "too loud" and asks repeatedly for *Team Umizoomi* and *Peppa Pig*.

- Child C gets leg stuck between the fold up seat. Two people required to extract him.

- Child C asks to go home twice. The second time, gathers his stuff, sits on the steps and tells me "me wait for you here".

- … then shouts "wee wee" and demands I take the travel potty to row G. Explain in the darkness that he has to go to the toilet and that not everyone wants to see him doing a wee on the staircase.

- Child C says that next time he wants a "smaller TV – not a big TV".

Other than that. Fab.

12.50 Short drive from cinema to Husband's office as he "just needs to do something quickly". Child C needs a wee two minutes after setting off. Stop. Do wee. Set off again. Child C falls asleep. No lunch out planned, as loads of popcorn etc. and under impression that visit to office will be a short one. It isn't. Visit lasts two hours.

Make bed for Child C to sleep on in Husband's office. Out for the count. Probably just as well.

Child A and B amuse themselves in the office with the following programme of activities:

1. Writing on wipeboard – motivational phrases including:
   - You can do it if you do it.
   - Go on Daddy. You can do it if you try hard.
   - Step one. Get out of bed and have a quick shower.

2. Tinkering with everything on the desk.

3. Spinning on chairs.

4. Spinning each other on chairs.

5. Cleaning wipeboard.

6. Roaming around looking at gadgets on other people's desks.

7. Looking under people's desks (particular amusement at the shoes they find).

Child A and B become increasingly hungry and bored. Husband not fully aware what it is like to have hungry children. How they turn to The Dark Side. What starts as "Are we going to get something to eat?" becomes a series of wails and groans, and complaints about how unfair we are. Remind them that at least they are not starving in Africa. Child A replies that if he had a choice between how he feels now and Africa, he'd choose the latter. Child B clutches his stomach and wails. Child C wakes and keeps telling me he's "hung hung". Not a McDonald's Drive Thru in sight. Where is one when you need one? Try pointing out that there is no point going anywhere else as by time we've ordered I could have cooked something. Child A insists that it needs to be "proper cooked meal". Fantastic photo moment obliterated.

15.15 Arrive home. Husband stalls them in the car for a bit. Put pizza in oven and noodles onto cook. Food served within eight mins. Barely eaten by Child A. "So hungry", he'd "rather be in Africa", was demanding a cooked meal and hardly eats a thing.

Child A and B make loom band bracelets, and mostly empty the bands all over the floor. Child C plays cricket with Husband, then *Jack and the Beanstalk*, then jigsaws with me.

17.40 Serve sandwiches which no one really wants.

18.10 Child B becomes totally vile and tired and irrational. While giving Child C a bath, can hear him declaring how much he hates us all, why Husband is the "worst Daddy in the world". Storms upstairs and throws bean bag over bannisters (which "worst Daddy in the world" makes him retrieve). Eughhhh. Bedtime pleeeeeeeaaase. Refuses to wear the pyjamas which are out. Refuses to get different ones.

18.50 Child A and B declare they are hungry. This is all because they didn't have a proper lunch. Give them some fruit.

Point out that they should have been in bed half an hour ago. Was aiming for early night to get them back on track and behaviour better for tomorrow, so am not left with vile children. Husband, Child A and B start indoor cricket match. Give up. Tell the three of them to sort themselves out. I'm out of it. Do puzzles with Child C who doesn't seem very tired.

19.30 Husband gets injured in the cricket match. Child A and B come to get me. Tell them should have been in bed an hour ago. Get cross. Fed up with them stringing Husband along and him doing more fun stuff which makes them even more tired, while he wants to compensate for not seeing them. Don't disagree with fun, but they need a bit of routine or it all just goes a bit wrong. As today totally demonstrates.

And to make it all worse ... payback for having had a nap afterwards in the car, and in Husband's office, Child C is very not sleepy and is still up. And I have the song *Everything Is Awesome* going round in my head. Clearly everything is very much *not* awesome.

Finally get Child C upstairs with offer of chocolate cake in the morning.

Husband asks if I want to play on the Xbox. No. I do not.

20.46 Called up by Child C. Wants chocolate cake now. Threaten to take toys away.

20.50 Child C trots downstairs complaining that "Daddy's TV wake me up". Turn it down. Shut the door.

Cook dinner. Serve up. Put on movie that we only watched thirty-one mins of last night. Three mins in Child C appears again, wanting to play / read books / do anything which isn't sleeping. Refuse to read, and eat our dinner while he sits and climbs. Asks where the reindeer is in the movie. Explain no reindeer in this one, and that that was a different night when he refused to go to bed. Asks us in turn (twice) if we like reindeer.

21.15 Take Child C up to bed. Husband lies down on sofa to demonstrate to Child C that really is bedtime. "You need to sleep in your bed, Daddy" Child C says. Am guessing he might not make it that far.

Settle Child C. Two further escape attempts, but quickly aborted once reminded I'm in the room. He's got to give in at some point.

22.10 Wake up in Child C's room. Go downstairs. Husband asleep on sofa. Eat Duck Death and clear up. Have to do last bit of clearing with button undone on my trousers. Such is the extent of my over-indulgence today. Oh dear.

22.48 Put blanket over Husband. Go to bed. Shattered. Thighs and stomach feel stacked full of Minstrels and popcorn and chocolate. Can't even face washing my face. Bed.

Diet Cokes: 3 (though suspect the cinema one counts as more than 1 since it was huge).

Chocolate: Too much. Lost count.

Glasses of wine: 1.25.

Day Eighty-Four
(Sunday)

5.45 Child C comes in.

6.00 Husband takes pillow and says he's going to the spare room to get more sleep.

6.15 Child C wants feeding. Stretch, grab dressing gown, tell him to be quiet on the way downstairs and off we go. Don't mind getting up early in the week, or when you know everyone else is up, or when you're feeling fresh as a daisy, but when you're already serving cereal at this time, and you've been up for a while already, the day that stretches ahead of you can seem like a really really long one.

Child A and B have cricket match today. Conscious that I'll need to occupy Child C for the duration. Am estimating one and a half hours. Start planning in my head the equipment with which I'll need to occupy him.

6.20 Child A appears as I'm serving breakfast for Child C. Child B shortly afterwards, due to the noise made by Child A and C.

Post breakfast, put on kids' TV and normal sofa wars commence. Along the lines of: "I was on that cushion" / "He pushed me" / "I was here first" / "He is taking up more space than me" / "I want to lie down" / "It was my blanket" / "I'm not moving" (followed by a kick to whichever other child is closest). Imagine that same argument has been happening the world over since sofas began. Drives me insane. Move Child B to a two seater sofa. Pitch it as comfiest sofa in the room.

Advise Child A and B to speak to Husband if they are unhappy about us not having Sky Multiroom. Until then, tell them they can watch their programme at 8.00. *Bullseye* (the 1980s gameshow) is on then, so they are excited about that.

8.00 *Bullseye* goes on. Child C goes off to watch *Thomas And Friends* DVD in playroom. Then gets scared and wants to switch it off.

8.45 Take Husband a cup of tea and his phone, which has new emails, which I figure he might need to action.

9.00 Husband comes downstairs. Mention to the children that we need to leave in about twenty mins. Husband looks alarmed and says he'll get in the shower. Agree that we'll meet at the cricket club as he needs to get ready for a cricket match he's playing in / night away too. Pack up toys, Child C packs up toys, ensure Child A and B get changed, teeth cleaned, bats in the car, snacks in my bag, changes of clothes for Child C, deckchair for Child C all on board. Sorted.

9.30 Leave. 9.40 Arrive. Everyone already there. Am guessing we were meant to get there for 9.30. Ooops. Didn't see that in the email. Child A and B rush off. Get Child C and bags.

Child A and B do well and, more importantly, enjoy themselves. Child C gives me one of the most unpleasant three hours spells of my life. A few other mums there, so it's lovely to see them. Child C takes a shine to some toys belonging to another little boy and is so unbelievably testing without a break I am really pleased when the match comes to an end and we can go home.

Just find it so exhausting that his whole being is centred around eight really challenging core values:

1. If it's mine, it's mine.

2. If it's yours, it's mine if I want it.

3. If anyone tries to talk to me I don't want their help, or even general words of guidance / encouragement.

4. If anyone tries to help me I will deem it a threat, and that you might be taking away the thing I am playing with.

5. Even if you wipe my nose, I will smear snot all over my face shortly afterwards. And then get stuff stuck to it without trying (mud, food, anything grubby looking).

6. When I say "wee", I mean it now, and the potty needs to come to me, not the other way round.

7. If you don't listen to me, or acknowledge my utterances the second the words leave my mouth then I will scream at you louder and louder until you do take notice.

8. Food will only occupy me for a limited window of time. Then I will revert to displaying the behaviours shown in points one to seven.

13.15 Arrive home. Feel like crying. Child A going on about how he wants sandwiches for lunch. Child B saying he doesn't want pasta. Child C wants to eat everything out of the treat cupboard. Insist they have a square meal. They ask what a square meal is. Not impressed by my reply.

13.30 Lunch served. After minor tantrum about Child C being in

Child B's seat at the table, and Child C saying "finished" after three pieces of pasta, children are fed and normal temperaments resumed. Ice lollies for everyone outside. A moment of peace and smiling all round. Happy tummies. Happy children. Happy me.

Clear up from lunch. Child A and B want to devise their own board games, and request card, pens, dice and Sellotape. Child C has different approach. Sandpit. Painting. Playdoh. Train track. Shops. At least he is big on clearing up whatever he has finished with (thank preschool for that) so not too much damage done. Hang paintings on the washing line and accidentally get paint all over it. Must remember to remove that before next lot of washing goes out.

16.30 Mission to get kids in bed by 18.30 starts now. Oven on. Bottle of cava in the fridge. Tea planned for 17.00. Bath planned for circa 17.40. Next bath circa 18.00 and just after. Teeth brushing planned for 18.20. All under control. Just have to hope there isn't a craft related meltdown between now and then. Otherwise, all on track to be sorted.

Strategy goes to plan. All in bed by 18.42. Child C makes three escape attempts, one call for water and one call to talk to me. Meanwhile, Child A and B swap pyjamas and beds to see if I notice them impersonating each other, causing much hilarity for them and minor confusion for me. All settled by just after 19.30. Cork popped at 19.35. Cava for one.

Hear from Husband. Has scored fifty runs … yay! Tell Child A and B who are still up. Smiles from ear to ear. Such pride. Lovely to see. They go to sleep happy with the news.

20.05 Feel tipsy already. Put dinner on. At this rate will get early night by the very fact I'm drinking cava, and will be unable to do anything useful by about 20.30.

20.06 Make mental note to get the washing in.

22.18 In bed. Not done any exercise. Not achieved anything great. But kids in bed on time. I'm in bed earlier than I would normally have been. Ordered Fathers' Day present from Child A and B for Husband, and had nice dinner. And washed up before bedtime. So not all bad. Plus day out with the boys tomorrow before Husband gets home, and another day out the next day so need to gather my strength.

22.30 Remember the washing is still outside. Am too snuggly to get it now.

Diet Cokes: 3.

Chocolate: 1 bag of buttons, lots and lots of Duck Death, 1 mini mint ice cream.

Glasses of wine: 2.

Day Eighty-Five
(Monday)

First day of half term holidays.

6.35 Play *Gingerbread Man* board game with Child C. He totally makes up the rules, has no interest in playing correctly, and I can't be bothered to argue.

Play *Top Trumps* with Child C. After about half an hour agree to end it there. Otherwise has the makings of going on for ever and ever and ever. Learn a lot about cars.

Child B wants me to give him a tutorial on how to crop images on the computer. Explain that will have to wait until later.

8.20 Tesco order arrives. Am reminded, on this occasion, of the perils of online food shopping:

- Baguette which was meant to feed all of us for lunch, is shorter than my forearm.

- Forgot to order the important stuff, like milk and bananas. Serves me right for doing it in a hurry.

- Veggies not necessarily the ones I would have picked.

- Inadvertently ordered five bags of carrots rather than five carrots.

8.58 Place Tesco order for all the things I've forgotten on today's order.

Child A and B start a match of balloon tennis. Child C wants to play a variety of different games, do drawing, get loads of stuff out. Eventually settles on Playdoh.

10.40 Leave to meet friends at local mini trains. Pouring with rain. Could be a short trip.

Enjoy a few train rides. Children enjoy going on by themselves a few times. At least no crowds in the rain.

12.00 Children hungry and rain getting heavier so all head back to ours. Child A keen to have picnic in the lounge, so put out blankets and tuck in. 12.15 Husband calls to say he's half an hour away and can he have some lunch as hasn't eaten for twenty-four hours. How can that even be possible? Food first, everything else second. Put the oven on, and stick nuggets and chips in.

Kids eat quickly then go off to play. Husband comes home. Walking like an old man. That's what sport does to you.

12.45 Friends head off. Serve lunch for Husband. Child C super demanding.

Go for a wee. Child C yanks on door handle and turns off light when I don't let him in.

Tearfully tell Husband have had enough of Child C. He suggests putting him up for adoption. Presume he is joking. "I'll take him out for a walk" would have been better.

Child A and B and Husband play on the computer. I play various games with Child C. Eyes feel so heavy during game of *Knickerbocker*

Glory that I would happily sleep on the carpet if I thought would get away with it.

15.00 Just so tired. Ask Husband if he minds watching the children while I have a sleep. Set alarm for an hour's time.

16.00 Alarm goes off. Feel like I could sleep all day long. Downstairs and sort tea.

17.25 Child C calls me upstairs to open window to let spider out, which he has caught in a beaker. Go to his aid. Has no pants or trousers on. Less Bear Grylls. More Bare Bum. Laughs heartily but in a way that suggests he hasn't actually got my joke.

18.00 Child A and B and Husband have a thirty minute warning on game of *Monopoly*. Child C charges round with umbrella (up). Stressed Husband tells him not to, and that it is bad luck. Tell Husband that there is absolutely no point going down that route. Tried it. Doesn't work.

18.56 Game still going. Apparently "nearly finished". Not going to end happily, I'm sure.

19.30 Child B is out of the game. Kindly gets changed and goes to bed. Put Child C to bed too.

19.43 Game ends. Feel so desperately tired. Feel like it has all caught up with me. The unrelenting nature of it all and the interminable demands.

Diet Cokes: 3.

Chocolate: 2 bags of buttons, 1 line of Fruit and Nut.

Glasses of wine: 0.

Day Eighty-Six
(Tuesday)

3.44 Child C thinks it is Morning Time. Go and lie in his room. Remind him every time he so much as moves that I can't take him to meet friends at the farm later if he doesn't sleep.

It's getting light when I wake up in Child C's room. And the birds have started singing. Head back to my room and wait for Wake Up Take Two, which comes at 5.52. Wake from the middle of an unpleasant dream, so a bit confused / relieved that it isn't true. Child C piles books and teddies on my head and brings in a mountain of Little People. Everyone else sleeps on. Not so for me. No doubt this is the source of my fatigue. It's the gradual wearing down and the continual never quite a full night's sleep.

6.16 Child B comes in. Child C plays with the Little People on the floor, in the dark. Invite Child B to lie down. Alarm goes off four mins later. Shower time. Child C decides to join me in the bathroom and keeps getting stuck behind the bath. Child A and B come in too. Encourage them to go and read a book – do anything – rather than me be on show while I have a quick shower. Child A asks for a hug, and I feel a bit bad.

Child C goes on and on and on about wanting breakfast. That'll be because he hardly ate any of his dinner last night, but not much point telling him that. Head downstairs and sort it out. Child C still snotty after about two weeks of snottiness. Feel like I'm getting another cold on top of a cold. And it's raining. A lot. And we're going to a farm.

7.20 Kids fed, Husband fed. Start sorting picnic for later. Wonder how it can take so long to source and pack food for a picnic. Child A and B have learnt that it means Mummy can't get involved in anything when the process is underway. Child C doesn't get it. Wants to play board games and undertake jigsaw puzzles which require adult assistance. Slows the process down even further.

7.50 Husband leaves.

8.00 Husband calls to say he's missing us.

8.02 Massive squeals break out from downstairs (while I'm on the phone). Enter the room to see Child A beating Child B (who is lying on the floor) with a huge stick (which was formerly in the shape of an archery bow). Flip. Send them both to their room. Xbox rights confiscated for the day. Tears. Child B claims he didn't do anything to Child A and that Child A called him "ugly". Child A denies all knowledge. Don't know who to believe but point out that calling your identical twin "ugly" (which, I point out, is mean and I don't want to hear again) means that you are calling yourself the same thing. The penny drops and they both look amused / alarmed.

8.25 Ask each child what happened. Still none the wiser. Let them come downstairs, but Xbox ruling remains. Instead Child B reads, and then does some jigsaw puzzles with Child C. Makes a lovely change. Though shame about the circumstances.

9.45 Leave for the farm. Later than planned but all shoes on, changes of clothing packed, wees done. All set. Have enough spare clothes to be going away for three days.

Lovely time at the farm. Child A, B and C, and their friends spend over four hours looking at the animals, climbing, bouncing, pedalling, running and sliding non-stop over and in everything. Brill time. Spend most of the day calling Child A and B by the wrong names, as I can't tell the difference at speed with their sun hats on, and we have a few minor strops from Child C, but the latter a lot better than he would have been at home.

14.33 Home. Xbox rights returned. Child A and B behaved really well and were uncharacteristically kind to Child C. Helped him loads and loads on the soft play equipment and were really thoughtful towards him. Play board games with Child C. To his rules, since he's not interested in the proper ones.

Feel shattered. Fed up with not having the oomph that I'm used to having. Maybe this is just getting old. Focus on getting to bed as early as possible.

15.45 Work email comes through that I need to action tonight. Grrr. There was me hoping to go to bed as soon after the kids as possible.

16.00 Xbox rights revoked again after Child B being kicked in the "peanuts" by Child A. And Child A claiming similar crime, though not sure about validity of that. Cries of "can we earn it back?". Nope.

16.20 Serve up tea (another slow cooker delight). Child C has other plans. Had a massive breakfast, not much lunch, ate a banana mid-afternoon, and barely touches his dinner. But did lick some tomato ketchup from a small bowl and drink some milk. How different my life will be when he sleeps like a normal person, eats like a normal person, and can be left in the same room as normal people without me being concerned for their safety.

16.34 Child C just so annoying. Starts ranting "I want a blue car. I want a blue car. I want a blue car now". Respond with what seems to work the best. Decide to fight fire with (equally immature) fire. "I want a pink car. I want one now. Please can you get me one". Stops ranting. Moves on to the next thing, namely running the tap in the downstairs loo, flushing the chain repeatedly when it hasn't had time to fill up again and sliding down the stairs on a large cushion.

16.40 Child A and B shattered and ask for their dressing gowns to wear over their clothes. Child C still being annoying, which I put down to tiredness. Tell him not to climb the TV stand and voice that he's being an "annoying pants". Replies "No. You an annoying pants". Euggggh. When can I put him and me to bed?

Grandma calls to let us know they are back from hols. Put Child C on the phone to tell Grandma where we've been. "To the farm" he says "Cows a bit yuk. Bird poo". Great lasting impression of the day then.

17.00 Bath for Child C. He puts the cold water on and leaves it for too long so have to run again for Child A and B. Child B shirty about having a bath. Loses thirty-five mins of computer time for tomorrow, in five minute increments.

18.45 All in bed. 18.50 Child C calls me up to do a wee. Goes back to bed reading *You Choose* book to a bear which sings *That's What Makes You Beautiful*. Both belong to Child A, but in true Child C style, he presumes they are his. Like everything.

19.00 Child B says he can't get to sleep as he's had a bad dream. Reassure him and send him on his way. Don't think for one minute that he can have been asleep, but don't labour that point.

Cook dinner. Do long overdue work report. Cash in Tesco vouchers which run out any day now, for day at Chessington.

21.41 Need to go to bed. Husband out for dinner.

Google "vitamin C deficiency". Conclude that I haven't got that, but possibly that shouldn't take so many vitamin C tablets. Then google "sleep deprivation". Helpful article outlines all my symptoms (thinking of sleep the whole time, clumsy, forgetful, grumpy etc.) and then suggests that one tackles sleep deficit by "tacking on a couple more hours e.g. at the weekend to begin with". Advises that "you will probably find you sleep for ten hours or so at the beginning". No hope here then. When on earth will I ever get the chance for ten hours' sleep? … just over half that is about the norm.

21.55 Husband calls to say he's en route. Chat for a bit then tell him I'll see him when gets home. Doze until then. Finally lights out proper at 22.36.

Diet Cokes: 4.

Chocolate: 1 bag of buttons, 1 hot chocolate (partly for defrosting reasons), 1 corner of Mars Bar cake, 1 bag of choc chip cookies, quite a lot of Minstrels (to try and feel better).

Glasses of wine: 0 … feel sleepy enough without it.

PART FOUR: DAY EIGHTY-SEVEN

"Love life. Engage in it. Give it all you've got. Love it with a passion because it truly does give back many times over what you put into it."

Day Eighty-Seven
(Wednesday)

Today starts no differently from most other days. But while I am clearing up from breakfast, sorting the piles of laundry and wondering what to serve for dinner, the world becomes a little bit less colourful for everyone.

12.00 At the age of eighty-six, Maya Angelou passes away.

Later, the children will come home from school, possibly bicker, probably not eat their tea, may or may not go to bed as requested. Whatever they throw at me (literally, and metaphorically), whatever the rest of the day, and the rest of their childhood years bring, Maya's words will stay with me. And it strikes me as poignant that she should pass away as I reach the end of this three month snapshot, built on the foundations of her words that I read all those years ago.

One day, if they stop reading books solely about football, I hope that Maya Angelou's wit and wisdom will give Child A, B and C the courage in the face of adversity that they have me. And if they lead *their* lives "hoping for the best, prepared for the worst, and unsurprised by anything in between" (and if they have managed to not totally annihilate each other) then I will have done my job.

* * *

12.45 Grandma calls about a funny clip she's seen on the internet. Asks how the ironing is going. Mention I'm writing an account of my life as a twin plus one mummy. She laughs. "What are you going to do with that? Publish it?"

You know what, Mum? I just might.